The Good Life *and*

Its Discontents

THE AMERICAN DREAM
IN THE AGE OF ENTITLEMENT
1945–1995

Robert J. Samuelson

TIMES 𝕿 BOOKS

RANDOM HOUSE

Grateful acknowledgment is made to the following for permission to reprint previously published material:

THE AMERICAN ENTERPRISE INSTITUTE FOR PUBLIC POLICY RESEARCH: Excerpt from "Party
'Reform' in Retrospect" by Edward Banfield, published in *Here the People Rule* (The AEI
Press). Reprinted with the permission of The American Enterprise Institute for Public
Policy Research, Washington, D.C.
AMERICAN ECONOMIC REVIEW: Excerpt from "Agency Costs of Free Cash Flow, Corpo-
rate Finance, and Takeovers" by Michael C. Jensen (May 1986). Reprinted by permis-
sion of American Economic Association, Nashville, TN.
THE BROOKINGS INSTITUTION: Excerpt from "Can Bureaucracy Be Deregulated? Lessons
from Government Agencies" by James Q. Wilson from *Deregulating the Public Service*, edited
by John J. DiIulio, Jr. (1994). Reprinted by permission of The Brookings Institution.
Commentary AND JAMES Q. WILSON: Excerpt from "A Guide to Reagan Country" by James
Q. Wilson (*Commentary*, May 1967). All rights reserved. Reprinted by permission of
Commentary and James Q. Wilson.
Harvard Business Review: Excerpt from Melvin Ashen, "The Management of Ideas,"
Harvard Business Review (July–August 1969). Copyright © 1969 by the President and
Fellows of Harvard College. All rights reserved.
THE ROPER CENTER: Excerpt from "The Polarization of America: The Decline of Mass
Culture" by Paul Jerome Croce (*The Public Perspective*, September–October 1992).
Copyright © The Public Perspective, a publication of the Roper Center for Public
Opinion Research, University of Connecticut, Storrs. Reprinted by permission.

Library of Congress Cataloging-in-Publication Data
Samuelson, Robert J.
The good life and its discontents: the American dream in the
age of entitlement, 1945–1995
Robert J. Samuelson.
p.   cm.
Includes bibliographical references and index.
ISBN 0-8129-2592-0
1. Entitlement spending—United States. 2. United
States—Economic conditions—1945–   I. Title.
HJ7543.S26   1995
336.3'9—dc20   95-21594

Manufactured in the United States of America on
acid-free paper

24689753

First Edition

Book design by Brooke Zimmer

To Judy, Ruth, Michael, and John—the best chapters of my life

Acknowledgments

This is a short book with a long history. I first decided to write about postwar America in the early 1980s and, in the ensuing decade, abandoned the project no less than three times. The final, irrevocable abandonment occurred in late 1991. I then distilled my message into a long cover story for *Newsweek*—it ran in the magazine's March 2, 1992 issue under the headline, "Behind the Voter's Revolt: America's Lost Dream"—and afterward I washed my hands of the whole project. I had learned much from exploring the economic, political, and social evolution of postwar America, but I could never quite master the tone and organization that would satisfy my own informal rule: never write a book you wouldn't want to read.

Almost by accident, I have now finished a book that passes that test. It is not exactly the book that I first imagined, because over the years, much has happened and my thinking has evolved. But that this accident happened at all is mainly due to my editor at Times Books, Steve Wasserman. After abandoning my project on postwar society, I resolved to do a short book consisting of selected columns of mine from

Newsweek and *The Washington Post*. Steve bought the proposal, and as he edited the columns, suggested that I could usefully combine some columns that had similar themes. As I did so, I began to drift back to the larger project, which is what really interested me. I soon set aside the book of columns and began, once again, to construct the story of postwar America. This time, the material coalesced. For giving me the right shove at the right time—and for championing the book in many other small and large ways—I will always be grateful to Steve.

As I wrote and rewrote, I had the help of three people, each of whom read all (or most) of the book in repeated drafts: Richard Thomas, my colleague at *Newsweek*; Joel Havemann, my best friend of many years and an editor at the *Los Angeles Times*; and my cousin Richard Samuelson, a Ph.D. candidate in American history at the University of Virginia. Looking back, I cannot understand why each spent so much time on someone else's work. Rich and Joel, each in his own way, helped me see better exactly what it was I was trying to say; each showed me how to be more precise and concise. My cousin Richard improved my understanding of the historic context of postwar politics and, at several points, refined the logic of my argument; I constantly marveled how someone half my age seemed to have read twice as much. It is not easy to be honest in criticizing without being discouraging. Rich, Joel, and Richard all managed that feat. There is no way I can repay their attention.

Others also helped. Evan Thomas, *Newsweek*'s Washington bureau chief, edited my cover story, and our discussions clarified my thinking. Michael Barone of *U.S. News & World Report*, an old friend and one of the nation's wisest political commentators, read an early draft and provided many detailed insights. Frank Levy, a friend and economist at the Massachusetts Institute of Technology, read the section on the economy and, though not agreeing with it all, helped me put matters in better perspective. Mike Wines of *The New York Times*, who had prodded me for years to finish the book, read the final draft and told me where to cut (I did). My brother Richard read an earlier draft and gave me some needed encouragement.

My agent, Rafe Sagalyn, has been with this project from the start and is surely surprised to see it finished; his advice has always been good, even when I haven't taken it. At Times Books, Robbin Schiff designed a handsome and provocative cover. My copy editor, Trent

Duffy (whom I have never met), did a truly superb job of cleaning up my messy manuscript and making it presentable and clearer. He is top-notch. A decade ago, George Hatsopoulos, chairman of the Thermo Electron Corp., allowed me to spend some time at his company, interviewing him and other top executives; even though the visit was short, I learned a great deal about how businesses operate, and I will always be indebted to George for his courtesy and candor. Over the years Karlyn Bowman of the American Enterprise Institute has provided me with much public opinion polling data and, more important, helped me understand their meaning; I am mystified by her generosity but grateful for it.

At *Newsweek*'s Washington bureau, I regularly benefit from the superior library staff. William Rafferty, the head librarian, may not be the best in the country, but I doubt there is anyone better. His predecessor, Sandra Fine, was almost as good, and they have been ably aided by Kevin Lamb and Shirlee Hoffman. In the wire room, Lindy Leo and Steve Tuttle helped on several occasions avert computer catastrophes that threatened to consume large parts of my manuscript.

Finally, there is Ed Banfield. If you are lucky, you will have at least one great teacher. Ed was my bit of luck. Among modern political scientists, Ed has been a towering thinker. His essays and books (among them, *The Unheavenly City* and *The Democratic Muse*) have been unfailingly prescient in illuminating the dilemmas of contemporary American democracy. As a teacher, Ed demanded a rigor of thought and taught a method of inquiry that—to anyone who was paying even modest attention—were permanent gifts.

This project began with an Alicia Patterson Fellowship in 1982; I am grateful to the foundation for the time it provided me for extended reporting.

In what follows, you will notice that I am a generous user of statistics, though (I hope) always in a context that makes them easily digestible. A few of these numbers will inevitably prove to be wrong. For these, I apologize in advance. For larger errors of judgment, I have reflected long about who must be to blame and can, unfortunately, think of no one but myself.

Bethesda, Maryland
September 4, 1995

Contents

Introduction

This is the story of the postwar American Dream. I call our era—from the end of the Second World War until now—the Age of Entitlement. By entitlement, I mean the set of popular expectations that arose about the kind of nation we were creating and what that meant for all of us individually. We had a grand vision. We didn't merely expect things to get better. We expected all social problems to be solved. We expected business cycles, economic insecurity, poverty, and racism to end. We expected almost limitless personal freedom and self-fulfillment. For those who couldn't live life to its fullest (as a result of old age, disability, or bad luck), we expected a generous social safety net to guarantee decent lives. We blurred the distinction between progress and perfection. Up to a point, we made progress on all fronts. But of course, we did not fully attain any of our goals, because they all required perfection. Our most expansive hopes were ultimately unrealistic. We transformed the American Dream into the American Fantasy. How this happened is the subject of this book.

Although not a memoir, this book is in some ways the story of my life. I was born in late 1945, only a few months after the end of the

Second World War, and I have spent most of my adult years as a reporter and columnist (for *The Washington Post, Newsweek,* and the *National Journal*) probing these matters. This is first and foremost a reporter's book. It asks the basic reportorial questions: What happened, and why? In searching for answers, I borrow from history, economics, and political science. As a child of the postwar era, I also aim to capture on paper the silent assumptions of the early postwar decades that, once they took hold, became a central part of the national consciousness. Throughout, I have heeded the dictum of popular historian Frederick Lewis Allen, who noted that "few things are harder than to observe the life and institutions of one's own day." The focus is on what Americans have taken for granted, often without realizing it.[1]

As you read, you will notice that the labels "liberal" and "conservative" hardly appear at all. These labels are political and polemical conveniences. They frame political debates and create conflict as much as they reflect it. Indeed, the growing acrimony of public life—not just politics, but popular discourse of all types—flows in part from a ritualistic categorization of people as antagonistic stereotypes. There are indeed "liberals" and "conservatives," but in my view, such true believers exist mainly in the relatively small population of political activists. By contrast, most Americans are too busy leading their lives to involve themselves passionately in politics.* The larger point is that, whatever Americans' particular political views, the ideas I am describing here don't belong exclusively to either the liberal or the conservative camp. They depict a general postwar consciousness that affected a large majority of Americans, regardless of party or political outlook. It is the confounding of this consciousness that is a common source of disappointment and disorientation.

You will also notice that I do not talk much of generational differences. I do not distinguish sharply between the Depression and World War II generation, the postwar baby boom and the so-called Generation X, today's twenty-somethings. This is not because I believe there are no differences. All Americans have obviously had varied life experiences, depending on when they were born. But I believe

---

*This is not mere conjecture. In a recent poll, respondents were asked how often they discussed politics. About 70 percent said a few times a week or less.[2]

that too much can be made of generational contrasts—differences of class, race, religion, or region mean more in most people's daily lives—and specifically, I believe that most Americans have been subsumed by entitlement. They have come to it by different paths, but they have still come to it. For older Americans, it emerged from the heady early postwar years and contradicted earlier doubts and social disruptions; for the baby boomers, it was simply the extension of a childhood when Americans imagined few limits; and for Generation X, it was already an established norm by the time they were born. One way or another, most Americans are prisoners of entitlement and its disappointments.

We feel that the country hasn't lived up to its promise, and we are right. But the fault lies as much with the promise as with the performance. Our present pessimism is a direct reaction to the excessive optimism of the early postwar decades. It stems from the confusion of progress with perfection. Having first convinced ourselves that we were going to create the final American utopia—an extravagant act of optimism—we are now dismayed that we haven't—a burst of unwarranted pessimism. In the United States today, things are much better than they seem or are routinely portrayed. Americans are now richer and freer than at any time in history. Prosperity, modern technology (from jet travel to personal computers), and the outlawing of racial and sexual discrimination have been profoundly liberating. We can go more places, "be ourselves" more easily, and enjoy life as never before.

Yet, we fixate on societal flaws: crime, family breakdown, persisting racial and ethinic tensions, and a loss of civility. Our faith in the superiorty and power of the American economy has faded. These feelings reflect real problems, but the problems have been so magnified in popular consciousness that they obscure America's very real successes. What has consistently been missing is a sense of proportion. Perhaps as a people we are incapable of that. But perhaps not. One motive for this book is the belief that we'd be better off with a more balanced view of our present condition. We need a clearer understanding of our strengths and shortcomings, because we are ill served by either excessive optimism or excessive pessimism. The first regularly leads us into romantic schemes that are doomed to failure, while the second may condemn us to hopelessness and continued paralysis.

Our extravagant postwar vision formed from a series of historic events: the Great Depression, the Second World War, and the early surge of postwar prosperity. The fact that we overcame the first two tragedies (and the fact that they *were* such great tragedies) gave us confidence that we could do almost anything, if we set our collective minds to it. And the spectacular and unexpected nature of the early postwar boom reinforced our self-confidence, because we seemed to be eliminating all traces of human want. The trouble was that a central pillar of our postwar optimism—our faith that we could ensure constant economic growth—was fundamentally mistaken. Our mastery was incomplete, but before that became apparent, we had reconstructed our politics on the false assumption of unbounded material prosperity. Government came to make more commitments than it could possibly keep. As a result, political leadership and national institutions have inevitably fallen into disrepute.

History matters. Each element in our postwar experience relates to the other. If we had not had the Depression and the Second World War, we might not have abandoned some of the social and political conventions of the first 150 years of our history. Until the 1930s, we were essentially a nation of small government and largely unregulated economic markets. The Depression and the world war that followed seemed to discredit these traditions; but without the early postwar boom, the drift toward bigger government and more regulation might not have continued. And without the faith that we could easily engineer ever greater wealth and economic well-being, we might not have made so many political promises. All these events combined to give us a sense of a limitless future, in which all possibilities, both for the nation and for individuals, were within our grasp. This is what I mean by entitlement: the conviction that we could completely control our economic, social, and political surroundings. Too sweeping, it was bound to disappoint, and we are now experiencing its bittersweet legacy.

I HAVE ORGANIZED this book into three sections to show how entitlement affected different parts of our national life. The first section ("The Entitlement Society") deals with entitlement's historic origins and the overblown belief that sufficient prosperity would solve almost any social ill; the second section ("The New Capitalism") shows how economists and corporate managers falsely believed they could ensure entitlement through constant, rapid economic growth; and the third (" The Politics of Overpromise") traces how this economic optimism led to an undisciplined expansion of government that involved more public promises than could possibly be kept. Although I believe that the disappointment of these hopes is the main cause of today's disillusion, it is not the only explanation. There are others, and if my story is to be convincing, you need to understand why these other explanations are either wrong or greatly exaggerated.

Let me explore four popular theories: (1) the end of the Cold War, which supposedly left a spiritual void; (2) the effects of the global economy, which allegedly lowered U.S. wages and spawned economic pessimism; (3) the capture of politics by "special interests," which is said to have weakened Americans' faith in democracy; and (4) the disintegration of the American family, which supposedly reflects—and reinforces—a breakdown in basic moral values. Each of these changes is, to some extent, genuine. But none has caused today's widespread disillusion.

Historian Ronald Steel has eloquently expressed the idea that the conclusion of the Cold War created a spiritual void in America. In a recent book, he writes, "During the Cold War we had a vocation; now we have none. Once we had a powerful enemy; now it is gone. Once we had obedient allies; now we have trade rivals. Once we used to know how to define our place in the world and what our interests were; now we have no idea." Although Americans won the Cold War, Steel says, it "weakened us: in our ability to compete with our allies, in meeting the needs of our people, in honoring our political values."[3] Clearly, the end of the Cold War has jolted our foreign policy, because containing Soviet expansionism was its main aim. But otherwise, it is hard to blame the triumph in the Cold War for today's discontents.

It didn't trigger popular moodiness. Public opinion polls show that the decline of confidence in national institutions and leadership started in the late 1960s and early 1970s. Nor did the Cold War fundamentally weaken our ability to compete with our allies or to meet the needs of our own people. Indeed, the Cold War's economic burden consistently declined. In 1955, defense spending constituted 62 percent of total federal spending and was 11 percent of our economy's output, the gross domestic product (GDP). By 1965 (even in the midst of the Vietnam War), those figures were 43 percent of federal spending and 7.5 percent of GDP; by 1975, they were 26 percent and 5.7 percent, respectively. (In 1995, they were 17.6 percent and 3.9 percent.)[4] With lower defense spending, we could have spent even more on domestic programs. But it's not clear that we would have or that, had we, we would now be more "productive" or less poor.

Most poor people are poor because they lack skills, and they can learn skills producing military goods as easily as civilian goods. Likewise, it is doubtful that Americans would be better educated. In this entire period, education spending and graduation rates rose. In 1960, 41 percent of adult Americans were high school graduates and 8 percent were college graduates; by 1990, those figures were 82 percent and 22 percent, respectively. (College graduates are also counted with high school graduates.) Similarly, social spending (on everything from Social Security to food stamps) has constantly risen. In 1955, government "payments to individuals" were 21 percent of the budget; by 1995, they were 57 percent. If anything, the end of the Cold War should have made us feel better, because it eased the conflict between rising social spending and stingy taxpayers. If defense's share of the federal budget had been the same in 1995 as in 1985, military spending would have been $150 billion higher. There was a "peace dividend," but no one seems to have enjoyed it.[5]

The global economy is another miscast villain. By now, its alleged evils are well known. A flood of "cheap" imports is said to be "deindustrializing" America and depressing wages. Companies subsidized by their governments are supposedly eroding U.S. technological leadership. Together, these global forces are allegedly crippling the economy. None of these arguments is entirely true. We are not deindustrializing and never have. In 1995, industrial production was more than 40 percent higher than in 1980, more than 90 percent higher than in 1970, and more than 350 percent higher than in 1950. Granted, manufacturing employment has stagnated. It's less than 19 million, which is slightly lower than in 1970; but this signifies enhanced productivity—the same number of workers making more goods. We are producing things now (computer chips, CT scanners, fiber optic cable) that were barely imagined in 1970. Growing trade does mean that we depend more on imports. For example, imports constitute 77 percent of our toys and 56 percent of our TV tubes. But trade has to be a two-way street. The United States makes other things and remains the world's largest exporter, ahead of both Germany and Japan.[6]

This doesn't mean that we don't have economic problems, that the expansion of the global economy isn't genuine, or that some workers don't suffer from global competition. But it does mean that our economy's strengths are routinely underestimated and that the effects of globalization are routinely exaggerated. The United States still has the world's most productive economy, enjoying income levels 15 to 30 percent higher than Japan or Western Europe; and U.S. industries are still the leaders in many important technologies (biotechnology, aerospace, computers, software). A White House review of twenty-seven critical technologies in early 1995 concluded that the United States lagged in none, though other countries did lead in some subsectors (Japan, for instance, in robotics and computer display screens). American wages and incomes aren't declining; but if they were, trade wouldn't be the main cause. In the context of a $7 trillion economy, it simply isn't large enough. Trade mainly influences manufacturing, which accounts for less than one fifth of all jobs.[7]

Another favorite explanation for Americans' distemper—that politics has been "captured" by "special interests"—suffers from a similar myopia. Anyone who has lived in Washington more than a few weeks (and I have done so for a quarter century) knows that the place is overrun by lobbyists, lawyers, and public relations consultants, all pleading some cause or other. Nor is it any secret that much legislation is decisively influenced by interest groups, whether these be bankers or environmentalists. Special interests are, in this sense, plentiful, and there are more of them now than there used to be. All this reinforces the impression that politics has become increasingly insulated from what the "people" want and is dominated not only by special interests but also by "insiders," "elites," and "career politicians." Again, the impression *is* partially true. As government has grown, it has become more complicated, and as that has happened, lobbyists, bureaucrats, congressional staff members, career politicians, and experts of all varieties have an advantage in influencing what it does.

But, in the main, the impression is false, because it implies that the main contours of politics—not all its details, but its general direction and tone—are not firmly rooted in public opinion. They are. The great explosion of federal spending has not been for allegedly unpopular causes like the poor or foreign aid but for the highly popular cause of the elderly, who now account for more than a third of all outlays. Environmentalism is highly popular, even if regulation isn't. Budget deficits persist because Americans like government benefits and dislike taxes—and politicians fear offending either preference. Nor do special interests, despite their lobbyists and campaign contributions, always get their way. After the Cold War, the reputedly powerful military-industrial complex was notably unsuccessful in preventing a dramatic decline in weapons procurement. American politics, for better or worse, is highly sensitive to public opinion and popular demands. Indeed, one argument of this book is that indiscriminate and sweeping public demands, coupled with the political system's unwillingness to choose among them, is a major source of popular irritation.

Finally, there is family breakdown. This is an all too real and socially destructive phenomenon. Almost everyone knows the trends. Divorce rates have soared, as have out-of-wedlock births. By the 1990s, more than a fifth of white births and more than two thirds of black births were to unwed mothers.[8] For some years, these trends were dismissed, ignored, or even regarded favorably: evidence (it was said) that women were no longer trapped in unsatisfying or violent marriages. By now, this reasoning is seen as too simplistic. Raising children is hard work. Two parents are generally better than one. Two-parent families usually have higher incomes and are better able to provide the time, love, and attention children need to develop self-confidence, independence, and personal skills. This is common sense, and I subscribe to it.

Still, I doubt that most of Americans' present complaints can be traced to family breakdown. Even for children, the importance of family can be exaggerated. A good family is better than a bad family, but not all two-parent families are good and not all single parents are bad. Some couples are indifferent, selfish, or abusive; some single parents are heroic and angelic. Children themselves have an astonishing capacity to defy their parents' best intentions or overcome their parents' worst faults. Anyone who has children (and my wife and I have three) also knows this: every child is different. I believe that America would be a better society if its family structure were stronger. Schools would do better, because students would have more supervision. Neighborhoods (and especially poor neighborhoods) would be more cohesive, because families provide a stabilizing influence. There might even be less crime. But family breakdown is not an explanation for every political, economic, or cultural anxiety. It does not explain soaring health costs or slowing income growth. It is not even the cause of every family problem, from adolescent rebellion to drug use.

The abundance of pat theories for our present distemper is no accident. It reflects the American tendency to seek out clear villains to slay. Each theory serves as a stalking horse for some political or intellectual agenda. Those who blame the Cold War say it diverted us from pressing domestic problems, which now dispirit us and need to be addressed effectively. Critics of the global economy often favor protectionist policies. The condemnation of special interests or career politicians is meant to inspire fundamental political reform, whether tighter limits on campaign fund-raising or congressional term limits.* Attacking family breakdown is intended to encourage "pro-family" government policies. Personally, I distrust many of these solutions. Protectionism would harm our economy; our industries will be stronger if exposed to vigorous competition, domestic or foreign. Although politics is often seedy, I believe that rigid attempts to reform it (and both campaign finance reform and term limits are rigid) would ultimately make it less representative and less effective at resolving conflict or creating consensus. As for reversing family breakdown, I'm in favor, but I doubt that this can fundamentally be accomplished by government policy.

My story of postwar America aims mainly to say what happened, not what we should do about it. Still, I cannot pretend that the story has no implications for the future. So I end the book by placing the postwar era in a larger historic context and making some common-sense suggestions. We need to be more disciplined in our use of government. Balancing the budget would be a good start. A good second step would be altering some of our government programs (Social Se-

---

*In May 1995, the Supreme Court ruled that states could not unilaterally adopt term limits for their senators or representatives. Term limit advocates have now vowed to press for a constitutional amendment to legalize such restrictions on the federal level.

curity, Medicare) to reflect the fact that we are an aging society; we need to raise retirement ages and be somewhat less generous toward the more affluent elderly. An ethic of responsibility needs to replace an expectation of entitlement in government policies and private behavior. To some extent, this change is already under way, though no one can say how far it will go or how successful it will be.

WHATEVER HAPPENS, something is now ending—the period in our history that began at the end of the Second World War and gave rise to a distinct vision of the American Dream. The fact that the phrase came into such widespread use is itself a good measure of our postwar ambitions. In earlier eras, Americans did not talk about the American Dream, though the ideas that underlie it have always been part of the national consciousness. The phrase was apparently coined by historian James Truslow Adams, who wrote of it in his 1931 popular history *The Epic of America*. To Adams, the American Dream was the "dream of a land in which life should be better and richer and fuller for every man, with opportunity for each according to his ability or achievement. . . . It is not a dream of motor cars and high wages merely, but a dream of social order in which each man and each woman shall be able to attain to the fullest stature of which they are innately capable, and to be recognized by others for what they are, regardless of the fortuitous circumstances of birth or position."[9]

But Adams's phrase was not a prominent part of the national vocabulary until the past few decades. Even Adams could not define the American Dream precisely, because it meant to him not only the existence of economic opportunity and abundance but also the establishment of a new set of values that would involve a "communal spirit and intellectual life . . . distinctively higher than elsewhere," values that would transcend "selfishness, physical comfort, and cheap amusement." The more Adams discussed it, the grander and vaguer the Dream became. And so, perhaps, it has always been. By whatever label, the American Dream implies that tomorrow should be better than today. If better is the destination, then there is no arrival and there is continual frustration at the endlessness of the journey. That is how it has often been, and that is surely how it was in the Age of Entitlement.

I

The Entitlement Society

I

The Postwar Paradox

⚑ ⚑ ⚑ ⚑

THE PARADOX OF OUR TIME is that Americans are feeling bad
about doing well. By most objective standards, the last half century in our national life has been enormously successful. Americans
have achieved unprecedented levels of material prosperity and personal freedom. We are healthier, work at less exhausting jobs, and live
longer than at any time in our history. Job security has vastly improved, and government provides a safety net for the poor, disabled,
and elderly that never before existed. Many old discriminations—
based on race, sex, or religion—have diminished dramatically, even if
they haven't entirely disappeared. In short, America today is a far
wealthier and more compassionate society than fifty years ago, and
on a personal level, most Americans appreciate these achievements.
When surveyed, about four fifths of us say we are satisfied with our
own lives. But when asked about the country—whether it's "moving
in the right direction"—Americans are routinely glum. Despite occasional bursts of hopefulness (for example, when the economy booms
or after a unique triumph, such as the Gulf War), a majority of us

(usually about 60 percent) express pessimism about the country's prospects. This has been true for at least two decades. Somehow, a society that satisfies most of us most of the time has also convinced many of us that it's rolling inexorably toward the edge of a cliff.[1]

The paradox is not just a curiosity, normal discontent, a testament to human inconsistency, or a fluke of surveys (a willingness to complain about the country, but not about ourselves). In part, it may be about all these things, but something larger is occurring. Americans are an optimistic people, always have been, and—in their personal outlooks—still are. But the nature of our society since the Second World War somehow seems to have created an almost permanent state of public grumpiness, which transcends Americans' historic suspicion of government or distrust of political leaders. Rather, we seem to have concluded that most of our major institutions (government, business, the press) are somehow failing us and that we have lost our capacity as a nation to reach cherished goals. This loss of national confidence affects how we feel and talk about ourselves—through television, newspapers, and politics—and how we govern ourselves. There's a resentful, accusatory edge to much public debate and commentary, as if someone (the list of suspects constantly changes) must be held responsible for the country's sorry state. The startling thing about this ongoing moodiness is that it contrasts with a record over the past half century that, though far from perfect, boasts many successes and compares favorably with earlier periods in our history.

The reason for this paradox is *entitlement*: a postwar word and concept. By entitlement, I mean more than the catalogue of well-known government benefits (Social Security being the most prominent) or various modern "rights" (such as the "right" of those in wheelchairs to public ramps). Entitlement expresses a modern conviction, a broader sensibility, that defines Americans' attitudes toward social conditions, national institutions, and even our role in the world. Increasingly, we have come to believe that certain things are (or ought to be) guaranteed to us. We feel entitled. Among other things, we expect secure jobs, rising living standards, enlightened corporations, generous government, high-quality health care, racial harmony, a clean environment, safe cities, satisfying work, and personal fulfillment. On the world stage, we think the United States should be the dominant political and economic power. Our political ideas ought to inspire societies everywhere; our industries should be the most efficient and innovative. Entitlement captures the full sweep of our feelings about America and its role in the world.

With only slight exaggeration, it can be said that the central ambition of postwar society has been to create ever expanding prosperity at home and abroad. This is not because Americans worship materialism, though it sometimes seems that way, but because prosperity has seemed to be the path to higher goals. At home, it would end poverty and the associated ills of crime, slums, and racial conflict. It would underwrite more generous government to support the elderly and the disabled. It would expand personal choice and freedom. Relieved of material wants, Americans would have more opportunity to express their individuality and enjoy themselves. Abroad, global prosperity would contain communism, spread democracy, and solidify U.S. global leadership. The United States would be the world's role model; our democracy would be the most admired, our economy the wealthiest. Other countries would emulate our political institutions and management practices. Our domestic and foreign ambitions have been spiritual twins. Both rested on a deep faith in the power of prosperity to improve the human condition.

The economy did so well for the first few decades after the Second World War (especially in contrast with the Great Depression) that Americans began to assume that Big Government and Big Business could guarantee its performance and, more, that the resulting improvement would effortlessly lead to more social justice, personal fulfillment, and greater world order. This evolving sense of entitlement became the modern embodiment of American "exceptionalism"—the recurring belief, going back to the earliest days of the republic, that America is a better society than ever has been or will be. This new exceptionalism, though, departed from the old. In general, our forebears understood that life was full of chance and uncertainty. They recognized that getting ahead and leading a fulfilling life involved periodic setbacks and inevitable risks. Even then, there were no guarantees of success. Some people were lucky, some weren't. The core of the American belief system, as William Whyte, Jr., wrote several decades ago, was the "pursuit of individual salvation through hard work, thrift and competitive struggle." In 1908, a banker told a group of Yale students: "You may start in business, or the professions, with your feet on the bottom rung of the ladder; it rests with you to acquire the strength to climb to the top." Implicit, even for elite students, was the possibility that not everyone would "acquire the strength" or "climb to the top."[2] Today, at the close of the century, we have quietly adopted different assumptions. Without denying the role of individual effort, the modern view presumes that people who "play by the rules" should prosper. And because most of us do (or think we do), we are therefore "entitled" to security, stability, and well-being. Entitlement means that almost everyone deserves to succeed.

But not everyone does. Nor are there universal security and stability. Measured against our idealized society, today's America is indeed a mess. It suffers from periodic recessions, corporate failures, inept government, and too much poverty. Government taxes seem too high and government services seem too low. Ongoing federal budget deficits are a disgrace. There is no racial peace and (many would argue) not enough racial justice. More broadly, social harmony has eluded us. Tensions along lines of race, ethnicity, and sex are increasingly palpable. New waves of immigrants seem culturally and economically disruptive—and less and less controllable. Crime is too high (much higher than half a century ago), with murder rates near all-time records. Divorce and out-of-wedlock births have exploded, jeopardizing children. Similarly, our position in the world seems—despite our triumph in the Cold War—increasingly besieged. Foreign companies sometimes flail our industries, while foreign leaders often ignore our advice or, worse, demonize us. The world is still a dangerous place, full of ancient hatreds and modern scourges: tribal vendettas and weapons of mass destruction, from nuclear bombs to poison gas. And we seem less able to influence, let alone dominate, events.

What upsets us, in short, is that we have inherited a country and world different from those that we felt were our due. The disillusion is not simply that we have problems; it is that these problems confound expectations that were widespread and were considered realistic. We felt and feel entitled, and so someone must be held accountable for our disappointments. The fault must lie with our larger institutions (whether political, business, or cultural) or with specific groups. We feel betrayed and righteously indignant about our betrayal. Someone or something has sabotaged the American Dream, and the villains deserve to be pilloried and punished. To some extent, of course, the anger is normal. Our leaders and institutions are hardly perfect; Americans would not be American if they didn't complain. But much of the recrimination obscures a deeper reality: our expectations were not realistic. We thought we were entitled, but we weren't. It is not that all our postwar ideas and strivings were utterly foolish. Many were (and are) sound—within limits. The trouble is that they were stretched beyond their limits and, having been imbued with possibilities they did not possess, generated unattainable ambitions. The result is much free-floating discontent, even though the record of the past half century, both at home and abroad, is mainly one of success.

IF WE REVISIT AMERICA before the Second World War, even briefly, we find a country that seems almost primitive by present standards. In 1940, more than a fifth of Americans still lived on farms; less than a third of those farms had electric lights, and only a tenth had flush toilets. The majority of Americans (56 percent) were renters. More than half of households didn't have a refrigerator, and 58 percent lacked central heating. Although use of oil and natural gas was rising rapidly, coal—for stoves and furnaces—was still the dominant fuel (in 55 percent of households), followed by wood (23 percent of households). In many families. women "spent six hours every week dusting floors, furniture and sills and more hours still washing wood ash or coal dust from curtains, blankets and clothing," according to economist Stanley Lebergott. In 1940, about 30 percent of households didn't have inside running water; in rural areas, the proportion was more than 60 percent among whites and more than 95 percent among blacks.[3]

Work was harder, longer, and much less secure. Nearly half the labor force had grueling farm, factory, mining, or construction jobs. Until the 1930s, the typical workweek in manufacturing for men averaged nearly fifty hours. In industrial cities, factory shifts typically began between six and seven-thirty in the morning; in working-class families, wives were usually up before 5:30 A.M. Spells of unemployment were frequent. When orders slackened, even seasonally, companies laid off workers. Because private pensions were skimpy—and Social Security didn't exist until 1935—many families lived in dread of the day their breadwinner would no longer be considered strong enough to hold a factory job. Compared with this, America today is a much better place. We did build a welfare state (though Americans dislike the term) that provides for the aged, the disabled, the sick, and—to a lesser extent—the poor. In 1992, 42 million Americans received Social Security, 35 million received Medicare, and 25 million received food stamps.[4] Our welfare state supports the middle class; it does not serve just the poor.

Prosperity also promoted national, as opposed to regional, sensibilities and in the process fostered the other great postwar advance: a huge drop in discrimination—racial, religious, ethnic, and sexual. Even now, it seems astonishing that in the South blacks were denied access to the same schools, lunch counters, public toilets, and swimming pools as whites until the Supreme Court outlawed school segregation in 1954 and Congress barred discrimination in public places and employment with the Civil Rights Act of 1964. Outside the South, racial discrimination was also widespread. The first black basketball player didn't enter the National Basketball Association until 1950, three years after Jackie Robinson broke the color line in major league baseball. When Bryant Gumbel hosts *Today*, it is worth recalling that the television networks didn't hire a black reporter until 1962. In 1964, there were fewer than 100 black elected officials nationwide; by the early 1990s, there were nearly 7,000.

Moreover, other groups suffered from prejudice as well. Anti-Semitism was widespread before the Second World War. Jews were kept out of certain neighborhoods, occupations, or companies. One poll asked non-Jewish respondents: "Have you heard any criticism or talk against Jews in the last six months?" In 1946, 46 percent answered yes. Ten years later, the figure had dropped to 11 percent. In prewar America, positions of power in business, finance, the professions, and cultural institutions were held disproportionally by WASPs (White Anglo Saxon Protestants), as the late Robert Christopher noted in a 1989 book. "When I left . . . to enter the Army in late 1942," Christopher wrote, "my hometown of New Haven, Connecticut, was a place where marriage between Irish and Italian Americans was still uncommon enough to occasion raised eyebrows on both sides, where social intercourse between WASPs and Italian or Jewish Americans was still minimal and generally awkward, and where no one of Polish or Greek heritage could sensibly hope ever to win the presidency of a local bank or brokerage house."[5] After the war, intermarriage and the expansion of education battered these barriers; WASP ascendancy declined. Blacks, Jews, Catholics, and women have all benefited from a shattering of stereotypes that, along with sanctioned discrimination, constricted lifestyles and careers.

Finally, the well-being of the poor has also improved substantially. As recently as the late 1960s, teams of doctors found hunger and extreme malnutrition, especially among children, in poverty-stricken areas of the Bronx, Appalachia, Mississippi, and Texas. A decade later, the doctors reported vast change. "Nowhere did I see the gross evidence of malnutrition among young children that we saw in 1967," one said. "It is not possible any more to find very easily the bloated bellies, the shriveled infants, the gross evidence of vitamin and protein deficiencies in children." One reason was the food stamp program, which barely existed in the 1960s but served 16 million people by 1975; by 1993, about 27 million people received food stamps (10 percent of the population and 69 percent of those officially classified as poor). Similarly, federal health programs have enhanced medical care for the poor. None of this means that the poor have an easy time of it or that, in some respects, poverty doesn't seem more entrenched than a few decades ago. But, inarguably, government programs have sharply relieved the worst aspects of suffering.[6]

Our foreign policy achieved comparable success. The guiding impulse was, in the apt phrase of Harvard historian Charles Maier, "the politics of productivity"—the belief that rapid economic growth would create stable democracies capable of withstanding communism. Military alliances and nuclear diplomacy constituted only the policy's high-profile aspects. They provided protection and bought time for prosperity to work. Americans believed in the "American Century"—a concept coined in 1941 by Henry Luce, the founder and editor of *Time* and *Life*. A passionate internationalist, Luce wanted the United States to wage war against Hitler. But he believed that Americans needed a "vision of America as a world power . . . which can inspire us." His choice of mission was spreading the American way of life—free enterprise and democracy—around the globe. The United States would support free trade and free speech, dispatching our "engineers, scientists, doctors . . . builders of roads [and] teachers" to other countries to promote prosperity and American ideals: "a love of freedom, a feeling for the quality of opportunity, a tradition of self-reliance and independence and also of cooperation."[7]

This blend of moral fervor and faith in prosperity became the hallmark of postwar American foreign policy. Victory in the Cold War vindicated its central strategy: one system survived and prospered; the other did not. Economic growth in the postwar period, even considering recent slowdowns, has outstripped that in any other era, not only the period between the world wars (which was ruined by the Great Depression), but also the so-called golden age of growth before the First World War. In France, income per person has grown 3 percent in the postwar period compared with 1 percent in the three decades before 1914; in Germany, growth has averaged 4 percent compared with 2 percent; in Japan, 6 percent versus 2 percent; in Brazil, 3 percent versus 1 percent.[8] Some of the higher growth, of course, reflected rebuilding from the Depression and the war that followed. But much of it stemmed from the expansion of international trade and investment that American policy consciously promoted. That policy spread technologies and managerial techniques worldwide. (The proof that trade has been an engine of growth is that, in the entire postwar period, it increased faster than overall economic output.) And, in turn, prosperity bolstered democracy. Europe, Japan, and much of Asia have never been more democratic than they are today.

OUR ERROR WAS not in trusting prosperity, but in trusting it too much. The illusion of the early postwar decades (say, through the early 1970s) was that we had unlocked the secret of perpetual economic growth. People began to feel that the "economic problem"—meaning society's ability to generate all the wealth it needed to satisfy its wants—had been solved, or soon would be. But in fact, we had not unlocked the formula. Since 1970, there have been four recessions; economic growth has slowed and, with it, the rise of incomes and living standards. Moreover, we now discover (or rediscover) that prosperity also imposes costs. The economist Joseph Schumpeter once described economic growth as "creative destruction," because new technologies and business methods obliterate the old.[9] In practice, growth creates winners and losers. It spurs the expansion of some industries, cities, and regions—and the decline of others. It confers and revokes status. It undermines tradition. It empowers some nations and imperils others. It disrupts settled ways and compels people (and institutions) to alter comfortable habits. It generates insecurity.

Our postwar history brims with these contradictory consequences. In the early postwar decades, suburban life seemed a relief from crowded cities, but the urban exodus often stripped cities of industry and middle-class neighborhoods, making them increasingly enclaves of poverty, crime, and drugs. And ultimately, the suburbs too lost some charm; they acquired some of the cities' congestion, grime, and even crime. More recently, industrial upheavals have shattered many communities. In the 1970s and 1980s, the steel, auto, and machine-tool industries—once the pride of American manufacturing—contracted sharply. Between 1980 and 1992, for example, steel industry employment dropped from 400,000 to less than 180,000. Change leaves deep scars, but it is precisely the pressure to change, as Schumpeter noted, that leads to a more productive economy and higher living standards. Steel employment is down, but efficiency is up. In the 1990s, the industry makes about the same amount of steel as it did in 1980 with less than half the workforce.[10] Our goals have been at loggerheads. We can't enjoy all the benefits of greater economic growth (higher living standards, improved technology) unless we also suffer some of the drawbacks.

In our foreign affairs, there was a similar naïveté. Prosperity is not a magic potion that, when applied to nations, induces conformity and calm. What we sought was not empire, but dominion. We assumed that other nations, once exposed to American-like affluence, would become more American. They would increasingly share our values and institutions. What happened was different. In Europe and Japan, prosperity brought a justifiable feeling that their success reflected their own efforts, not just American help. Economic convergence (European and Japanese living standards approached the American by the late 1970s) did not bring cultural or political convergence. Germans, Japanese, and Italians might drink Coca-Cola and wear Levi's, but they did not become Americans. They retained distinctive national interests, traditions, perceptions, and prejudices. And they also resented being dependent on the United States for nuclear protection in the Cold War. We imagined the Cold War, if won, would secure American leadership. It didn't.

The postwar era's mixed record leaves us confused and contentious. Although successes overshadow failures, it seems just the opposite in our mind's eye. Somehow, the shortcomings seem more compelling; they offend our sense of entitlement. Our attitudes are shaped more by unattained ambitions than actual achievements. We seem to have lapsed into a selective view of the American condition and into tortuous self-criticism. We are hypersensitive to all of America's flaws and limits. In theory, self-criticism is healthy for societies as well as individuals. Learning from mistakes is a time-proven method. But our self-criticism has not been of this type. It has mainly been of the complaining and whining variety. Our societal performance is judged against impossible standards and, naturally, found wanting. This is not a constructive corrective, a stepping back, a regaining of perspective that balances what's desirable with what's doable. But it is probably the inevitable consequence of the sensibility that informs the nation's psyche. Countless millions of Americans feel, in one way or another, that they have been deprived (or might be deprived) of something they deserve or have been promised.

These fears and anxieties penetrate deeply into everyday life, because entitlement is one way Americans deal with their dependence on large institutions—government bureaucracies, business corporations, huge universities, and medical systems. The less credible entitlement becomes, the more we resent these immense institutions. Americans have never liked them. Before the Second World War, there was a long history of intense hostility toward large corporations, which were viewed as destroying small business and exploiting workers. There was even a longer history of hostility toward government and "handouts." Even in the Depression, when many Americans worked on relief (government work projects), the antipathy was strong. The first question ever asked by the Gallup Poll, in 1935, was whether the government was spending too much money for "relief": 60 percent of the respondents thought so, and only 9 percent thought spending was too little (31 percent said it was "about right").[11]

But by the 1950s, Americans had reluctantly come to terms with these huge institutions: a point made brilliantly in William Whyte's *The Organization Man*, published in 1956. We projected onto them demands for improving our personal well-being. Inherently impersonal, these institutions had to justify their social usefulness by becoming more humane, and they could do so by making us better off. To use modern jargon: they had to empower us, not enslave us. Their social and political legitimacy would depend on how well they succeeded. Our confidence that they could succeed flowed from the faith in prosperity, which would enable big companies and big government to deliver mass economic and social benefits to individuals. Their size was inevitable because group production was society's "source of creativity," and only big institutions could organize progress through the "application of science," as Whyte put it.[12] But their size was also acceptable, because their power had been democratized. Ultimately, the new benefits they provided would become "entitlements," signifying they were due individuals as much as a matter of right as a matter of organizations' benevolence.

People altered their thinking. It was okay to be dependent on government or corporations, because we really weren't dependent. These institutions were our servants; we weren't their serfs. Government-provided welfare was, of course, still stigmatized. But it was narrowly identified with only a few unpopular programs—mainly help for unmarried mothers through Aid to Families with Dependent Children (AFDC). Otherwise, Americans have rationalized their growing reliance on government aid. Social Security is the best example. Many recipients feel they've earned their benefits—that they are entitled to them—because their past "contributions" in payroll taxes, having been saved, are merely being returned. In fact, the amounts of their benefits—for Social Security and Medicare—vastly exceed the amounts of their past taxes, even if these had been saved (which they weren't). In this respect, Social Security resembles ordinary welfare. It is an income transfer program organized by government to move funds from some people (taxpayers) to others (beneficiaries). Yet, this is widely denied. "Handouts" (pejorative) have become "entitlements" (neutral or deserved).*

---

*Even if Social Security taxes had been saved and credited with interest, they would not cover the benefits of typical retirees. Workers with average wages retiring in 1980 would have recovered their entire contribution (employee taxes, employer taxes, plus interest) in about three years. By 1993, the hypothetical recovery period had jumped substantially to about eleven years, which is still just over half the life expectancy (nineteen years) of someone at age sixty-five.[13]

The case of Social Security is straightforward, but similar rationales (based on various unwritten "contracts" or alleged inequalities) have arisen to explain or justify a whole array of official and unofficial entitlements. To some extent, these rationales were devised and promoted by governmental and business leaders seeking to make themselves or their institutions more powerful or popular. When President Franklin Delano Roosevelt signed the Social Security Act, he said of the taxes: "We put these payroll contributions there so as to give the contributors a legal, moral, and political right to their pensions and unemployment benefits."[14] Some changes evolved simply through custom. But the cumulative effect is to make government, business, and many other institutions (courts, school systems) responsible for delivering certain benefits to mass constituencies.

Thus, entitlement is not only a set of expansive (often impossible) expectations. It is also a set of specific demands and expectations imposed on identifiable institutions and, in turn, justified by more accepting public attitudes toward dependence. Government, business, and other institutions—and their leaders—are judged not only by how well they fulfill their historic functions (say, providing defense or making profits) but also by how well they provide all the entitlements that people have come to expect. Unsurprisingly, popular esteem for these institutions and leaders has fallen, because dependence—the end result of entitlement—spawns a love-hate relationship. People often regret or detest being dependent on someone or something else, although they can't imagine surrendering their dependence. As a result, these providing institutions inspire considerable ambivalence, even when they perform their expected duties and, predictably, great anger toward them when they don't. And that happens increasingly, because many are overcommitted. They are expected to perform many more social functions than they can.

NO ONE FAMILIAR WITH American history can say that our present predicament is altogether new. We go through cycles of strenuous striving, followed by periods of disenchantment and disillusion. Ironically, what creates these cycles is an enduring national optimism. Tocqueville long ago noted that Americans believe in "the indefinite perfectibility of man." In modern jargon, we are progress junkies.

Progress, we think, is the natural order. All problems ought to have solutions. We view our social shortcomings in moralistic terms. It's good guys versus bad guys, and if the good guys persevere, they will triumph. We believe in happy endings and react sullenly when they don't arrive. The late historian Richard Hofstadter, writing in the mid-1950s, put it this way: "A great part of both the strength and weakness of our national existence lies in the fact that Americans do not abide very quietly the evils of life. We are forever restlessly pitting ourselves against them, demanding changes, improvements, remedies, but not often with sufficient sense of the limits that the human condition will in the end insistently impose on us."[15]

The trouble is not that we strive but that we cannot discipline our strivings: we cannot temper our underlying optimism and enthusiasm with a proper sense of what's within our grasp, and what's not. In this sense, the fatal defect of our postwar vision—entitlement—is that it rested on an almost dreamlike concept of progress. We expected a continual and mechanical process by which life in all its aspects would constantly improve. No one actually put it that way, of course, because to do so might seem foolish or even utopian, and Americans, by and large, have considered themselves to be practical and hard-nosed. But our fuzzy vision was, in fact, quite utopian, because it silently presumed that we might somehow purge life of all uncertainty, upset, or insecurity. Life no longer needed to be a struggle; it could simply be enjoyed. Whatever hard personal or national choices that previous generations of Americans had faced would mostly vanish, because in a richer and more stable society, we could "have it all." Never before had Americans so indulged their faith in "indefinite perfectibility."

The rise of entitlement has also logically contributed to something else that is, on the whole, undesirable. It is a decline in the sense of responsibility. This does not mean that all Americans have become lazy, unethical, or selfish. But there is a growing tendency to blame others for whatever national or personal problems we might have. We feel entitled both as a society and as individuals, and if the entitlements—whether they are specific government benefits or more general expectations, such as a constant rise in income or airtight job security—are denied, then we embark on a search to find the culprit. The responsibility lies elsewhere, we seem to feel, not with us. The ease with which this occurs is novel. Sixty or seventy years ago, Americans by and large subscribed to the notion of the "rugged individual." People considered themselves responsible for their own fates. The promise of America was to give everyone an opportunity to achieve the good life and, if you didn't make it, well, America wasn't to blame. Now, the spirit has shifted. If something's wrong, it's someone else's fault. Government, business, the schools, or the courts are responsible. Or we are brought down by racism, sexism, ageism, or some other "ism." What is now called "victimology" has become widespread and respectable.

Quite obviously, these stereotypes are overdrawn. Even when the rugged individual was an accepted ideal, it never fully described reality. Few Americans were ever completely in charge of their own fates. They were always, to some extent, held in the grip of events and forces beyond their control, whether these were economic cycles, crop failures, new technologies, or wars. Similarly, Americans have throughout their history found a variety of villains (bankers, robber barons, immigrants) to blame for their troubles. We have identified causes for our discontents and pursued the scoundrels through newspapers, courts, or legislatures. By the same token, most Americans today have not entirely abandoned the faith that what they do as individuals matters. There is plenty of striving and plenty of rhetoric about the importance of personal effort and responsibility. Finally, it is simply untrue that every social or personal complaint is excuse-making. Complaints often reflect legitimate grievances, and the effort to address them has generated much social progress. Still, the stereotypes accurately describe a change in spirit. We have become adept at rationalizing failure—personal, institutional, and national—and assigning responsibility to some hostile group, distant organization, underlying social pathology, or foreign country. This frame of mind ultimately undermines the moral basis for individual effort and responsibility, without which no society can function successfully.

Entitlement is the modern American Dream and, because it is so unattainable in so many of its details, it is also the American Fantasy. But entitlement did not materialize in an instant. It slowly stitched itself into the national psyche over the course of several decades, beginning in the Great Depression and ending in the late 1960s. A succession of experiences gave it form and meaning. Americans barely understand this process, because they suffer an almost willful historic amnesia. "I've never brought up the Depression to my children," a suburban car dealer remarked to Studs Terkel in his 1970 oral history of the Depression. "Never in my life. Why should I? What I had to do, what I had to do without, I never tell 'em what I went through, there's no reason for it. They don't have to know bad times. All they know is the life they've had and the future they're gonna have."[16] By nature, Americans are forward-looking, and in some ways that is a huge national advantage: we don't get trapped in the past. But it is also a great disadvantage, because, being ignorant of the past, we can't learn from it. The future we have entered is not the one we imagined; and we will never understand why unless we grasp when and how the notion of entitlement arose.

2

History's Chasm

❧ ❧ ❧ ❧

THE GREAT DEPRESSION, stretching from late 1929 to 1939, and the Second World War represent a chasm in American history. On the one side lies one set of popular ideas and national institutions, and on the other lies another. Of course, the two sets are connected by many enduring national beliefs and traditions. Still, the gulf between what came before and what came after is enormous. We take many things for granted today—the large role of government in our lives, the expectation that most middle-class children will go to college, the belief that most of us will enjoy retirement—that were unimaginable to Americans of the 1920s. Likewise, the notion that the United States ought to reign as the world's major economic and military power would have struck most prewar Americans as far-fetched and, on the whole, undesirable. At the end of the First World War, the United States had flirted with such a role; the effort had left most Americans cold. By the early 1930s, "the country was in an overwhelmingly isolationist mood, convinced that it could live in safety and satisfaction behind a wall of neutrality, regardless of what was going on in the rest of the world," as popular historian Frederick Lewis Allen aptly put it.[1]

Together, the Depression and the Second World War shattered prevailing attitudes about the economy, the role of government, and America's place in the world. The Depression discredited private business and the faith that the normal workings of capitalism—what we now customarily call "the market"—would automatically improve Americans' well-being. But the Depression did not firmly establish government as an alternative source of authority, because Roosevelt's New Deal did not end the Depression—in 1939, the unemployment rate was still 17 percent.[2] The wartime boom ended the Depression and, in so doing, created an economic and political model that seemed to work. Afterward, government and business could collaborate, as they had during the war, to engineer prosperity and progress. Likewise, the war convinced most Americans that isolationism, though appealing in spirit, was self-defeating. Americans could see that isolationism had abetted war by creating a vacuum of power that had been filled, catastrophically, by Germany and Japan. Victory showed Americans their country could lead. We did not have to become "entangled" in foreign alliances; we could engineer the alliances. In the span of one and a half decades, two of the basic working assumptions of American life—that government would remain small and focused and that America would keep itself one step removed from the world's major quarrels—were effectively repudiated.

It is in this sense that the Depression and the war represent a chasm. Although they did not alter many basic values (for example, the love of freedom), they irrevocably refined some others (for example, the faith in self-reliance). The fact that the Depression and the war were sequential events gave them a far greater significance than either might have had alone. Both were pervasive upheavals that affected most Americans and had a profound impact on popular attitudes. Likewise, each altered the other's meaning. No one will ever know where the Depression would have led without the war. In the late 1930s, Americans were deeply divided over the New Deal. Worse, the disagreements occurred along class lines. Business leaders blamed the New Deal for the Depression, and Roosevelt blamed business. Without the war, Roosevelt might have pursued a more aggressive overhaul of private enterprise. Or disillusion with the New Deal might have led to its collapse; indeed, some polls indicated that Roosevelt would have lost the 1940 election without the threat of war.[3] Similarly, the war didn't inevitably create bigger government. Government had expanded massively during the First World War—and then contracted rapidly. This did not happen after 1945, because prewar America was despised; almost no one wanted to return to the Depression. A more active government was one way to prevent that. Moreover, a larger international role virtually required bigger government. To examine the history of these years is to appreciate why they had such a huge impact.

WHAT WAS SO TERRIFYING about the Depression was not the economic collapse but its apparent permanence. This, more than anything else, sapped morale. The economy is sometimes now said to be in a "depression" or "quiet depression" when there's a slump. This use of "depression" dilutes the word's historic meaning. Before the Second World War, "depression" connoted a steep drop in prices and economic activity, and in this sense, nothing like the Great Depression has occurred since the war. Between 1929 and 1933, the U.S. economy's output declined roughly one quarter; prices dropped nearly 30 percent. By contrast, the deepest postwar recessions (1973–1975 and 1981–1982) have involved declines in output of 4.9 and 3 percent, respectively. Prices have not dropped at all since 1945. Unemployment reached its highest level (10.8 percent) in the postwar era at the end of the 1981–1982 recession. In 1933, joblessness averaged 25 percent; for the entire decade, it averaged more than 18 percent. Before the 1930s, Americans were used to hard times; periodically, the economy experienced a bust. In 1920–1921, industrial production had dropped 20 percent; thousands of businesses (including the haberdashery owned by future President Harry S Truman) went bankrupt. But the economy had recovered. By contrast, the Depression persisted.[4]

Stocks crashed in the autumn of 1929. By 1931, the early optimism that the economy would revive had dissipated. What remained was fright and mystification. Farmers, unable to repay loans because crop prices had declined (a bushel of wheat worth $1.32 in 1928 sold for 49 cents in 1932), had farms repossessed. Industry was crushed. In

1932, U.S. Steel operated at 19 percent of capacity. One of its major customers, the American Locomotive Company, had sold an average of six hundred locomotives annually in the 1920s. In 1932, it sold one. Breadlines formed in cities; homelessness grew. In the 1920s, the country had gotten visibly richer, and the effect was to fortify the power and prestige of business, which was credited for the economic boom. (Two conspicuous examples of the boom were automobiles and radios; the total of registered cars increased from 8 million to 23 million, and the number of radios rose from virtually none in 1920— the year of the first commercial radio station—to 12 million by 1929.) In the 1930s, business lost all its luster. Many of the shabbier speculative excesses of the 1920s came to light. There were embarrassing congressional hearings; the president of the New York Stock Exchange was jailed for embezzlement. More important, business leaders could not explain, or cure, the Depression. "As for the cause of the Depression or the way out," one banker said in a newsreel talk, "you know as much as I do." Charles M. Schwab, the head of Bethlehem Steel, once confessed fatalistically: "I'm afraid, every man is afraid."[5]

It was hard for ingrained beliefs to withstand the Depression. In general, individual self-reliance had been the national creed. Americans attributed persistent poverty, as opposed to bouts of bad luck, to character flaws—laziness, irresponsibility, or an inability to acquire useful skills. To the extent that people needed help, extended families, private charities, and churches were the chosen instruments. Government was not a preferred alternative. These ideas crumbled under the pressure of the Depression. Everyone could see that vast numbers of people were suffering through no fault of their own. When a quarter of the labor force was unemployed, and most of the jobless were desperate for work and had long histories of hard toil, it was hard to claim that there had been a sudden outbreak of mass shiftlessness. In 1934, the average person on relief was a thirty-eight-year-old man, a head of household who was from "a relatively experienced group of workers," reported one national study. Even families that had jobs felt the pinch and fear. Maids and butlers were let go. (This was not insignificant; in 1930, 7 percent of the nonfarm labor force were household servants.) "Wives who had never before—in the revealing current phrase—'done their own work' were cooking and scrubbing," Frederick Lewis Allen wrote in 1939. "Husbands were wearing the old suit longer, resigning from the golf club." Anyone who had been heavily invested in the stock market in the late 1920s had taken a beating. At its 1929 high, General Motors stock sold for $72.75 a share; its 1932 low was $7.63.[6]

There was a void in political values, and new ideas and political groups rushed to fill it. Among some college students and intellectuals, communism seemed compelling. If capitalism (private ownership of property) inflicted such misery, maybe communism (collective ownership) could create social justice. There was a surge in union activity, and many union leaders also were Communists or sympathized with collectivist approaches. Populist movements mushroomed, though it was often hard to say whether they were of the left or right. The Townsend plan (after a California health official, Francis E. Townsend) proposed that everyone over age sixty receive $200 a month as a way to revive the economy. Father Charles E. Coughlin, a preacher in a Detroit suburb, had a huge following and proposed even more radical share-the-wealth schemes, while also railing against "godless capitalists, the Jews, Communists, international bankers, and plutocrats." There was an almost "universal hobby of looking for the Depression scapegoat," as Alistair Cooke later noted, whether the scapegoat be greedy bankers or the President. Below this ferment lay much confusion and hopelessness. "My father spent two years painting his father's house. He painted it twice," one man raised during the Depression recalled to Studs Terkel. "It gave him something to do."[7]

It is almost impossible for us now to evoke the widespread despair of the time or to appreciate how much people's innate sense of "how things worked" was shaken. One of the many letters that poured into the White House conveys a sense of shame and disorientation felt by many Americans.

> Goff, Kansas
> May 10, 1935
>
> Mrs. Franklin D. Roosevelt:
> My Dear Friend:
>
> For the first time of my lifetime I am asking a favor and this one I am needing very badly and I am coming to you for help.
>
> Among your friends do you know of one who is discarding a spring coat for a new one. If so could you beg the old one for

me. I wear a size 40 to 42 I have not had a spring coat for six years and last Sunday when getting ready to go to church I see my winter coat had several very thin places in the back that is very noticeable. My clothes are very plain so I could wear only something plain. We were hit very hard by the drought and every penny we can save goes for feed to put in crop.

Hoping for a favorable reply.

Your friend,

Mrs. J.T.[8]

The New Deal tried to dispel the gloom and give the country a renewed sense of purpose and coherence. Roosevelt offered not so much a new program as a different approach: a willingness to use government more forcefully both to end the Depression and to preserve the nation's democratic and private enterprise institutions. There is little doubt that the New Deal's many agencies and laws alleviated suffering and helped to overcome the climate of extreme panic of the winter of 1932–1933, when runs on banks were endemic and unemployment was near its peak. By one estimate, more than 10 million Americans ultimately worked for New Deal relief programs (the Works Progress Administration, the Public Works Administration, the Civilian Conservation Corps, and other agencies). Home mortgages and bank deposits were insured. Farm production was regulated. Yet in the end, the New Deal did not fill the country's spiritual void or create a new political framework for governing, mainly because the Depression endured. Although the economy had significantly improved during Roosevelt's first term, it entered a new slump in late 1937 that reversed the decline of unemployment and ended optimism that the country was fully recovering. "This was the first depression in an America supposedly fortified against depressions by the economic control legislation of the early New Deal," wrote Alistair Cooke. "If there was a time in the thirties when wobbling Marxists were strengthened in their fatalist doctrine that depression is the wages of boomtime sin, and that salvation lay only in Communism, this was it." The New Deal didn't identify a formula for success or create a new political consensus. Just the opposite: it ignited fiery disagreement.[9]

Politics grew increasingly acrimonious. In the 1936 election, Roosevelt had inveighed against "economic royalists"—business leaders, bankers, and the upper classes—whom he blamed for the Depression. Roosevelt's opponents despised him. Although many business leaders had initially welcomed Roosevelt, the mood had changed. Many came to believe that his inflammatory rhetoric and meddlesome policies undermined economic confidence and prolonged the Depression. It is doubtful that this was true—the main cause of the 1937 recession seems to have been the mistaken credit policy of the Federal Reserve Board—but it was certainly true that the New Deal was a confused bundle of policies with little intellectual consistency. In the beginning, Roosevelt had tried to prop up prices and incomes with a variety of programs. Farmers were paid not to plant; the National Industrial Recovery Act attempted to revive spending by allowing competing businesses to hold up prices and wages (the theory was that collapsing wages and prices were undermining business profits and consumer purchasing power). But other New Deal programs attacked business price fixing. Big relief programs aimed to prop up incomes through spending, and new banking and stock market regulations tried to restore confidence. In 1935, Congress passed the Social Security Act creating unemployment insurance, old-age pensions, and Aid to Families with Dependent Children (what we now call "welfare"). Despite continuous budget deficits, Roosevelt said he favored balanced budgets. One presidential adviser was asked publicly in 1940 whether he thought "the basic principle of the New Deal is economically sound." He confessed he couldn't answer. "I really do not know what the basic principle of the New Deal is," he said. "I know from my experience in the government that there are as many conflicting opinions among the people in Washington under this administration as we have in the country at large."[10]

None of Roosevelt's policies had really worked, and had it not been for the war, it is conceivable that the economy would have continued to drift—recovering only slowly from the Depression—and that politics would have become increasingly polarized. Roosevelt, always the experimenter, might have tried more radical measures; his opponents would almost certainly have become more embittered. It is impossible to know what might have happened, in what direction Roosevelt might have moved, or whether a concerted and continuing reaction to the New Deal would have led to its repudiation. The social and political significance of the war was that all these questions became moot. Suddenly, Americans' concerns were directed elsewhere. The fractious debates of the 1930s became largely irrelevant, because the economy was booming and the war demanded everyone's attention. The war allowed people to edge away from the uncompromising positions taken in the thirties. By 1942, Roosevelt had ditched many of his more radical economic ideas, to the dismay of New Dealers. If they felt betrayed (as they did), they were an isolated minority. In any case, there was really no choice; in 1942, Republicans gained 46 seats in the House of Representatives. Congress was in no mood to perpetuate the New Deal. Americans did not blot the Depression from their minds. But the Depression's lessons, whatever they might be, would now be modified by the wartime experience.

IT SIMPLY OVERSHADOWED everything. In war, government's power expanded well beyond anything previously known. The War Production Board set broad production allocations between military and civilian goods. Most Americans had ration books entitling them to scarce supplies of gasoline, meat, tires, sugar, and coffee, among other items. A nondefense worker was allowed only three gallons of gasoline a week. The Office of Price Administration controlled prices. The War Labor Board regulated working conditions and labor disputes. Government agencies expanded dramatically, and Washington became a big, bustling city. This vast growth of government was made acceptable not only by the war but also by the manner in which the expansion was conducted. Business leaders were sought for their skills, and the legitimacy of business accomplishment was once again acknowledged. Donald Nelson, an executive vice president of Sears, ran the War Production Board, though his leadership was often criticized as ineffectual; dozens of other executives assumed top positions. Some business leaders became popular heroes for their feats of production. Henry Kaiser, the shipbuilder, ultimately succeeded in reducing the time needed to build a new cargo ship to seventeen days. In general, Roosevelt abandoned the contentious politics of the 1930s and assumed, as Michael Barone has recently put it, "that the way to mobilize labor and business and the farmer was to allow each to make a hefty profit out of the war effort."[11] Of course, there was lots of grumbling during the war over rationing, price controls, and profiteering. But the complaints were generally subsumed by the resurgence of prosperity and, ultimately, the collective sense of triumph.

Even five decades later, the economy's wartime performance seems awesome. The United States did serve as the "arsenal of democracy"; about one eighth of U.S. armaments production was exported to the Allies. Beyond this, the economy created a standard of living that, on average, was probably higher than during the 1930s. True, a lot of civilian production was halted. Americans couldn't buy new cars, new appliances, or new houses. Anyone with a secure job in the 1930s was, considering these restrictions and rationing, worse off. But lots of people hadn't had jobs at all, and they were better off. Unemployment virtually disappeared; by 1943, the jobless rate was 1.9 percent. Food production soared. Between 1940 and 1944, it rose by more than one fifth, even though the number of farm workers dropped by 16 percent. One reason was enhanced mechanization; tractor use was up 25 percent. On top of all this, the war production itself was phenomenal. In the end, the United States simply overwhelmed both Germany and Japan with a war machine that—effectively removed from enemy attack—could not be matched. Between mid-1940 and mid-1945, armaments output included the following:

Warplanes	296,229
Tanks (including self-propelled guns)	102,451
Artillery pieces	372,431
Trucks	2,455,964
Warships	87,620
Cargo ships	5,425
Aircraft bombs (tons)	5,822,000
Small arms	20,086,061
Small arms ammunition (rounds)	44,000,000,000[12]

To historian William Manchester, a marine who served in the Pacific, the huge prosperity strengthened the nation's patriotism. "For tens of millions the war boom was in fact a bonanza, a Depression dream come true, and they felt guilty about it," he later wrote. "Not so guilty that they declined the money, to be sure . . . but contrite enough to make them join scrap drives, buy war bonds, serve in civilian defense units and once in a while buy a lonely soldier a drink." Manchester's point is too sweeping. Wartime patriotism was more than an artifact of prosperity. But prosperity did fundamentally alter the social climate. A Gallup Poll at the beginning of 1945 asked whether "you had to make any real sacrifice for the war." Almost two thirds of the respondents (64 percent) said no; among those who said yes, the most common reason was having a relative in the military.[13] The simple point is that the Depression's main economic problems had disappeared. So had the poisonous social and political climate of the 1930s. To be sure, there were plenty of wartime disagreements and disappointments. Allegations of war profiteering stirred outrage, as did occasional union strikes. But hardly anyone questioned the war's necessity or impugned the motives of the nation's leaders. There was a coming together in common goals, universal experiences, and shared joys and sorrows.

With hindsight, of course, we know that many of the popular lessons drawn from the war were oversimplified and romanticized. They were partial truths or self-serving myths. Social memory of war, for good or ill, is inevitably colored by triumph or defeat. Victory inevitably created a selective and self-serving recall of what actually had happened. At greater remove now, we can, perhaps, resist the impulse to sentimentalize or sanitize. In a recent book, historian William O'Neill of Rutgers University reminds us that the war was far from a universal success. The fact that it occurred at all represented a failure, because the war almost certainly could have been prevented if the United States, France, and Britain had acted earlier and more forcefully to Hitler's threat. It is worth recalling that 405,000 Americans died and that total worldwide deaths were probably somewhere between 40 million and 60 million. Though our mobilization was ultimately awesome, it was inexcusably tardy. As late as 1941, American soldiers trained with wooden guns. Even later, there was fierce bickering among government agencies over production goals. During the war, our strategy was often ill conceived. In the Pacific, interservice rivalry caused the Army (under General Douglas A. MacArthur) and the Navy (under Admiral Chester W. Nimitz) to have separate theaters, resulting in unnecessary island invasions and loss of life. Strategic bombing of Germany was largely a failure, and our conduct of the war was blotted by huge moral blind spots, from the mass internment of Japanese-Americans to ignoring the Holocaust.[14]

For individuals, the war was often a mix of horror, boredom, and fear—especially for those who fought it. In another recent book, the literary critic Paul Fussell, an army lieutenant and platoon leader who was wounded in France, noted dryly: "One reason soldiers' and sailors' letters homes are so little to be relied on by the historian of emotion and attitude is that they are composed largely to sustain the morale of the folks at home, to hint as little as possible at the real, worrisome circumstances of the writer. No one wrote: 'Dear Mother, I am scared to death.' " In one division, a quarter of the men admitted that at one time or another they had been so scared that they had vomited; a quarter said that at terrifying moments they'd lost control of their bowels and a tenth said they'd urinated in their pants.

Among combat veterans, there was little enthusiasm for more combat. Quite the opposite. The more combat soldiers had experienced, the more they dreaded it. A 1943 survey asked frontline troops about how they felt "about getting back into actual battle." Less than 1 percent of ordinary riflemen said they wanted "to get into it as soon as possible"; among winners of the Silver Star (the second highest decoration for valor), almost none did. About another 5 percent said they were "ready to go anytime." Just about everyone else disdained more combat: 29 percent said they hoped they wouldn't have to go but felt "if I go, I think I will do all right"; another 22 percent hoped they wouldn't have to go, because "I don't think I would do very well"; 15 percent felt they "had done their share—let others do theirs"; and 11 percent said they "couldn't stand more—afraid, nerves shot." Aside from the fact that soldiers kept these things to themselves, one reason that knowledge of the horror didn't become more widespread is that only a minority of those in the military were actual combatants. Of those in the Army, only about 20 percent were in combat divisions.

The more common wartime experience of soldiers, sailors, and airmen was what Fussell calls "chickenshit." This was more than the "inevitable inconveniences of military life: overcrowding and lack of privacy, tedious institutional cookery, deprivation of personality, general boredom." It was instead the "behavior that makes military life worse than it need be: petty harassment of the weak by the strong; open scrimmage for power and authority and prestige; sadism thinly disguised as necessary discipline; a constant 'paying off of old scores';

and insistence on the letter rather than the spirit of ordinances." In response to a questionnaire in 1942, one soldier gently protested: "We are entitled to the respect we have worked for and earned in civilian life." Military historian John Keegan has concluded that the war exposed 12 million U.S. servicemen to "a system of subordination and autocracy entirely alien to American values."[15]

Still, these traumatizing or bitter experiences did not alter the war's dominant lesson. This was simple: we won. With hindsight, the war was a transforming event in many large and small ways. It disrupted established institutions and habits of thinking. During the war, perhaps 27 million Americans moved for one reason or another, roughly 40 percent because they had to serve in the military and the rest because they wanted work in war plants or government. Considering that the U.S. population in 1940 was 132 million, this meant that roughly one in five Americans moved during the war. Some cities and localities were turned into boomtowns overnight. By 1944, more than 10 percent of California's population consisted of new arrivals, who had been drawn mainly by sprawling aircraft plants, busy shipyards, or bustling ports that were the disembarkation points for the Pacific theater. On the eve of war, California (like much of the West) seemed—by both those who lived there and those who didn't—to occupy a "colonial status" in relation to the economic and political power centers in the East. The West exported raw materials (foods, minerals) and imported manufactured products. Most major institutions were located in the East. By war's end, the situation had changed dramatically. California accounted for 17 percent of war production. Between 1939 and 1947, the state's manufacturing output more than tripled.[16]

Similar stories could be told about many aspects of American life. War enlarged and energized the nation's research establishment, creating—for the first time—an explicit partnership between the academy (university scientists and laboratories) and government. The atomic bomb was only the most visible product of this partnership. Radar (originally developed in England), antibiotics, numerically controlled machine tools, and computers were among the notable wartime advances. Women flooded the labor markets to relieve crippling shortages of workers and, in the process, performed jobs that had previously been considered off limits—as crane operators, welders, assembly workers. Although most women happily returned home after the war, a precedent had been set. The pressures to produce stimulated entirely new industries; at war's end, aluminum production (needed for aircraft) was 600 percent higher than it had been in 1929. Race relations, though not revolutionized, were permanently changed. In June 1941, President Roosevelt signed—after a threatened Negro demonstration in Washington—Executive Order 8802, which barred government contractors and agencies from job discrimination. In 1940, blacks' overall share of manufacturing jobs was actually lower than it had been in 1930; in the aircraft industry, blacks held only 240 jobs out of 100,000. But labor shortages and government pressure changed matters. In 1942, only 3 percent of war workers were black; by 1945, it was 8 percent. The federal government, for its part, increased its employment of blacks from 60,000 to 200,000. Government agencies moved against discrimination. In 1943, the War Labor Board outlawed wage differentials based on race; later that year, the National Labor Relations Board refused to certify contracts that excluded minorities.[17]

What the war demonstrated, in simple and stark fashion, was that the country was working again—both in a literal sense and in the larger sense that its institutions and ideas seemed to be succeeding. The war was for many Americans an all-consuming event, and there were many small and large shared experiences. In 1943, a Gallup Poll asked whether families had done any home canning of fruits and vegetables from victory gardens. Three quarters of the respondents said they had, with the average number of cans or jars being 165. With only slight exaggeration, the historian Geoffrey Perret has written of the war: "Without knowing it or intending it, the American people in the six years from 1939 to 1945 refreshed the springs of authority in society and politics, from the lowliest local school to the most imposing seats of power. It was a renaissance of the spirit and carried home to ordinary people the legitimacy of American ways, beliefs, aspirations and institutions. It was the supreme collective social experience in modern American history. Nothing like it has happened since, for in the unity of wartime a disparate people was fused into a community."[18]

But the satisfaction of victory did not translate into an explicit agenda for social or political action. People were impatient to get on with their lives. They wanted the troops home, and inconveniences that had been tolerated with relative cheer during the war—housing shortages, no nylon stockings—quickly became intolerable. Simply getting from war to peace was a mammoth leap. There were strikes as workers pressed for higher wages. There was confusion about the end of price controls. And there were fears of another depression, once the postwar spending spree was exhausted. In 1946, 60 percent of Americans rated a depression a strong possibility within a decade. As late as 1947, President Truman declared that "the job at hand today is to see to it that America is not ravaged by recurring depressions and long periods of unemployment." Yet, few Americans desired social experimentation. In 1944, the Democratic Senate had rejected legislation that would have improved unemployment insurance coverage for war workers during the reconversion period. Two Gallup Polls (one in August 1943 and the other in April 1945) asked whether respondents wanted reforms after the war. In both cases, majorities said no; support for reform was only 32 percent in the first poll, 39 percent in the second. But ill will toward government was not so great that Americans weren't willing to use it if necessary. In a 1945 poll, 42 percent of respondents said government would have to provide jobs for the unemployed within the next five years.[19]

WHAT THE WAR fostered was a vague pragmatism that recognized few hard lines between governmental and private responsibilities. By and large, Americans did not want to revert either to the 1920s, when business had been the nation's dominant institutional force, or to the New Deal, when government had played that role. They wanted something in between, and the wartime model of business-government collaboration seemed workable. The war's prosperity had refurbished the reputation of business without restoring the twenties' luster. Big corporations, though not adored, were seen as an essential source of material goods and technology. "For the majority of Americans by 1945," as historian John Morton Blum has written, "size and abundance appeared to march hand in hand." But having lived through Depression and war, most Americans knew they often couldn't control their own destinies. A twenty-two-year-old bombardier put it this way in 1944: "The more I think about it—and I've thought about it a lot lately—the more it looks as if I've been a cog in one thing or another since the day I was born. Whenever I get set to do what I want to do, something a whole lot bigger than me comes along and shoves me back into place."[20] In short, Americans had accepted, with some regret, the need for both Big Business and Big Government to protect them against large tragedies.

In the end, the war provided a metaphor for all our social problems: war itself. Once a problem had been identified, it became the enemy and could—as the Second World War had shown—be defeated with the right tactics and weapons. Sometimes the metaphor was applied explicitly, as with the 1960s War on Poverty or the 1980s "war on drugs." More often, it was simply a frame of mind that Americans adopted when confronted with society's imperfections. Deciding what problems existed, how they might be solved and by whom (whether government, private business, individuals, or some combination of all three) slowly became the substance of politics. To some extent, of course, this has always been true. The change after 1945, however, was that many more areas of national life became potential subjects for discussion and possible action. The political and social arena became more open-ended, unbounded by past notions of what could (or should) be done. Both the war and the Depression seemed to discredit the notion that "just leaving things alone" was the best way to proceed. The postwar style of politics would blend the two experiences into the "politics of problem solving." The phrase conveyed a faith that, as a nation, we might solve whatever problems presented themselves. This approach belonged to neither party and was ultimately shared by both.

But none of this was obvious at the end of the war. If Americans had more confidence in their collective problem-solving capacity, most did not have a master list of problems that needed to be solved. Plenty of ambitious schemes floated about—from national health insurance to guaranteed jobs for everyone—but none commanded a majority among the public or Congress. In general, the spirit of reform that had characterized the Depression had ebbed. Democrats had suffered severe congressional losses beginning in 1938, when their majority had dropped by 70 seats. There were more losses in 1942, and Republicans captured both the House and Senate in 1946. Even among many ardent New Dealers, the failed experiments of the thirties and the wartime experience had had a chastening effect. Most had abandoned the "efforts to create cooperative associational arrangements [i.e., the National Recovery Administration], the vigorous if short-lived anti-monopoly crusades, the overt celebration of government, and the open skepticism towards capitalism and its captains," as historian Alan Brinkley has noted.[21]

Americans didn't yet feel entitled. Postwar ambitions were more modest. Most Americans simply hoped for a period of prosperity and tranquility as a respite to the turmoil and uncertainty of the previous fifteen years. They wanted to be rid of the fears and frustrations of Depression and war. They yearned for private pleasures, not public agendas. But what had changed was the popular willingness to abide obstacles to those pleasures. Tolerance for passivity in the face of social collapse had diminished. Confidence in the ability of collective action to deal with national problems had increased. The seeds of entitlement had been planted, even if it would take the infectious prosperity of the early postwar years to make them grow.

3

The Cult of Affluence

※ ※ ※ ※

IF YOU GREW UP in the 1950s (as I did), you were a daily witness to the marvels of affluence. There was a seemingly endless array of new gadgets and machines. At home, you watched television. At school, you were vaccinated against polio, until then a dreaded disease. Outside, you could occasionally gaze upward and catch the distant vapor trail of a new jet. You watched in wonder until it vanished. Cars were becoming ever bigger, fancier, and more powerful. Atomic energy seemed to promise an inexhaustible source of cheap energy. No problem seemed beyond our power to assault and conquer. Good times and the ingenuity of American technology: these were not lessons learned, they were experiences absorbed. The presence of so much prosperity impressed almost everyone and had the effect of cultivating a new postwar consciousness. The seeds that had been planted during the Depression and the Second World War germinated, grew, and blossomed in the first two decades after 1945. Our everyday experience seemed to confirm the lessons of war and shaped a new set of popular expectations.

The judgments of the 1950s, both at the time and in hindsight, have tended to miss the decade's true significance. At the time, it was dismissed by its critics as boring and complacent. College students were termed "the silent generation," because they rarely complained and seemed to lack a social conscience. President Dwight D. Eisenhower, it was said, played too much golf. By contrast, the 1950s have more recently acquired a nostalgic glow and a funky reputation. Cars had fins, rock 'n' roll began, and Elvis reigned. American self-confidence and power were at their peaks. In popular memory, it was a blissful time, but in fact, the 1950s seem more tranquil now than they did then. The decade started with the Korean War and ended with its third recession (these occurred in 1953–1954, 1957–1958, and 1960–1961). Along the way, jarring events regularly punctured the presumed calm. In the early 1950s, there was McCarthyism. In 1957, the Soviet Union launched *Sputnik*, the first space satellite, rattling Americans' sense of superiority and security. Also in 1957, Eisenhower dispatched troops to Little Rock, Arkansas, to integrate Central High School; that was a disturbing evidence of smoldering racial tensions that, in the 1960s, would explode.

But these headline events, for better or worse, omit the decade's most important development: we began—as never before in American history—to take prosperity for granted. Certainly, most middle-class children (the core of the postwar baby boom) did. Prosperity was all that they had ever known. Their parents, too, were increasingly convinced because the depth and duration of postwar prosperity seemed to prove that something new (and basically wonderful) had happened. To be sure, there were those inconvenient recessions. But they were trifling compared with the Depression of the 1930s, which, of course, was the comparison that most adults made. The 1957–1958 recession was the decade's worst. Yet, unemployment averaged only 6.8 percent in 1958 (for the decade as a whole, the average was 4.5 percent), a far cry from the Depression.[1] We seemed to be erasing the evils of the business cycle and engineering a constant rise of living standards. Because economic want and insecurity had been so central to most people's ordinary anxieties for so long, the sense that we were slowly subduing them contributed to a general optimism that other national problems might be similarly overcome.

These notions came to full fruition in the 1960s, as the advance of prosperity continued and actually accelerated. All during these years, millions of Americans were moving into more spacious suburban homes, which—though they had their critics—represented a real and much desired improvement for most of their owners. When the political scientist James Q. Wilson described how early suburbanites felt in Southern California (where he grew up), he might well have been talking about the residents of most new postwar suburbs:

> The important thing to know about Southern California is that the people who live there, who grew up there, love it. Not just in the way one has an attachment to a hometown, any hometown, but the way people love the realization that they have found the right mode of life. People who live in Southern California are not richer or better educated than those who live in New York; the significant point about them is that they don't live in New York, and don't want to. If they did, they—the average Los Angeleno (my family, for example)—would have lived most of their lives in a walkup flat in, say, the Yorkville section of Manhattan or not far off Flatbush Avenue in Brooklyn. Given their income in 1930, life would have been crowded, noisy, cold, threatening—in short, *urban*. In Long Beach or Inglewood or Huntington Park or Bellflower, by contrast, life was carried on in a detached house with a lawn in front and a car in the garage, part of a quiet neighborhood, with no crime (except kids racing noisy cars), no cold, no smells, no congestion.[2]

It was not just suburbia. The movement into new homes with lawns, garages, and privacy was simply a part of the larger mosaic of material progress. The proliferation of new conveniences made ordinary life less demanding and less physically exhausting. As factories grew more automated, they became less punishing on their workers. Indeed, factory automation meant that a rising proportion of Americans found cleaner, safer, and less arduous jobs in offices and stores. By 1970, about 60 percent of the workforce consisted of white-collar or service jobs (managers, administrators, teachers, professionals, sales workers, office workers), up from 39 percent in 1930. The whole fabric of everyday life was undergoing a massive transformation, driven mainly by an enormous surge of prosperity and technological advance. The effect was to foster a sense of mastery, because so many old worries and conflicts seemed to be receding. As early as 1952,

Frederick Lewis Allen contended that "an incredible expansion of industrial and business activity" in the first half of the twentieth century had led to a historic subordination "of capitalism to democratic ends." Big Business, which had once seemed threatening to average Americans, had—by its very bounty—actually had a profoundly liberating and leveling effect on their lives.[3]

In 1966, John Brooks made much the same argument in *The Great Leap: The Past Twenty-five Years in America*. Brooks found that the quarter century since 1939 had brought "rapid and far-reaching changes" in American life that were "unprecedented" in the nation's history. "Everybody is someone," he wrote. Mass production and rising incomes seemed to be reducing class-based distinctions. "The comfortably off have become our great central mass," he found. Allen had noted the same phenomenon fourteen years earlier, in his book *The Big Change*, calling it the "all-American standard" and observing that "millions of families in our cities and towns, and on the farms, have been lifted from poverty or near-poverty to a status where they can enjoy what has been traditionally considered a middle-class way of life: decent clothes for all, an opportunity to buy a better automobile, install an electric refrigerator, provide the housewife with a decently attractive kitchen, go to the dentist, pay insurance premiums, and so on indefinitely."[4]

Reading between the lines, the drift of things seemed clear. Economic concerns would fade from ordinary worries, and our growing wealth would, spontaneously or otherwise, overcome other social or personal problems. Since its beginnings, for example, America had been a country of vast regional differences and conflicts. These now seemed to be narrowing, as television, new highways, and long-distance telephone service drew the nation—in time, income, and lifestyle—closer together. In 1958, the Brooklyn Dodgers moved to Los Angeles and the New York Giants moved to San Francisco. For the first time, the West Coast had major league baseball. Likewise, the South had long been the nation's poorest region, regarded with suspicion and condescension by outsiders. Yet by the 1960s, its living standards were rapidly approaching the national average, and by the 1970s, it was being lauded as part of the Sunbelt. By the latter decade, its per capita income, which had traditionally been 50 to 60 percent of the national average, had risen to 75 to 85 percent of the national average. Air-conditioning, among other things, enabled the South to enjoy living standards comparable to those of the rest of the country, as historian Raymond Arsenault has noted. "Can you conceive a Walt Disney World over in the 95-degree summers of central Florida without its air-conditioned hotels?" asked a southern columnist in 1978. Or would any other corporation open "a big plant where their workers would have to spend much of their time mopping brows and cursing mosquitoes?"[5]

It was changes like these that made the 1950s and the 1960s seem so alive with possibilities. Even now, the most impressive advances in material well-being of the past half century seem disproportionately bunched into the first twenty-five years after the Second World War. Consider a list of what are, arguably, the ten most influential changes in consumer products and services since the war:[6]

1. *Television*: In 1945, almost no one had one. By 1960, nearly nine of ten households did (the exact figure was 87 percent). Although color TV was first approved by government in 1953, there wasn't much of it until the late 1960s; even in 1963, NBC—the leader—had only 40 hours a week of color programming. By 1994, almost all homes (97 percent) had color TVs.

2. *Jet travel*: Introduced in 1958, commercial jets made flying faster and less expensive. In 1940, U.S. airlines carried 3.5 million passengers. Thirty years later, the number had risen to 154 million, and in the mid-1990s, the total exceeded 400 million.

3. *Air-conditioning*: Except in major public buildings, it hardly existed before the Second World War. By 1980, nearly three quarters of homes in the South had it, as did more than half of all homes nationwide. The proportion has steadily risen since, as more new homes came equipped with central air-conditioning or old homes were refitted with window or central units. More than 70 percent of homes now have air-conditioning.

4. *Long-distance phone service*: In 1945, only a minority of households (46 percent) even had a phone. Long-distance calls were expensive and relatively rare; they were still placed by operators, and waits on holidays were long. Direct dialing began in 1951, but it wasn't until 1965 that a majority of calls were dialed directly. Between 1940 and 1970, the average number of daily long-distance calls rose from about 3 million to nearly 26 million. By the mid-1990s, it exceeded 150 million.

5. *Interstate highways*: Passed by Congress in 1956, the interstate highway program made driving quicker and safer. Though interstates constitute only 1 percent of all roads, they carry about a fifth of all traffic. By and large, they're also much safer than other roads with accident rates half the overall national average.

6. *Automatic washers and dryers*: In 1940, dryers barely existed, and only a minority of households had cumbersome wringer-washers. By 1960, nearly three quarters of households had modern electric washers—and many of those who didn't lived in apartments. Today, about 70 percent of households also have automatic dryers.

7. *Antibiotics*: Only in the Second World War was penicillin, the first modern antibiotic, used widely in military hospitals. After the war, it—and, later, other antibiotics—became a staple of modern medicine, used to treat everything from pneumonia to sore throats and wounds.

8. *Social Security and private pensions*: Although Social Security was created in 1935, the expansion of benefits and coverage didn't really occur until after the war. In 1945, only about half a million Americans received benefits; by the mid-1990s, the number exceeded 42 million, of whom more than 26 million were retirees. (The others received benefits under Social Security's disability program or were widows or the children of beneficiaries.) In 1940, private pensions were negligible; by 1990, about half of full-time workers had coverage.

9. *Health insurance*: In 1940, patients paid roughly four fifths of their medical costs directly. By 1990, private and government insurance paid nearly three quarters of all health costs. There was a gradual expansion of private coverage, and in 1965, the government created Medicare (insurance for the elderly) and Medicaid (insurance for the poor).

10. *The Pill*: Introduced in 1960, oral contraceptives revolutionized birth control. They made it easier for families to plan their children and for unmarried couples to engage in sex without having children.

A list like this, of course, is subjective. It's certainly possible to quarrel with what should and shouldn't be on it. For example, the GI Bill of Rights, passed in 1944, subsidized veterans' college tuition and popularized the notion that middle-class Americans should attend college. Subsequently, there was a vast expansion of colleges and universities, and the porportion of Americans going on to some type of post-secondary education sharply increased. In 1940, there were fewer than 1.5 million college students, and only about one in twenty Americans had a college degree. Fifty years later, there were nearly 14 million in institutions of higher learning, and about one in five Americans had a college degree. Perhaps this qualifies as one of the ten most important changes.[7] But that's not the point. Nor is it important that there have been other major new products since the 1960s—personal computers and VCRs, to name but two. The real point is that the advances of the early postwar decades had a profound impact on how we lived and how we thought about our life prospects.

What was routine and unremarkable altered. Social Security and pensions meant that retirement became commonplace; as late as 1948, nearly half the men over sixty-five worked. Washers and dryers radically reduced the burden of housework, making it easier for women to take paid jobs. Antibiotics meant that common cuts and infections were no longer, as they had been, life threatening. Disease (and the anxiety associated with disease) declined dramatically. The spread of health insurance made medical care seem a "right": something due people when needed. The Pill was so convenient that it opened new vistas of sexual freedom or experimentation. Television, jet travel, long-distance phoning, and new highways created new experiences. Even in the early 1960s, only a third of all Americans had ever flown; by the late 1980s, the proportion had risen to three quarters and included most adult Americans.[8] And these changes merely skimmed the surface of what was occurring. In 1986, Consumers Union published a book called *I'll Buy That!* appraising the most significant consumer products of the previous half century. Much of what we now take for granted dates from these early postwar years. The original modern detergent, Tide, was first marketed in 1947. National credit cards began with the Diners Club card in 1950, followed by the American Express card in 1958. Synthetic fibers, led by nylon and polyester, boomed after 1945. Before the war, there had essentially been no synthetics (nylon appeared in the late 1930s).[9]

It is hard now to think of ordinary life without these changes, and, naturally enough, so many conspicuous advances had a huge impact on popular consciousness. In 1958, economist John Kenneth Galbraith of Harvard published *The Affluent Society*, whose title captured the new sense of expectation. The overriding social problem, it seemed, had become how the country might spend its newfound wealth. On this, sharp disagreements remained. Although Galbraith and others argued that more government spending (on education, culture, and the environment) would most improve the nation's quality of life, there was no real consensus. Rather, the consensus was more narrow: that the country could turn its attention to these larger questions precisely because it could count on prosperity. The confidence in ongoing prosperity was not so much a conscious conceit as a reflexive generalization of postwar experience. Progress had triumphed; ever broadening affluence would continue indefinitely. This was an enormous revolution in domestic psychology and politics.

NOT SURPRISINGLY, prosperity worked a comparable revolution in foreign affairs. The old orthodoxy crumbled and was replaced by new ideas that also presumed great confidence in the power (and certainty) of prosperity, this time global rather than domestic. The then prevailing analysis of the causes of the world war assigned a large role to the Depression, which had (the argument went) abetted the rise of Hitler. In turn, trade wars—intensified by high tariffs and competitive currency devaluations among nations—had, it was thought, worsened the Depression.* American officials were determined not to repeat these mistakes. Open trade would bolster global prosperity. In 1942, American and British economists had begun work on postwar international trade and payments systems. The onset of the Cold War simply added urgency. When Americans examined Europe, they saw a series of small, protected markets that contrasted vividly with the vast and open U.S. market. To Americans, the huge U.S. market made possible large-scale investments with long production runs and low costs. This efficiency led to higher living standards, which fostered social peace and political stability. Americans felt that Europe should follow the same formula: merge its markets and ex-

*Recent scholarship casts doubt on some of these ideas. Although the Depression abetted Hitler's rise to power, it is less clear that trade wars and competitive devaluations were major causes of the Depression. More likely, they were consequences. My view is that the futile defense of the gold standard was the primary economic cause of the Depression. For a fuller discussion, see pages 92–95.

pand trade. Countries that traded together wouldn't fight each other. Commercialism was better than nationalism. American leaders repeatedly expressed confidence in these ideas. Here is Dwight Eisenhower in 1951 speaking to a London audience: "Once united, the farms and factories of France and Belgium, the foundries of Germany, the rich farm lands of Holland and Denmark, the skilled labor of Italy, will produce miracles for the common good."[10] Here is Will Clayton, a principal architect of the Marshall Plan, lauding free trade: "Nations which act as enemies in the market place cannot long be friends at the council table."

The Marshall Plan, named after Secretary of State George Marshall, the wartime chief of staff, became the proving ground for these theories. In the winter of 1946–1947, Europe had suffered exceptionally cold weather and severe snowstorms. Food and fuel stocks were depleted; deliveries of scarce supplies were impeded. The following summer's harvest was the worst in a century. Large Communist parties in Italy and France were gaining strength. The Marshall Plan poured $13.3 billion of aid into Europe between 1948 and 1951 (a comparable effort today would total more than $300 billion), enabling Europeans to buy—mostly from America—the food, fuel, raw materials, and machinery necessary to restart their economies and rebuild their war-ravaged societies. There was a conscious effort by American officials to promote a common market in Europe and to bolster those Europeans (most prominently, Jean Monnet) who advocated such an arrangement. As a condition for receiving U.S. aid, European countries were required to explore ways to remove the continent's pervasive trade and economic restrictions. The plan succeeded—between 1947 and 1951, industrial production in Europe grew 37 percent, triggering a long expansion that lasted through the 1950s and 1960s. The practical possibilities of Communist takeovers in France and Italy soon receded.[11]

By and large, Americans justifiably congratulated themselves. The Marshall Plan's success reinforced popular attitudes toward the world. Though devised by diplomats, the plan's basic approach was rooted in American ideas and ideals. Despite some opposition, it passed Congress with overwhelming bipartisan support. An opinion poll taken just after Marshall's proposal in June 1947 showed 57 percent of the public in favor (21 percent disapproved, 22 percent had no opinion). American businesses, confident of their superiority, opened their factories to European industrialists who wanted to learn better management techniques. The Acme Galvanizing Company in Milwaukee stretched a sign across its shop door reading: "Welcome to U.K. Specialist Team No. 6." An executive of Midvale Company, a maker of machine tools, wrote after a visit: "We here at Midvale hope that we were able to import to the Norwegian Delegation some of the many benefits of our American way of life and our free enterprise system." The Europeans, for their part, were stunned. "The detailed information placed at our disposal by all these firms has been astonishing," marveled one British executive. A French visitor wrote: "We wish to thank very sincerely all the American manufacturers who opened their doors, and sometimes their accounting books so widely; they can be assured of our discretion."[12] *

The significance of the Marshall Plan was that abstract convictions—the belief in the political benefits of prosperity—were proven in practice. The ideas behind the plan became the model for postwar foreign policy. Although ordinary Americans did not debate them in detail, the policies fit the broad contours of public opinion. The United States' immediate economic interests were subordinated to the larger foreign policy goal of a prosperous world. In trade negotiations, the United States often granted more concessions than it received. At the initial talks in 1947 establishing the General Agreement on Tariffs and Trade (GATT)—the umbrella agreement setting rules for global trade—American negotiators made trade concessions worth about 50 percent more than those they obtained. The idea was to strengthen the economies of U.S. allies by keeping American markets open, and any danger to U.S. industries was seen as minimal. The same approach was adopted toward Japan. In the early 1950s, a National Security Council study concluded that "increasing access to markets in the United States" was needed by Japan to stem the "eco-

---

*Some modern scholars question whether the Marshall Plan was so pivotal. In this view, the economic "crisis" of 1947–1948 was less grave than portrayed and Europe would have recovered spontaneously. That being so, Communist takeovers in France and Italy would not have happened even if the United States had done nothing. Perhaps. But American economic historians Charles Kindleberger, who was involved in devising the Marshall Plan, and Barry Eichengreen both argue that the Marshall Plan was critical. Regardless of the economic verdict, the political verdict is unequivocal: people at the time—in Europe and the United States—thought the Marshall Plan was decisive.[13]

nomic deterioration and falling living standards" that made it a "fertile ground for communist subversion." Americans felt no threat from Japanese industry. The United States would always enjoy a trade surplus with Japan, Secretary of State John Foster Dulles said in 1955, because Japan's products were so inferior.[14]

IN OUR DOMESTIC and foreign policies, the importance of the early postwar decades was not that they were problem-free. It was that problems were faced and apparently surmounted. Thus did the politics of problem solving, which was the immediate postwar impulse, evolve into a wider sense of entitlement: an ill-defined feeling that any and all problems could and should be solved. The two concepts blurred and blended. Success at home fed confidence abroad, and vice versa. In foreign policy, Americans began to think of the supremacy of the United States as part of the natural order of things. The Second World War was increasingly seen as a seminal event that confirmed the inherent superiority of American ideas and institutions and, as a result, meant that the United States was destined to lead the world along the path of progress. Americans thought of themselves as less selfish, more idealistic, and more productive than other peoples. Coupled with a reflexive fear of communism, these ideas bred the overconfidence that led to Vietnam. In his prizewinning biography of John Paul Vann—an American colonel who fought in Vietnam from the early 1960s until his death in 1972—Neil Sheehan captured the prevailing mood. Vann embraced, Sheehan wrote,

> the set of beliefs characteristic of the United States that had emerged from World War II as the greatest power on earth. . . . He was convinced that having gained the preeminence it was destined to achieve, the United States would never relinquish the position. He did not see the United States as using its power for self-satisfaction. He saw the United States as a stern yet benevolent authority that enforced peace and brought prosperity to the peoples of the non-communist nations, sharing the bounty of its enterprise and technology with those who had been denied a fruitful life by poverty and social injustice and bad government.[15]

What entitlement meant at home was that, as never before, Americans would be free to do what they had always been promised—to join in the "pursuit of happiness." In the 1960 presidential campaign, John F. Kennedy pledged that he would "get the country moving again," as if it hadn't already been moving fairly well in the 1950s. (Of course, the worst recession of the decade had ended two years before.) To some extent, the election was a referendum on the future. On the one hand were those who were inclined to let well enough alone and to continue haphazardly along a path of gradual social improvement. On the other were those who felt that this approach was too lazy and complacent toward America's remaining faults. The election was close, but it was decided in the direction of greater exertion. That was the point. Good was no longer good enough. All problems should be confronted and conquered. The frontiers of progress were limitless. Once in office, Kennedy was far more cautious than his rhetoric, going slowly, for example, on civil rights and economic policy. But his enduring historic significance may lie more in his rhetoric than his actions. "Man holds in his hands," he said in his inaugural address, "the power to abolish all forms of human poverty."

The journalist and novelist Tom Wolfe has suggested that the new mood has become more or less permanent and can be ended only by a major economic collapse or social catastrophe. America has "enjoyed one of the most stupendous economic booms in all of history. It started about 1943 . . . [and] has continued, unabated really, [with] a few little blips up and down" ever since, he said in 1989. It "has given us . . . a sense of immunity to ordinary dangers." To Wolfe, the permanence of prosperity had shattered many old taboos and allowed Americans to explore and flaunt their individuality as never before. Prosperity shook family stability, because people felt less needy of the family's sheltering. It encouraged more sexual openness and partnering, because if people had their material wants satisfied, they could pursue other pleasures more easily. It relaxed the moral and financial stigma against debt, because unending prosperity would enable most borrowers to service their loans forever. Permanent prosperity, in short, meant (or seemed to give rise to) endless possibilities. "We are in a period," Wolfe reflected, "of every man and every woman as an aristocrat. In every walk of life people more and more feel free to indulge themselves in the whims, the instincts, the freedoms that formerly only aristocrats dared to assume."[16] Although he overstated the case, he caught its essence. People thought (and continue to think) they deserved aristocratic opportunities, even if they didn't always have them.

JUST WHO COINED the word "entitlement" and when precisely it came into common usage isn't clear. William Safire noted that the term was used in an obscure 1944 law, to no apparent effect. It made little impression until the early 1980s.[17] Norman Ornstein of the American Enterprise Institute found the word "entitlement authority" used in the 1974 Budget and Impoundment Control Act and observed that Ronald Reagan was the first president to use the word extensively, possibly because he was "tired of getting beaten up every time he mentioned Social Security, and wanted a broader and more neutral term." In April 1981, *U.S. News & World Report* referred to a "revolution" in entitlements; later in the year, *Time* and *Business Week* used the word. In this sense, entitlement refers to specific government programs, whose benefits are promised if people (or institutions) meet explicit legal standards.[18]

But the word has also acquired a broader meaning—namely, a firm popular expectation that some specific or general outcome will occur, whether or not it is formally embodied in law. The distinction of introducing this broader use may belong to Yale Law School professor Charles Reich. In a 1965 law review article, he wrote:

> Society today is built around entitlement. The automobile dealer has his franchise, the doctor and lawyer their professional licenses, the worker his union membership, contract, and pension rights, the executive his contract and stock options; all are devices to aid security and independence. Many of the most important of these entitlements now flow from government: subsidies to farmers and businessmen . . . and channels for television stations; long term contracts for defense, space and education; social security pensions for individuals. Such sources of security, whether private or public, are no longer regarded as luxuries or gratuities; to the recipients they are essentials, fully deserved, and in no sense a form of charity.[19]

It was in this sense that Americans began to feel themselves entitled in the early postwar decades. They expected to have "security" and "independence," which would somehow be provided or guaranteed by someone or some institution, but which was also "fully deserved." Entitlement, in Reich's formulation, was bestowed, extracted, or perhaps extorted. It rarely if ever seemed to be earned. It simply happened. Americans began to expect things from their government, their businesses, and other social institutions that they had never previously expected—though they may have wanted them. The public agenda of politics and government became more open-ended. If we were getting ever richer, then we could eliminate the last remnants of poverty and racism. If the environment was getting dirtier (or a dirtier environment seemed less tolerable), then we were wealthy enough to clean it up. And finally, if America was wealthy enough and imaginative enough to accomplish these feats for itself, then it could show the rest of the world how to do the same.

Such expansive notions affected Americans' personal expectations. People shouldn't have to worry about job security as long as they did their jobs adequately. Moreover, work should be satisfying and rewarding, not just remunerative. When people got sick, they should receive the best care that modern American medicine was capable of providing. All Americans ought to have the opportunity to go to college, own a home, and enjoy a good retirement—not just a period of vegetating before death but a time ("the golden years") to reap the fruits of their labor. Women, once confined to the home, should be able to pursue careers. No one should be trapped in loveless or perhaps hateful marriages by tradition; if a mistake had been made, then easier divorce would give couples a second chance or, at least, freedom. Those less inclined to traditional relationships (homosexuals, for example) should be able to pursue their own lifestyles without being ostracized or penalized. Not all these ideas were embraced by everyone everywhere; but they achieved widespread acceptance.

By the end of the 1970s, pollster Daniel Yankelovich began to discover in his surveys (and he was not alone) that assured affluence was driving a new ethic of "self-fulfillment" that often discarded "many of the traditional rules of personal conduct." The new rules of self-fulfillment permitted "more sexual freedom . . . [and] put less emphasis on sacrifice 'for its own sake.' " It also valued self-expression and meaningful work. In some ways, the demand for self-fulfillment became the ultimate entitlement.[20] At some point, entitlement —this bundle of broad and ill-defined feelings—became an independent sensibility in its own right. It became disconnected from the experiences that produced it and assumed a meaning and momentum all its own. It didn't belong to any one generation or group. It affected almost everyone in some way, and it altered Americans' attitudes toward the country's major institutions.

Americans increasingly recognized that their well-being depended on their relationships with large commercial, cultural, and political institutions. Prosperity depended on government economic policy and corporate performance. Job security depended on companies. Retirement depended more on Social Security and corporate pensions than on private savings. Health care depended on employer-paid or government insurance. Americans increasingly defined their well-being in terms of how well large institutions were performing and how well such institutions were delivering on their explicit or implicit promises. Individual effort and responsibility were diminished and, to some extent, devalued. Institutions were expected to deliver. If problems weren't solved and promises weren't kept, then some institution or set of leaders was at fault. So much prosperity was, as Wolfe suggested, intoxicating. We were entitled.

4

Prosperity's Broken Promise

⚓ ⚓ ⚓ ⚓

ENTITLEMENT IS A MIRAGE. Its essence is the quest for control. Americans do not want to be at the whim of unpredictable events or destructive social trends. No one ever does, of course, but the postwar illusion has been that we might attain such bliss. We could create prosperity, eliminate poverty, cure disease, advance social justice, foster racial harmony, and ensure global peace. Enlightened thinking and rising wealth would confer control over most of the social, economic, and political conditions that might threaten us. Our overall sense of entitlement is the sum total of all our individual entitlements—and then something more, a larger social calm. Our present letdown stems from the gap between our idealized society and the one we actually experience. Most of us do not suffer from the most visible defects of modern America: crime, poverty, homelessness, unemployment, corporate failures, or any number of others (say, AIDS or lack of health insurance). But all these problems are unnerving reminders of national imperfections seemingly beyond our capacity to repair; and what's worse, no one can be absolutely sure of being spared some or many of them. Americans are hypersensitive to life's insecurities, precisely because we have imagined that we were banishing them.

The absence of this ultimate entitlement—peace of mind—helps explain the postwar paradox: If American society has, by and large, been so successful, why do so many Americans feel so dejected about the results? The answer is that most Americans expected to be unburdened of their anxieties and insecurities, or at any rate many of them. People still feel entitled to this sort of relief, but they are regularly rebuffed—sometimes by daily experience and, more often, by the images of a flawed society that flash before them on television, in newspapers, and in magazines. We feel shortchanged, and the constant presentation of society's defects and dangers makes us feel more vulnerable to them. These anxieties and frustrations then discredit our major institutions (Congress, the presidency, business, the media), which are blamed for society's shortcomings. There is an undercurrent of betrayal that makes people willing to believe the worst of our institutions and leaders. Entitlement signifies a set of false expectations, whose open-ended nature means that—like a mechanical rabbit—it can never be caught.

The first contemporary American social theorist to recognize this predicament was Daniel Bell, who described it in his 1976 book, *The Cultural Contradictions of Capitalism.* To Bell, it was already obvious that American society (and, indeed, all advanced democratic societies) had generated an outpouring of new demands that were "not just the claims of the minorities, the poor or disadvantaged; they are the claims of *all* groups in society, claims for protections and rights—in short *entitlements*" (Italics in the original). At some point, he noted, the "revolution of rising entitlements" (a phrase he derived from Tocqueville's "revolution of rising expectations") might overwhelm society's capacity to satisfy them: "When everyone in society joins in the demand for more, expecting this as a matter of right, and resources are limited . . . , then one begins to see the basis for the tension between the demands in the polity and the limitations set by the economy."[1] Today, Bell's prophecy seems understated. Beyond economic claims, entitlement has also come to encompass a much broader category of claims—from job security to health insurance—that are legal, political, or psychological in nature.

When multiplied repeatedly, these unqualified claims create precisely the sort of economic and political congestion that Bell predicted. Many entitlements are mutually inconsistent: that is, the rights and benefits that some people expect cannot be met without infringing on the rights and benefits that other people expect. The crippling illusion of entitlement has been to portray most social, economic, and (sometimes) personal concerns as "problems" that can, therefore, be "solved." If they can be solved, then they *should* be solved; people are "entitled" to solutions. The trouble is that many important public and private concerns are not problems in this sense. Rather, they are often permanent conditions or distasteful choices. Some conditions can be mitigated; others must simply be endured. Choices force us to select among things that are inconsistent, though they all may be desirable individually. Americans have not adequately distinguished among problems that are genuinely soluble, those that aren't, and those that aren't worth the effort. We have wanted every wrong righted, every social or economic defect eliminated. We have not simply wanted prosperity: we have expected government and business to create it without interruption. We have not simply wanted better health care; we have expected everyone to have the best health care available. We have not simply wanted a cleaner environment; we have wanted a pure environment. And so on.

Failure and disappointment are preordained. Opinion surveys have asked for years whether Americans have a "great deal of confidence, only some confidence or hardly an confidence at all" in major institutions. As is well known, the declines have been dramatic. The following table gives the proportion of respondents who have a "great deal" of confidence in Congress, the executive branch (the presidency), major corporations, the press, higher education, and the medical profession.

Confidence in Institutions, 1966–1994[2]

	1966	1975	1985	1994
Congress	42%	13%	16%	8%
Executive branch	41	13	15	12
Major companies	55	19	17	19
The press	29	26	16	13
Colleges, universities	61	36	35	25
Medicine	73	43	35	23

This disillusion is often ascribed to specific events: Vietnam, Watergate, Iran-contra. To be sure, these episodes have generated plenty of popular anger and angst. Vietnam especially stands out as a source of wrenching social strife and national self-doubt. But these headline events only partially explain ongoing public pessimism, because the events have passed while the pessimism has persisted. The other pat theory for disillusion is that the economy and personal income have stagnated. The trouble with this explanation is that they haven't. As noted earlier, economic growth has slowed since 1970 and the slowdown has been demoralizing. In a country as diverse as ours, the obsession with prosperity is natural. Economic growth is the lowest common denominator: something that almost everyone endorses. It embodies the American Dream of "getting ahead." It appeals across class, racial, religious, and regional lines. When Frederick Lewis Allen praised the "all-American standard" and John Brooks declared that "everyone is someone," they meant that everyone's incomes were rising and that living standards were converging. The slowdown of income growth and an increase of inequality (those at the top have done better than those at the bottom) have dispelled some of that good feeling. Still, these trends need to be kept in perspective. They constitute a slowdown—not stagnation.*

In an evocative essay, Nicholas Lemann tracked down people he found in an archive of photographs of the 1940s. Interviewing them in the early 1980s, he found that "[they] thought, as a general proposition, that American life had gone downhill since those days, but their own lives had always gotten better."[3] So it still seems. Most Americans live better than their counterparts did in, say, 1970—let alone 1960 or 1940. Homes have gotten bigger; the typical new home now is 40 percent larger than its counterpart in 1970. They are stocked with more appliances (air conditioners, microwave ovens) and gadgets than ever before. In 1994, 37 percent of households had home computers and 58 percent had telephone answering machines.[4] (Neither was even available in 1970.)

Moreover, some commonly cited income statistics understate gains in living standards. For example, Americans now receive more health care than ever, much of it paid by employer-provided or gov-

* The slowdown is discussed in more detail in Part II, "The New Capitalism."

ernment health insurance. Family income statistics, which measure only cash income, miss this. Likewise, Americans enjoy cleaner air and water than a few decades ago and safer working conditions. These are gains in living standards that don't fatten paychecks and escape conventional income statistics.

Even the poor generally live better than they once did. Medicaid (enacted in 1965) has expanded their health care. Housing conditions for most of the poor have improved, despite increased homelessness. "The low-rent housing available in 1973 often lacked modern amenities, such as central heat and hot water," reports sociologist Christopher Jencks of Northwestern University. "Many poor tenants who came of age before World War II saw these amenities as luxuries they could survive without." By 1989, low-rent housing was less crowded and had more "complete bathrooms, complete kitchens . . . , modern plumbing, central heat and air conditioning." To some extent, greater homelessness is a visible manifestation of problems that always existed but were kept largely out of sight, according to Jencks. The destruction of "skid rows"—districts rarely visited by the middle class where the destitute slept on the streets or in cheap hotels—spread the homeless and the near homeless throughout the city, where they were more conspicuous. Likewise, the "deinstitutionalization" of mental patients put people on the street who would have previously been in state hospitals. The plight of these people was never good, and it is arguable whether they are better or worse off today. But what is not arguable is that they are now far more visible. Jencks estimates that, in the 1980s, the number of homeless probably increased from about 100,000 to 300,000 or 400,000. Exact figures, he believes, are almost impossible to get. But he dismisses estimates that put the numbers in the millions, and his larger point is that a lot of today's homelessness is not a new problem but a new form of old problems.[5]

The general complaint against the economy is that people "fear for the future." But what exactly do they fear? One frequently expressed anxiety is that today's young won't live as well as their parents; they won't be able to afford homes and will have lower incomes. These possibilities, though conceivable, are far-fetched. Consider housing. About 1 million new homes are built annually; the elderly die and vacate their homes. The overall home-ownership rate has remained remarkably stable (it was 64.4 percent in 1980 and 64.5 percent in 1993).[6] Similarly, average incomes should increase if productivity (average output per worker) continues to rise, as it has throughout U.S. history. It is true that the impending retirement, early in the next century, of the baby boom generation will put a huge strain on existing government programs and tax rates. Some income gains that might otherwise go to younger workers may be siphoned off (via higher taxes) to support the elderly. Even so, workers' aftertax incomes aren't likely to drop, because their pretax incomes will be much higher. It is also possible (even probable) that today's middle-aged workers, most of the baby boom, will work longer, as retirement ages rise. But their living standards won't drop; they will work longer, because they will live longer.*

The "fear of the future" is, in fact, mostly a clever catchphrase expressing disappointment that our institutions and leaders haven't fulfilled the larger and more shapeless promise of entitlement—to suppress all insecurity and build a predictable and placid society. In effect, they are held accountable for not creating a utopia. They are blamed for anything that makes tomorrow uncertain and anything that makes today less than ideal. They are blamed for not generating faster increases in incomes, for not providing greater job security, for not creating racial harmony, and so on. Up to a point, these criticisms seem fair, because politicians and business leaders boasted for decades that they could make good on all these promises. But the criticisms are unfair in the sense that the goals are often impossible. Although some may be realistic individually, they are not collectively. Still, our demand for entitlements expands constantly. (Some feminists, for example, contend women have an entitlement to a violence-free life. Surely this is desirable—and for men, too. But an entitlement? If so, how is it to be guaranteed?)[7] Although not all these declared entitlements are universally accepted, the ease with which they are enunciated is revealing of popular attitudes.

OUR ENTHUSIASM for entitlement has rested on a massive misunderstanding. It is the myth of the unbounded power of prosperity. We have thought that most social conflict and personal discontent stem

---

*Again, I discuss these issues more fully on pages 220–25.

from scarcity—poverty or a lack of resources. These, we think, prevent individuals or entire societies from realizing their aspirations. Frustrated people despair and quarrel; so do frustrated nations. Because prosperity can relieve scarcity, it can resolve conflict and dispel despair. It is the raw material of societal happiness; it can open wide vistas of personal fulfillment and social harmony. This logic is seductive, and there is certainly some truth to it, but it is a qualified and limited truth. It isn't that prosperity is bad or that the materialistic bent of American society is, as many social critics have long argued, somehow misconceived or even evil. Prosperity is good, and a richer society is better in many, many ways than a poorer society. But just because prosperity is good doesn't mean that it is the ultimate good or that it automatically leads to all other goods. Prosperity doesn't entitle us to entitlement.

Prosperity cannot smother all the foibles of human nature, starting with envy and longing. As a result, there can never be enough prosperity. Scarcity and all the conflicts it engenders are enduring, because material wants are infinite. Neither individuals nor nations are ever satisfied, because people always want more. This endless appetite may explain why today's living standards, the highest in U.S. history, inspire so little self-congratulation. Americans often find their rising incomes insufficient precisely because their demands seem to have risen still faster. The sense of deprivation comes not because we have so little but because there is so much to have and we cannot "have it all," all of the time. Yesterday's luxuries become today's necessities. They are what middle-class Americans think they "have to have" to qualify as being middle class. The VCR, once a luxury, is now a virtual necessity. By 1994, 81 percent of households had one, up from 1 percent in 1980. When old luxuries become necessities, people instinctively crave new luxuries. There is an unending quest for what the late Fred Hirsch called "positional goods" or, more simply, status symbols. If more people go to college, then more will want graduate or professional degrees to distinguish themselves from run-of-the-mill college graduates. If everyone has a car, then more people will want Mercedeses, Cadillacs, and Lexuses. If everyone can afford vacations, then having a vacation home will become more fashionable.[8]

By itself, prosperity will simply not ensure personal happiness or contentment. In a recent book, journalist Ellis Cose (who is black) interviewed many black professionals—lawyers, academics, corporate executives—who had done well economically. (In 1992, about one sixth of black families had incomes exceeding $50,000; the rate for whites was about twice that.) Yet, Cose found that "instead of celebrating, much of America's black privileged class claims to be in excruciating pain." According to Cose, many successful blacks feel they continue to be stereotyped and held back by prejudice, even though they enjoy the trappings of economic and social success. They still feel they aren't receiving the dignity, status, recognition, or rewards that they deserve. The larger point here is not that blacks are especially embittered, though they may be. The point is that economic well-being by itself only partially satisfies us.[9] Countless novelists have played this broader theme, and it is confirmed by opinion polls, as the table below shows. It gives results from surveys by the National Opinion Research Center (NORC) at the University of Chicago, which regularly asks respondents to rate themselves "very happy," "pretty happy," or "not too happy." Except among the poorest and wealthiest, differences don't vary much by income.

Money and Happiness

Income	Very Happy	Pretty Happy	Not Too Happy
$0–$14,999	21%	58%	21%
$15,000–$24,999	31	56	13
$24,000–$34,999	32	60	8
$35,000–$49,999	36	59	5
$50,000–$74,999	34	60	6
$75,000 or more	45	49	6

This is not as implausible as it seems. Consider a family that suddenly receives a $15,000 increase in income. Its members would almost certainly feel happier. But would the extra money fix all their life problems? Probably not. The sensation of greater contentment would probably be temporary. "It's family, friends and work that contribute most to well-being," concluded the political scientist Robert Lane after reviewing academic studies of happiness. Broadly speaking, this seems commonsensical. It also accords with the NORC surveys. These find that increases in income do temporarily make people feel happier. But the deeper causes of personal satisfaction seem to lie elsewhere. Married people, for example, consistently report higher happiness than singles; 39 percent say they're "very happy" compared with 24 percent of those living alone. (Those living alone include not only those who have never married but also people who are divorced or widowed.)[10]

Our infatuation with prosperity stems from the belief that it permits more personal choice, which is good. Up to a point, this is true. People who make more can buy more and, in theory at least, can trade some of their extra earnings for more leisure and relaxation. Our individualistic culture values extra choices. But more choices do not always mean better choices. A few years ago, the writer Steven Waldman coined the phrase "choice overload" to explain why ordinary shopping sometimes seems so oppressive. The proliferation of choices overwhelms, he concluded; buying things is too time consuming and too stressful, precisely because having more choices makes the job harder and multiplies anxiety over making the wrong choice. He found that

> A typical supermarket in 1976 had 9,000 products; today [1991] it has more than 30,000. The average produce section in 1975 carried 65 items; this summer it carried 285. . . . A typical Cosmetic Center outside Washington carries 1,500 types and sizes of hair products. The median household got six TV stations in 1975. [Thanks to cable TV], that family now has more than thirty channels. The number of FM radio stations has doubled since 1970. A new religious denomination forms every week. . . . In 1955 only 4 percent of the population had left the faith of their childhood. By 1985, one third had. In 1980, 564 mutual funds existed. [By 1991] there [were] 3,347.[11]

The anxieties of choosing cosmetics or a mutual fund, of course, are fairly inconsequential, but more important personal and social choices are fraught with similar confusions. Greater freedom for women to work outside the home—once imagined as unqualified "liberation"—has tormented many mothers, who would like both to stay with their children and to have outside jobs. The expansion of moral and social codes to accommodate more sexual freedom is one of the great postwar upheavals. In a 1939 poll, roughly 80 percent of respondents condemned premarital sex; now, fewer than one in five Americans under forty-four thinks "premarital sex is always wrong."[12] We talk about homosexuality with an openness unimaginable even in the 1970s. It is possible to favor (as I, personally, do) many of our new choices without believing they will always be wisely made or foster social peace. Couples who lived together before marriage, it was once thought, would have a better chance of staying married. Not so: just the opposite. "Cohabitation carries with it the ethic that a relationship should be ended if either partner is dissatisfied," writes sociologist Andrew Cherlin.[13] Lifestyle choices, whether over "working mothers" or "gay rights," sow personal and social conflict. The "cultural left" battles the "religious right"; disputes resist compromise, because they reflect intense personal or religious convictions.*

Americans seemed more satisfied in the 1950 and 1960s not only because their incomes were rising faster but also because these huge gains contrasted so vividly with Depression-dampened expectations. Because we bought into the idea of endless, ever accelerating affluence, we calibrated future wants to future incomes that, to our surprise, have not materialized. Although true of people individually, this is even more true of government. During the 1960s and 1970s, the federal government launched, or expanded, many programs on the casual belief that, sometime in the future, the money would be there to pay for them. Medicare and Medicaid were created in 1965. The food stamp program was dramatically expanded in 1970. Two years later, Social Security was sharply improved. But the money has not been there, because slower growth has meant lower than expected tax revenues and higher than expected costs. There are perpetual budget deficits, even while beneficiaries of many federal programs feel that spending is too low. Perversely, higher economic growth generated higher expectations, which, in turn, were disappointed by lower growth.

THE SAME UNCRITICAL FAITH led us wrongly to view economic growth as the solution to most serious social problems. "Solution" im-

---

*The abortion controversy is the most inflamed of these. But it merely epitomizes the bigger problem: one person's "choice" offends another's "values."

plies a perfect resolution, but many social problems do not admit to that. Race relations, poverty, and crime are conditions with which we must struggle, for better or worse. So are many other problems, ranging from immigration to environmental degradation. If prosperity cured crime, there would be less crime now than a century ago. In fact, there is more. In 1900, the murder rate was about 1 per 100,000 people. By 1930, it rose to about 10 per 100,000. During the Depression, it plunged to about 5 per 100,000 and stayed there until the 1960s. Since then—a period of constant, if interrupted, economic growth—it has risen again to about 10 per 100,000. Similarly, if wealth suppressed crime, a rich society like the United States would have a low crime rate. Instead, the U.S. homicide rate is eight times that of the next highest industrial country, Italy. Whatever the connection between poverty and crime, other causes (national culture, family breakdown, law enforcement) predominate.[14]

The logic that enough prosperity would support government programs capable of eradicating almost any social problem is simplistic. Consider the "underclass." Hardly anyone now disputes that it is sustained by rising out-of-wedlock births. The figures are well known. In 1991, 68 percent of black births were to unwed mothers, up from 35 percent in 1970 and 22 percent in 1960; among whites, the figure was 22 percent, up from 6 and 2 percent.[15] There are many theories to explain these increases: a decline in the stigma of illegitimacy (even the term has fallen into disuse); welfare's support for single mothers; the declining economic appeal, as husbands, of young, unskilled men. But whatever the cause, the explosion of out-of-wedlock births has fostered social conditions that government cannot easily overcome. Schools and social agencies can sometimes partially compensate for the worst cases of family breakdown—if the worst cases are few. But what might work for the few won't work well or at all for the many, as Judge Richard Neely has noted.[16] The capacity of individual caregivers and teachers to deal with the personal needs of multitudes of rootless children is overwhelmed. And economically, mounting costs strain the willingness of the wider public to pay.

The only solution is to reconstruct, somehow, families that provide the love, sense of self-worth, and discipline that children require to develop into responsible, self-sufficient adults. But no one really knows how to do this, and the implications, of course, transcend poverty and determine the condition of race relations. More than half of black children live only with their mothers; nearly half live in families with incomes below the government's "poverty line." On average, children of single-parent families have lower incomes, do worse in school, and have higher arrest rates. Blacks now account for nearly a third of all police arrests; roughly half of all murder victims are black.[17] These grim conditions poison race relations and, as long as they persist, will sow mutual recrimination. Blacks (not all, but many) identify historic and institutional racism as the basic problem. Whites (not all, but many) think blacks aren't doing enough for themselves. These worsening conditions and perceptions have defied rising prosperity or any obvious public solution. It is even conceivable that they were abetted by rising prosperity, because splintered families could (more easily than before) manage to meet their basic needs.

OUR OUTSIZED FAITH in prosperity also explains our disappointment in our foreign policy. World economic growth has reduced, contrary to Americans' expectations, the United States' global economic and political dominance. This was virtually an inevitable consequence of recovery from the war and the spread of well-known technologies and management practices, even though the United States remains the world's largest economy (it represents slightly more than a fifth of world output, compared with Japan's 9 percent).[18] Still, Americans no longer feel so rich, nor has prosperity proved to be a principle around which global order can be simply organized. In part, prosperity cannot mechanically be made universal. The notion, once widespread, that the success of the Marshall Plan could be duplicated in most poor countries was wrong. The Marshall Plan and its counterpart in Japan succeeded because those societies had the traditions, institutions, and knowledge to restore their productive prewar economies. American aid merely provided a catalyst. Countries without these strengths cannot instantly be imbued with them.

The larger problem is that global commerce has not brought global cohesion. The Cold War's illusion was that countries would "go over" to one side or the other and that, if one side prevailed, so would its system. In fact, the prism of the Cold War distorted our vision. It stripped nations and peoples of their separate identities and reduced them to pawns in a larger ideological struggle. With that struggle ended, the more complicated truth—that other peoples have their own histories, hatreds, principles, and prejudices—has emerged with a vengeance. "Western ideas of individualism, liberalism, constitutionalism, human rights, equality, liberty, the rule of law, democracy, free markets, the separation of church and state, often have little resonance" in other cultures, political scientist Samuel Huntington recently argued in an article predicting a "clash of civilizations" among Western, Asian, Islamic, Hindu, and Slavic-Orthodox cultures.[19] Global prosperity may actually increase the odds of war by bringing antagonistic cultures into closer contact and making them more able to afford modern weaponry, including weapons of mass destruction. Perhaps democratic nations will war less (at least against each other) than nondemocratic nations. But no one really knows, because democracy on a worldwide basis is a phenomenon of only the past half century and some countries (perhaps China?) may develop more rapidly economically than politically.

WHAT CONNECTS OUR disappointments abroad with those at home are their common emotional and intellectual sources and consequences. It is not just that our hopes have been dashed. Hopes are often and predictably dashed—every ball game has a loser—so that the disappointment, though genuine, is routine and manageable. Our present disappointments are of a different sort. The amalgam of our postwar hopes and expectations created for us a frame of reference. It constituted a psychic destination toward which we thought we were marching. The hardships of the journey seemed tolerable so long as the destination was known and desirable. At home and abroad, we thought we were building a new kind of order. That was our terminus. But our frame of reference has now vanished; it was but a figment of our idealistic imagination. So now the journey continues, but it is at once aimless and frustrating. Some Americans continue to believe that they are still advancing toward our imagined destination. But we never arrive, and so these travelers are repeatedly frustrated and disappointed. Others know that they are no longer going to the imagined places. But they don't know where they are going.

The overwhelming collective experience is one of disorientation, and the great casualty has been our confidence and sense of national cohesion. Ours has always been a noisy, messy, and splintered society. It still is. But we thought we were fostering social harmony by eliminating our most wrenching social and economic divisions. We thought we were securing a safe place for ourselves in the world by creating enduring alliances for global peace. Clearly, none of this has happened. The peace of mind that was to be the crowning glory of the problem-solving society has eluded us. Instead, we are left with a heightened sense of insecurity. Abroad, we quarrel with our former allies and wonder just how to classify our former enemies. At home, there is intensifying competition among groups for all their individual entitlements. The trouble is not that all the exertions of postwar society have failed. They haven't. Postwar society (to repeat the point once more) is much better than prewar society. America is a more successful society at home, and its engagement abroad is more realistic. But the questing for more than is possible has done more than disappoint; it has driven us apart.

In this sense, the problem-solving society has fallen prey to what Richard Hofstadter termed "absolutist aspirations." It is this spirit that has often animated America's past reformist impulses. As Hofstadter wrote:

> We go off on periodical psychic sprees that purport to be moral crusades: . . . [to] restore absolute popular democracy or completely honest competition in business, wipe out the saloon and liquor forever from the nation's life, destroy the political machines and put an end to corruption, or achieve absolute, total, and final security against war. . . . The people who attach themselves to these several absolutisms are not always the same people, but they do create for each other a common climate of absolutist enthusiasm. Very often the evils they are troubled about do exist in some form, usually something can be done about them. . . . [The] limitation of [our reform tradition is] that it often wanders over the border between reality and impossibility.[20]

Our entitlement society builds upon this tradition. It exhibits the same mix of moralism and faith in enlightened thinking that characterized the Progressive movement of the early twentieth century (about which Hofstadter was writing). And it has succumbed to simi-

lar excesses. Wandering over the border between reality and impossibility is more than a harmless exercise in excess enthusiasm. Our idealized goals become etched in popular consciousness. By expecting
our leaders and institutions to do the impossible, we overburden them
and hamper them in doing the possible. In a larger sense, we blame
them for larger failings and absolve ourselves of any responsibility.
No society can work unless there's a crude balance between what individuals must do for themselves and what they expect others to do
for them. We have created a collision between a well-developed set of
public expectations and social and economic conditions that prevent
those expectations from being realized. The question is no longer
whether the two will somehow be reconciled. They won't. Either we
reconstitute our expectations, or we condemn ourselves to perpetual
disappointment.

II

The New Capitalism

5

The Apostles of Control

⊭ ⊭ ⊭ ⊭

THE NEW CAPITALISM was the handmaiden of entitlement. It was the notion that the economy might be tamed and harnessed. The booms and busts that had occurred throughout history would be eliminated, and the process by which societies grew wealthier would be completely understood and ultimately mastered. Economic progress would become routine and predictable. It would form the foundation for personal contentment and social peace and justice. No nation had ever before so thoroughly subjugated capitalism without destroying capitalism, and yet—as we have seen—Americans came to assume after the Second World War that these feats lay within our grasp. The architects of this new capitalism were modern economists and professional corporate managers, who joined in an unspoken alliance. The economists, advising government, felt they could end booms and busts: the traditional business cycle. The managers, running big companies, felt they could guarantee constant increases in living standards through new technology and advanced management. Together, executives and economists convinced themselves and Americans at large that the economy could be manipulated for the larger social good. We now know that this was a huge conceit: it has not come to pass, and its prospects seem remote.

The glory of the new capitalism, Americans believed, was that it would achieve most of the virtues of socialism—a dreaded word and concept—with few of the vices. The gains from economic growth would be distributed widely, and the worst aspects of capitalism (job insecurity, poverty, vulnerability to economic dislocation or personal accident) would be eased or eradicated. Yet, these gains would occur without massive governmental interference, because private companies would serve as the main instruments for generating and distributing the benefits of economic growth. Government's role would be to set rules, care for stragglers (the elderly, the disabled, the incompetent or unlucky), and overcome the instability of business slumps. Most Americans would receive health insurance and old-age pensions through their companies. Governmental welfare would be relatively small, because it would protect mainly those who were somehow missed by the corporate safety net. Permanent economic growth and the triumph of enlightened management would give capitalism a face-lift and obviate the need for anything like socialism.

At the pinnacle of the new capitalism were "good corporations." They were companies like IBM, Delta Airlines, and Time Inc.— companies that dominated their industries, while also providing career jobs, high wages, comprehensive fringe benefits, and attractive working conditions. These firms married economic efficiency and social responsibility. They would be the models; other big companies would emulate them. Inevitably, many smaller firms would not be so stable or generous. Building contractors, local stores, and family-run companies would not necessarily endure forever. But ongoing prosperity—guaranteed by government's command of business cycles— would enable job losers to find new work quickly, and the spread of high wages and fringe benefits would compel even small firms to do better. Otherwise, they wouldn't be able to compete for workers. Gradually, almost everyone would enjoy better security and welfare benefits.

The new capitalism would also relieve us of discomforting political choices. We could have social justice without Big Government. By creating the first, the new capitalism would dispense with the need for

the second. Government might police the worst abuses of free enter
prise; but it would not be overbearing precisely because private enterprise would be resourceful and responsible. Though business
might object to the details of new regulations, it would accept their
existence in principle. It would support the idea that companies could
(and should) be used as mechanisms for achieving larger public purposes, from a cleaner environment to safer working conditions to better informed consumers (through, say, product labeling). In this sense,
the struggles between business and government that had dominated
politics in the late nineteenth and early twentieth centuries simply
ended. Business surrendered and conceded the superiority of the
state. But the surrender was not bitter, because it stemmed from a
shared conviction created both by the collaborative experience of
the Second World War and the phenomenal early postwar prosperity.
The conviction was that American business was so well managed
that, despite complaints about particular government regulations,
companies could comply without significantly impairing their efficiency. In the new capitalism, government would remain relatively
small, because much of the burden of creating an orderly and compassionate society could be quietly shifted to business.

IT HASN'T HAPPENED. Vestiges of the old capitalism endure. Economic life is often precarious, unfair, and unequal. Companies that
were once bastions of lifetime employment—IBM, General Motors,
Sears—have ceased to be. The "safety net" of private welfare benefits (mainly, health insurance, pensions, and job security) has bigger
holes than expected, and, therefore, we face the unappealing choice
of tolerating these gaps (which most Americans deplore) or enlarging
government to fill them (which many Americans oppose). Companies
now object that excessive regulations do hurt their efficiency. Nor
have we been able to control fully the economy's behavior and have
not completely reaped the psychic or political benefits of doing so.
Business cycles continue, and the rise of living standards has slowed
noticeably since the early 1970s. Likewise, income differences—
inequality—have widened.

Consider the following two tables. The first shows changes in median family income (half of families are above the median, half

below) between 1950 and 1990. As the table indicates, typical families nearly doubled their incomes between 1950 and 1970, but the increase over the next twenty years was only one seventh. (The figures adjust for inflation by being stated in constant 1993 dollars—that is, as if all incomes had all been paid in 1993.)

Median Family Income, 1950–1990[1]

	Income	INCREASE FROM PREVIOUS DECADE	
			Percent
1950	$18,305	—	—
1960	$25,220	$6,915	37.8
1970	$34,523	$9,303	36.9
1980	$36,912	$2,389	6.9
1990	$39,086	$2,174	5.9

In practice, these figures need to be qualified. First, there are more single-parent families now than in 1950, and these families typically have lower incomes. Their increasing number, therefore, has depressed the median (or middle) income. More immigrants have had the same effect. (Some of this downward pressure, though, is offset by more two-earner families, which have higher average incomes.) Second, the income figures exclude fringe benefits (such as employer-paid health insurance) and "in kind" government benefits (such as Medicare and food stamps). Because these have grown faster than cash income, true incomes have increased slightly faster than the figures show. Third, official inflation indexes overstate inflation and understate "real" income gains; over the past two decades the understatement may be 10 to 20 percentage points. Still, the income slowdown is pronounced, and the main cause is no secret: poor productivity growth. Productivity signifies the economy's overall efficiency—how much each worker produces in, say, an hour. Higher productivity raises living standards through higher wages, lower prices, or greater profits. Unfortunately, productivity grew slightly more than 1 percent annually between 1970 and 1990, down from nearly 3 percent a year between 1950 and 1970.[2]

The second table highlights the increase of income inequality. It is not merely that we are getting richer more slowly than before; the rich are also getting rich faster than the poor. The table shows the dramatic differences since 1970. It divides families into five income groups, from the poorest to the richest fifth. (Again the effects of inflation are eliminated by stating all incomes in constant 1993 dollars; the incomes given are the median figures for each group.) Incomes of the poorest fifth rose hardly at all, while incomes of the richest fifth rose nearly one third. This reversed the experience of the first two postwar decades, when the bottom half of the income spectrum claimed a greater share of income.[3]

Family Income Distribution, 1970–1990[4]

	1970 Income	1990 Income	INCREASE	Percent
Poorest fifth	$10,570	$10,871	$301	2.9
Second fifth	$23,704	$25,357	$1,653	7.0
Third fifth	$34,274	$39,051	$4,777	13.9
Fourth fifth	$46,233	$56,160	$9,927	21.5
Richest fifth	$79,503	$104,372	$24,869	31.3
Richest 5%*	$121,062	$163,764	$42,702	35.3

*Also included in the richest fifth.

Similar qualifications apply. More single-parent families and immigrants have aggravated inequality. For example, two fifths of the increase in poverty (as classified by the government) since 1980 has occurred among Hispanics—often immigrants or their children. With time, many will move into the middle class. Paradoxically, the increase in the number of elderly families has also worsened the reported inequality. Although their well-being has improved dramatically, the fact that more people live longer skews overall incomes because the elderly are past their peak earning years. Still, all the qualifications explain only part of the worsening inequality. The rest (probably half or more) reflects a widening gap in wages and salaries between the rich and the poor as well as the upper- and lower-middle classes.

The deterioration and unpredictability of the economy's performance since 1970 confounded the apostles of the new capitalism. They saw themselves as pragmatists who, in the great American tradition, were advancing the frontiers of human knowledge in the cause of social progress. To some extent, their sweeping vision was obscured by their technocratic style and language. In reality, they were evangelists for the power of rationality. Listen to the late Arthur Okun, a Yale economist who had been chairman of the Council of Economic Advisers under President Lyndon B. Johnson, writing in 1970 about the revolution in economic thinking:

> The experience of the sixties has made a marked and lasting change in the business cycle mentality. . . . Today few research economists regard the business cycle as a particularly useful organizing framework for overall analysis of current economic activity and few teachers see "business cycles" as an appropriate title for a course to be offered to their students. Now virtually no one espouses the fiscal formula that was most popular just a decade ago—that of balancing the federal budget over the course of a business cycle.
>
> In 1965 President Johnson was making a controversial statement when he said: "I do not believe recessions are inevitable." That statement is no longer controversial. Recessions are now generally considered to be fundamentally preventable, like airplane crashes and unlike hurricanes.[5]

The theology of modern management was no less confident. Almost everyone—critics as well as champions of business—assumed that the largest firms were economically impregnable. Their survival and prosperity flowed from their command of modern technology and machinery. Critics of business urged companies to use their huge productivity in more "responsible" ways, whether it was making safer products, paying more attention to the environment, or treating workers better. Modern executives felt they could cope with all these demands, as well as earn adequate profits, because improved managerial systems enabled them to anticipate economic and social change. A 1969 article by Melvin Anshen in the *Harvard Business Review* caught the grandiose tone of managerial thinking and even prophesied that corporate leaders would soon become "philosophers":

> New analytical techniques, largely quantitative and computer-based, are presenting a management opportunity that is unique in at least two important ways. First, they provide an adminis-

trative capability without parallel in breadth, depth, and speed. Second, for their full and efficient utilization, they press management to establish a unified command over the totality of business, including the dynamic interface of external environment and internal activities. These changes are defining a novel view of management itself as a universally applicable resource, readily transferred from one business to another, from one industry to another, from one technology to another, from one country to another. . . .

The main task of management [might be described] . . . as the management of ideas. Skill in manipulating ideas is precisely the skill of the great philosophers.[6]

THE NEW CAPITALISM emerged logically from the prewar experience. The Depression profoundly influenced a generation of economists. The Nobel Prize winner James Tobin, a member of President Kennedy's Council of Economic Advisers, once put it this way: "As a child of the Depression, I was terribly concerned with the world. It seemed then that many of the problems [of society] were economic in origin. If you thought the world ought to be saved, and I did, then economics looked like the decisive thing to study." The Depression had spawned the theories of the English economist John Maynard Keynes (1883–1946). Until Keynes, business cycles were viewed as deplorable but inevitable events, though economists in the 1920s had begun to consider ways of moderating them. "Of course, the Great Depression of the thirties was not the first to reveal the untenability of [old economic theory]," Paul Samuelson,* another Nobel Prize winner and sometime adviser to Kennedy, once said. "But now for the first time, it was confronted by a competing system."[7]

Inspired by Keynes, many economists felt they could subdue business cycles. After the Second World War, Congress passed the Employment Act of 1946, which committed the government to maintaining "full employment." But the promise was initially hollow. ("Full employment" was not rigorously defined, nor were there sanctions for missing it.) Four recessions occurred between the end of the

---

*No relation to the author.

war and the Kennedy administration in 1961. The economy was then recovering from a mild slump, and unemployment was 7.5 percent. Kennedy's economists, led by Walter Heller, chairman of the Council of Economic Advisers, felt that tax cuts would increase economic growth. Kennedy's own economic knowledge was skimpy, and to convince him, Heller showered the President with memos. (It is hard to recall now, but economic ideas were not then widely discussed and economists were generally treated as obscure academics. Keynes, though renowned in Europe, was little known to most Americans.) By mid-1962, Heller had triumphed. In a commencement address at Yale in June, Kennedy embraced what came to be called the "new economics"—American Keynesianism. Old economic rules ("mythology," Kennedy had said) were too rigid. Balanced budgets were not always good; the danger of inflation was often exaggerated. Government needed to discard platitudes and rely more on experts—economists. "What we need is not labels and clichés but more basic discussion of the sophisticated and technical questions involved in keeping a great economic machinery moving ahead," Kennedy said.[8]

Within a few months, he proposed the major tax cut his economists wanted. The speech's true significance, though, was its effect on public opinion and politics. Henceforth, the economy's performance was, for better or worse, to be attributed to government. The new assumption was that, if the "economic machinery" was not moving ahead, then government should act. It should avail itself of the tools offered by economists. Before, expectations had been vaguer. People didn't automatically exempt government from blame for the economy's troubles (in the recession year of 1958, Republicans had suffered large congressional losses). But neither did they believe that government could fix the economy's every problem. Moreover, any proposal (higher spending, or lower taxes or interest rates) for improving the economy had to contend with Kennedy's "myths"—that balanced budgets were generally good or that inflation was generally bad. By 1965, things had changed. The economy was growing rapidly. *Time* magazine put Keynes on its cover and noted a broad change in social climate. Even business leaders had "come to accept that the Government should actively use its Keynesian tools to promote growth and stability," *Time* said. "They believe that whatever happens, the Government will somehow keep the economy strong and rising."[9]

Indeed, the "new economics" was a godsend to business leaders, who were eager to demonstrate they could make companies good citizens as well as prolific producers. The impulse to do so dates at least to the 1910s and 1920s, when some major corporations—Standard Oil, International Harvester, and General Electric, among others—began adopting policies, including pension plans and compensation for industrial accidents, to treat their workers more fairly. After the Second World War, scattered change became more general. Corporate leaders wanted to obliterate the hostile climate of the Depression. They would rid big business of its ugly reputation. Modern managers didn't have to exploit workers or gouge customers to make adequate profits. Companies would show they were using their great power responsibly to advance widely held values and goals. The new postwar mood was never better reflected than in a full-page ad in the *New York Times* run by the General Cable Corporation in 1952:

> *I am Industry—1952.*
> *People were hurt when I first stirred in life;*
> *Then I grew and learned;*
> . . . . .
> *I am the people!*
> *With maturity, I have grown, too, in social responsibility*
> *To the people,*
> *   To America!*
> *And even those beyond our shores.*
> *My efforts are not in selfish interest;*
> *Rather, all my brains and brawn strain for the good of many;*
> *I am the American way!*[10]

WHAT UNITED THE "new economics" and modern management was a shared belief that problems could be distilled into scientific truths. Economics aspired to be a "hard" science like physics rather than a "soft" social science like history. It was in this sense that Okun could describe recession avoidance as more like preventing plane crashes than eliminating hurricanes—for a plane could be designed not to crash. Similarly, modern managers sought to extend the tradition of "scientific management" that dated to the early twentieth century, when Frederick Taylor pioneered "time and motion" studies. These claimed to show the best ways to do certain manual jobs, such as moving bricks. The larger message was that most business tasks could be analyzed and improved by adopting the most efficient ways of doing them. The central assumption of postwar managers was that capitalism had fundamentally changed, because its basic unit (the firm) had altered in size and character. Companies had grown so large that they might—unlike Adam Smith's atomistic firms—influence or even control the market. They could determine their own destinies, and new scientific techniques (the best known of which was "strategic planning") would enable them to do so in efficient and enlightened ways.

The failures of this vision are, by now, well known. Instead of taming the business cycle, the efforts to do so unleashed rising inflation and continual budget deficits. These were developments without precedent in American economic history. Inflation has persisted year in and year out for three decades. The highest inflation occurred in 1980, when it was 13.5 percent, but there were long periods of 5 or 6 percent. In earlier eras, prices never behaved this way. Wars typically triggered massive inflations, but these usually subsided in peace. Moreover, one period of inflation (rising prices) was typically offset by a later period of deflation (falling prices). During the Civil War, for example, wholesale prices had doubled; but by 1879, they had returned to their 1860 level. The story of budget deficits was similar. In previous times, budget deficits—sometimes huge—had materialized in wars or economic collapses. But otherwise, balanced budgets had prevailed. By contrast, the federal budget has remained constantly out of balance since 1960, with one exception (1969).[11]

Corporate America's faith in modern management also backfired. It led to companies that were overmanaged and, as a result, poorly managed. Many became rigid, costly bureaucracies that—insensitive to changes in technology or consumer tastes—were vulnerable to new competition. In other instances, managerial overconfidence produced a whole new class of underperforming companies: conglomerates, which were collections of separate (and often totally unrelated) businesses under a common corporate roof. These were new to America. In 1949, nearly 70 percent of the top 200 industrial companies confined their business to one industry. A steel company made steel, an insurance company sold insurance. By 1970, only 35 percent of similar companies restricted their business to one industry. Conglomerates arose on the theory that a good manager could improve almost any business. As a result, many conglomerates ran dozens of businesses— more than they knew how to. In the 1960s, ITT bought more than fifty companies, including Continental Baking, Sheraton Corp. (a major hotel chain), and Levitt & Sons, a major home builder.[12] Ultimately, many conglomerates were broken up; at least some of the resulting layoffs and plant shutdowns might have been avoided with less arrogant (and better) management.

Although the full costs of these economic mistakes can never be precisely calculated, they contributed to deeper recessions and slower income growth. It was no coincidence that the worst postwar recessions (those of 1973–1975 and 1981–1982) followed the worst inflations. Only deep slumps with large doses of unemployment and surplus industrial capacity could halt double-digit price and wage increases that had been caused by loose money. Inflation encouraged speculation and disguised inefficiencies (profits and incomes seemed to be rising when they were doing so only in cheapened dollars). Mismanaged companies also operated inefficiently. The impact of budget deficits is less settled, but it is likely they undermined growth by raising uncertainty and lowering private investment. Even if all these mistakes (high inflation, corporate mismanagement, and big budget deficits) reduced annual income and productivity growth by a scant 0.2 percent between 1970 and 1990, the impact would be to depress incomes by more than 4 percent from what they might have been. (Even without compounding, a 0.2 percent annual loss for 20 years equals 4 percent.) In a $7 trillion economy, that's $280 billion of lost annual production and income.*

The point is not that all would have been well but for these corporate and governmental blunders. It would not. There would still have been business cycles and corporate failures. But these blunders made matters worse in many ways. For example, high inflation was the underlying cause of both the savings-and-loan and the farm debt crises of the 1980s. Farmers took out loans at low interest rates based on rising prices for foodstuffs (wheat, corn) and land values; between

---

*This calculation is conservative. Some studies have estimated that the productivity loss from higher inflation alone is 0.3 percent a year.[13]

1975 and 1982, the price of the average acre of farmland went from $340 to $789.[14] Once interest rates rose—and crop and land prices collapsed—many borrowers couldn't repay their loans and had their farms repossessed. The savings-and-loan crisis occurred because savings associations specialized in long-term mortgage loans, which, until the late 1970s, were made mostly at fixed interest rates. In turn, the funds supporting these loans came from short-term deposits— usually at low rates—that could be withdrawn almost at will. Inflation sharply raised short-term deposit rates; savings associations suffered huge losses, because the rates they had to pay on deposits suddenly exceeded the rates on their preexisting mortgages. By 1981, roughly 85 percent of the savings associations were running losses. Because deposits were federally insured, the government had to cover the losses, which ultimately totaled about $175 billion.*[15]

Nor were the effects of these corporate and governmental blunders exclusively—or even mainly—economic. The promise of economic salvation was made so often by so many authorities and political leaders that the failure to achieve it was bound to dishearten millions of ordinary Americans. Every recession was taken as evidence of incompetence, bad faith, or both. The high and rising inflation of the 1960s and 1970s especially devastated public optimism and confidence in government. People couldn't believe in the future, because prices and values couldn't be predicted—and blame was (correctly) placed on government. By the late 1970s, as William Greider observed, Americans "had absorbed a new common wisdom." To wit:

> Steadily rising prices were considered a permanent fixture of American life, a factor to be calculated into every transaction. For years, a succession of political leaders in Washington had promised to do something about inflation, and the public became quite cynical about those promises. Each government campaign against inflation had eventually failed and, each time, prices had resumed their steady escalation. . . . It [made] sense

---

*Inflation can't be blamed for all the S&L crisis. Once the industry developed problems, Congress enacted ill-conceived "deregulation" to liberalize its lending practices. More bad loans were made, which—given federal deposit insurance—had to be covered by government. Had Congress acknowledged the problems of the S&Ls in 1981 or 1982, the government's cost might have been held to $25 billion instead of the ultimate $175 billion.

to borrow in order to buy things now. Even with higher interest
rates, a loan made today to purchase an automobile or television
set would be paid back tomorrow in dollars that were worth
less. . . . As consumers, people were compelled to focus more immediately on short-term decisions. . . . Daily chores as routine as
grocery shopping induced a sense of running on a treadmill that
was moving faster and faster. As voters, people expressed the
same insecurities. Their daily lives might be prosperous, but they
found themselves uncertain about the future, more skeptical of
distant political promises.[16]

NONE OF THIS means—emphatically not—that the postwar economy has been a failure. Quite the opposite. It is vastly superior to its
prewar counterpart. But there is a distinction between changes that
happen and changes that we make happen; and that is the relevant
distinction here. Many of the improvements in the postwar economy
were unplanned; they resulted from underlying economic and social
changes. In postwar America, business cycles have become milder. In
the late nineteenth century, Americans typically saw themselves as
whipsawed between prosperity and long-lasting depressions. "The
prevailing depression in business," *The Nation* magazine noted in
1879, had continued "for six years." Now, most Americans assume
that prosperity prevails most of the time. More exact studies confirm
a change. The National Bureau of Economic Research, a professional economists' group, estimates that postwar expansions (periods
of rising production and jobs) have averaged more than four years,
compared with only two years before the Great Depression (the Depression is typically excluded from comparisons because it is considered an exceptional event). Postwar slumps (falling production and
jobs) now last an average of less than a year, compared with eighteen
months before the war. In slumps, unemployment rose an average of
about 5 percentage points before the war; since 1945, increases have
averaged about 2 percentage points.[17]

Likewise, the new capitalism did arrive for many Americans. In
1940, few workers had employer-paid health insurance; now, about
four fifths do. In 1940, only about 17 percent of full-time workers had
employer-financed pensions; by 1970, 52 percent did—a proportion

that has stayed roughly stable since then. Career jobs have become the norm. About half the men between forty-five and fifty-four have been with their current employer for more than twelve years (and many will be there much longer before retiring). Despite corporate layoffs, most middle-aged workers still have fairly stable jobs.* This represents a huge historic change. On the eve of the Depression, "layoffs [in manufacturing firms] came without notice, seniority was often ignored, dismissals were regular and rehires were haphazard," writes labor economist Sanford Jacoby.[19] No one expected different. A century ago, farmers were at the constant mercy of the weather and creditors. About 30 percent of all men in the nonfarm workforce were unskilled laborers, who often had only seasonal jobs. With some admitted oversimplification, economic historian Claudia Goldin has noted that:

> The labor market in the nineteenth century was a spot market in which workers had considerable job insecurity, invested little in human capital [training and education], had trivial wage growth over their life cycles, were discarded as older workers, were subject to considerable discretion by foremen and supervisors, and were disciplined by "sticks," such as being fired or fined [docked for pay]. In contrast, the labor market of the post–World War II era is characterized by greater job security, investment in human capital . . . firm-related benefits, protection for older workers, strict personnel rules, and discipline by "carrots" and other incentives.[20]

The trouble is not that things haven't improved. They have. The trouble is that the improvements haven't continued effortlessly and haven't always resulted from our conscious efforts. There is a larger, more obscure, and less manageable process at work. Time passes; things change. The economy behaves differently, because it is differ-

---

*Put another way, the anxiety about increased layoffs is greater than the actual increase in layoffs. In 1991, men aged forty-five to fifty-four had typically been at their present jobs 12.2 years, up from 11 years in 1978 and 8.8 years in 1966. The explanation for the apparent contradiction between this stability and widespread stories of layoffs is that the stories—though true—involve only a minority of workers and that the past has, to some extent, been romanticized. There were always layoffs.[18]

ent. Companies now offer more career jobs and greater security to their workers, because—as jobs have become more specialized—businesses have a greater interest in keeping the same employees and keeping them content. Workers are not interchangeable parts: their skills are valuable; their knowledge of a company's products, practices, and customers represents an immense investment, which often can be duplicated only at a substantial cost and at the risk of lost sales and sacrificed reputation. This change in the character of the firm coincided with the new postwar sensibility—the sense that companies should be "fairer"—and made it more practical. Similarly, the quest to tame the business cycle benefited from gradual changes in production, finance, and the size of government that, in fact, made business cycles milder. In particular, two changes were critical: a decline in the relative importance of farming and manufacturing and the end of the gold standard and associated changes in the banking system.

In 1900, agriculture and manufacturing provided 55 percent of all jobs. By 1990, their share had dwindled to 17 percent, as greater efficiencies raised production with relatively fewer workers.[21] This shift toward a "service economy" abetted stability, because farming and manufacturing are both given to huge drops in income and employment. Bad harvests or sharp swings in crop prices can devastate farmers' purchasing power; manufacturing is always vulnerable to consumers' decisions to postpone big-ticket purchases (cars, appliances). By contrast, spending on services (repairs, education, health care) is more stable, because purchases are smaller and often harder to delay: people switch off the electricity only as a last resort. The nineteenth century's industrial and agricultural instability was also compounded by financial instability. Until the 1860s, there was no national currency. Money consisted mainly of gold and/or silver coin and paper banknotes (theoretically redeemable for gold or silver) issued by state-chartered banks. If people feared paper currency wouldn't be converted into coin, they clamored to redeem their notes and deposits. If such panics persisted, banks would exhaust their vault cash and be forced to suspend payments. Depositors could lose funds, and bank loans could drop.

During the Civil War, Congress tried to cure these problems by creating National Banks that could issue paper money (National Bank Notes) and effectively outlawing state banknotes. But the new system had many of the problems of the old. Banknotes were still backed by gold, and banks that needed cash quickly had no easy way of getting it. Bank panics continued, sometimes driven by overinvestment in land or railroads that caused business bankruptcies that fed back into the banking system. Between the Civil War and the First World War, there were at least five major panics: 1873, 1884, 1890, 1893, and 1907. Panics could in turn cause (or worsen) stock market crashes, because much stock was bought with loans. If these were called, securities had to be sold. Fear mounted. One account of the onset of the Panic of 1907 shows how panics spread public pessimism:

> With the coming of daylight, people congregating first by scores, then by hundreds, and later by thousands were herded by policemen into lines stretching away from the marble entrance to the Knickerbocker Trust Company, New York. . . . When the Knickerbocker's doors opened at nine A.M., October 22, the throng fought its way inside to the windows of the paying tellers. All day the run continued; at three o'clock, when the bank closed, hundreds were still in line. Next day witnessed a similar scene, which came to an end at noon, when the Knickerbocker's directors, their stock of cash almost exhausted, decided to suspend payments. The spectacle of the run on the Knickerbocker precipitated (with other causes, before and after) runs on other banks in New York and elsewhere throughout the country.[22]

In the twentieth century, many of these defects were repaired. Congress created the Federal Reserve System, a government central bank, in 1913 to issue paper currency and make loans to banks in need of cash. (A bank would use some of its own assets, such as Treasury securities, as collateral to borrow from the Federal Reserve. When the bank's cash squeeze ended, the Federal Reserve would be repaid and would return the collateral.) In 1933, Congress effectively ended gold backing for the dollar.* That same year, it enacted federal

---

*One reason the gold standard intensified downturns is that withdrawals of gold from the banking system—either because people didn't trust paper currency or because the gold flowed abroad to pay for imports—tended to reduce credit and the money supply. Both changes are contractionary; this mechanism helped cause the Great Depression, as the next chapter explains. See pages 92–95.

deposit insurance. Depositors wouldn't have to withdraw their funds because the government would guarantee their value up to a specific limit (initially $2,500, it has been progressively raised to the present $100,000).

ALL THESE CHANGES—lesser roles for manufacturing and farming, shifts in the banking and money systems—helped stabilize the economy. So did the growth of government, which, through a variety of programs (Social Security, unemployment insurance, food stamps), tends to maintain people's incomes and purchasing power. The mellowing of the business cycle reflects these scattered and protracted developments more than the conscious efforts by government to outlaw recessions through its instruments of economic policy (interest rates, taxes, spending), though these efforts surely have had an effect, for both good and ill. But they have been overshadowed by larger, historic trends and changes; the modern business cycle is the interaction of all these forces, and though it has generally grown less violent, there is no reason that future changes could not reverse the trend and make recessions longer and harsher. The larger lesson is that the economy is not, as the apostles of the "new economics" and modern management hoped, a "system" that could, with ever better theories and knowledge, be completely subordinated to human will.

It is not that our exertions have no effect; it is simply that the effects are limited and sometimes unintended. The scientific analogy is fatally false. True science allows precise prediction, because we are dealing with phenomena that, once understood, are constant and repetitive. When two chemicals are mixed together under the same conditions, they always form the same compound. In economics and business, there are few such ironclad laws. The raw ingredients are not chemicals but human emotions and institutions, the forces of tradition and history, the power of new technologies and ideas. The resulting reactions are far more complex than any chemical reaction, and they are forever changing in new and unfamiliar ways. The delusion of the new capitalism was that it could dispense with chance and unexpected change. But these are central characteristics of a market economy. Business cycles and corporate failures are part of a turbulent process that generates new products, technologies, and efficiencies—and, less conveniently, leads to repeated excess and upheaval. The quest to remove these uncertainties and insecurities, to entitle us to an anxiety-free and perpetually expanding prosperity, ran afoul of the nature of the economic system itself. The control sought by modern economists and managers seemed reasonable; but it actually defied reason.

6

Cheery Economics

⚐ ⚐ ⚐ ⚐

THE SELF-APPOINTED MISSION of modern economics to regulate and sanitize growth—desirable in the abstract—foundered on the erratic and usually spontaneous nature of the economic process. We talk of "the economy" as if it were a coherent whole, when the phrase is actually a convenient simplification. What we call the economy is merely the collective consequence of how millions of individuals and enterprises behave. It is the amalgam of all the institutions, ideas, customs, and attitudes that influence the production and distribution of wealth. And these, of course, are constantly changing under the pressure of new technologies, evolving commercial and governmental practices and policies, shifting public moods, and different international conditions. The essence of a market economy is its disorder. Its genius is its self-regulating mechanisms, which, in the face of all this disorder, maintain a fair amount of stability. The exaggerated promise of postwar economics has been that, through the rational manipulation of government policies, the disorder might be better understood and ultimately suppressed. The result has been to foster the illusion that economic growth emanates from government itself.

In America, this is not true and, except for wars, has never been true. Government is critical to growth but only loosely controlling of it. Through laws, regulations, and taxes, government establishes a climate in which growth will—or won't—occur and can affect individual industries and regions. But production and wealth flow mainly from personal and institutional ambitions and talents that drive work, investment, and risk taking. The chancy and uncertain quest for growth is one enduring reason that our economy has, up until now at least, exhibited periodic instability. People and companies miscalculate. They make mistakes, and mistakes cumulate into cycles of expansion and decline. The bad news about this is that such cycles (and all the adverse social consequences they cause) appear inevitable, because no one has perfect foresight. The good news is that the economy appears to have powerful self-correcting mechanisms (shifts in prices, wages, interest rates) that limit the adverse consequences. Government policies sometimes abet and sometimes compound the instability just as they affect selected industries. But they are not, as yet, powerful enough to eliminate it, in part because government is no more clairvoyant than anyone else.

The effort to make government more important (and the popular belief that it is more important) represents a logical culmination of modern economic thought. Economics labors under the pejorative label of the "dismal science," when it actually aspires to be the "cheery science." Since Adam Smith, economic philosophers have dared to imagine ways in which ordinary life might be made more tolerable and even enjoyable. Theirs has been a secular religion, an alternative to traditional religion that sought to reconcile people to their earthly (and often miserable) lots by promising a better afterlife. Smith argued that free markets, as opposed to those constricted by government, would best promote material well-being. Karl Marx believed that the economic system was evolving toward a higher and more enlightened stage of collective ownership and production. Keynes thought that deep depressions, with all their obvious suffering, might be avoided through a keener understanding of what causes total spending to rise and fall. But all these giants of economics were ultimately concerned with humanity.[1]

What separates our era from earlier periods is that economic ideas, having been aggressively incorporated into governmental policies, have risen beyond mere musings and have powerfully influenced the daily course of events. The Keynesians played the decisive role in this transformation, because they first conditioned the public, in the 1960s, to visualize the economy as a massive machine (Kennedy's exact analogy) that ought to be watched and, if not running properly, should be fixed and made to purr by government. In effect, sustained economic growth was converted into a mass entitlement: something that government was expected to deliver. It followed, then, that if one band of economic mechanics couldn't do the job, new mechanics should be summoned. When Keynesianism failed, other economists naturally promoted their doctrines, also with flawed results. Monetarism—the idea that steady increases in the money supply would maximize the economy's stability—proved unworkable. Subsequently, "supply-side economics" made wildly unrealistic claims about how tax cuts might raise economic growth. All these ideas were oversimplified and overpromoted. The transformation of economic performance into an entitlement ultimately debased popular economic discourse, because economic doctrines were increasingly merchandised as panaceas to popular anxieties.

TO CALL WALTER HELLER and like-minded economists Keynesians is, of course, to take liberties with labels. Keynes died in 1946, and it's impossible to know whether he would have endorsed those who invoked his name. That said, Heller and his contemporaries felt comfortable with the label and felt, too, that their policies were not especially risky. It is easy to see why, because the basic Keynesian framework still retains a strong, though superficial, appeal. The general idea was that the economy could be kept continuously close to "full employment": a level of production that would provide a job for everyone who wanted one and keep factories operating near peak capacity. Economists thought they could precisely estimate the economy's output, or gross domestic product (GDP), at "full employment." If the economy were below this ideal level, then government could cut taxes, increase spending, reduce interest rates—or some combination of the three. Consumers and businesses would spend more, economic growth would increase, and the economy would approach full employment. By the same token, if rapid growth threatened to breach the economy's limits, government could slow growth by raising taxes, increasing interest rates, or cutting spending. Otherwise, excess demand would collide with limited supply, and price inflation would occur.

This was all straightforward, and huge advances in economic statistics and forecasting techniques seemed to make it practical. For instance, we now take it for granted that government can tell us how much the economy's output has grown—or contracted—over a given period. But before the Second World War, this was not possible. The calculation of economic output (GDP) did not regularly become available until 1947.* It represented an enormous improvement over the selected economic indicators (steel production, railroad freight car loadings) that had previously been used to measure the economy's ups and downs. Similarly, new computer economic models seemed to make it easier to forecast economic changes—potential recessions or inflation—and to predict the impact of government policies. The computer models examined the relationships among scores or even hundreds of economic variables (say, interest rates and home construction). Economists were seemingly empowered as never before. They could detect tendencies of the economy to veer into recession or inflation and could then devise countermeasures whose effects could be, it was thought, precisely predicted.

Nothing contradicted this optimism for much of the 1960s. After Kennedy's assassination, Congress cut taxes in 1964. The economy expanded strongly, just as Heller said it would. By 1966, unemployment was 3.8 percent, which was slightly less than the 4 percent that the Council of Economic Advisers had defined as "full employ-

*Actually, the statistic that was given most publicity until 1991 was gross national product (GNP), not gross domestic product (GDP). GDP and GNP are nearly identical, though there are some small technical differences between them. References to GDP and such statistics as unemployment rates for earlier eras often involve after-the-fact estimates that did not exist at the time. I use GDP throughout this book to avoid confusion.

ment."* Heller and his associates were hailed as having brought America the wonders of modern economics. Economists relished their newfound prominence and and basked in the glory of public adulation. There was a "growing political and popular belief that modern economics can, after all, deliver the goods—that even if they never meet a payroll or carry a precinct [in an election], economists can meet a crisis and help carry an expansion," as Heller himself wrote.[2] But the triumph was short-lived, and by the late 1960s, rising inflation would shatter the claim that Keynesian policies could permanently reconcile "full employment" with stable prices. The "new economics" did not work for at least three reasons. Any one probably would have been fatal. Together, they were devastating.

First, economists had exaggerated their ability to forecast accurately—and, therefore, their ability to prescribe sensible policies. True, there had been big advances in economic statistics. But the improved statistics were still imperfect, subject to omissions and constant revisions. Computer models in turn relied on the flawed statistics and, worse, assumed fixed relationships among economic variables that were actually always changing. (For example, a cut in short-term interest rates may affect long-term rates—those on bonds and mortgages—differently at different times. In turn, these differences would affect interest-sensitive spending on housing and business investment.) Inevitably, forecasts erred. In 1969, most economists thought that the danger of a recession had passed; instead one started. In the 1970s, economists routinely underestimated inflation. On balance, economic forecasting has probably improved since 1945; but it has not attained the reliability and accuracy that many economists once envisioned.[3]

---

*The obvious question arises: How could there be 4 percent unemployment at "full employment"? During the Second World War, unemployment had fallen below 4 percent, and in the early 1960s, some economists said the full employment target should have been set lower. But most economists then regarded—and still regard—some unemployment as "frictional": workers voluntarily leaving one job to look for another with better pay or working conditions; or people looking for jobs just after entering the labor force (for example, ex-students or housewives); or some workers on layoff who expect to be recalled to their old jobs. The judgment of Kennedy's Council of Economic Advisers in the early 1960s was that, once unemployment got much below 4 percent, the fierce competition for workers would rapidly raise wages and trigger wage-driven inflation. Thus, 4 percent unemployment represented "full employment." With hindsight, we know that even this target was too optimistic; trying to drive unemployment down to 4 percent and keep it there increased inflation.

Second, even if accurate forecasting existed, Keynesian policies would have foundered. To succeed, they required political freedom—the ability to make needed policy changes quickly. The trouble was (and remains) that not all policy changes are popular, and unpopular changes encounter political resistance. This quickly became clear. By 1965, President Johnson's economists had recognized the dangers of higher inflation and believed that it would be aggravated by the military buildup for Vietnam. They urged a tax increase to curb spending. But convincing Johnson was hard and convincing Congress was even harder. It didn't raise taxes until 1968, and by then inflation had become much worse. The problem of timing is permanent. Practical politicians resist anything unpleasant until the need for it becomes obvious and overwhelming, and by then difficulties that might have been minimized may have mushroomed into something much larger and less manageable. (Conceptually, there's an escape from this dilemma. Although presidents and Congress may resist raising taxes or cutting spending, if economists recommend such actions, the Federal Reserve—whose policies affect short-term interest rates and credit conditions—can move on its own. That is, it can raise interest rates to avert inflation or lower them to prevent recession. Not surprisingly, the Fed carries much of the burden of responding to business cycles for precisely this reason. But the Fed also faces two practical problems. First, it may not know when or how much to change rates; its forecasting, too, is imperfect. Second, though it is nominally independent of Congress and the White House, it still encounters intense informal political pressure not to do things that will be seen as unpleasant.)

Finally, the basic theory was wrong. Keynesian economists misunderstood inflation by relying on an analytical device called the Phillips Curve (named after the economist A. W. Phillips, who devised it). It purported to show a fixed relationship between unemployment and inflation. Thus, 4 percent unemployment was associated with 3 percent inflation, and a 3 percent unemployment rate was associated with 4 percent inflation.[4] The Phillips Curve implied that if unemployment fell to very low levels, the inflationary consequences wouldn't be large. This, it turned out, was a mirage. The Phillips Curve showed past relationships between inflation and unemployment, and those relationships had been created, in part, by periodic recessions that had quelled inflation. But once government policies changed, relationships also changed. The constant effort to hold unemployment at very low levels resulted in constant increases of inflation: first to 3, then to 6, and, ultimately, to 12 and 13 percent. Most economists now believe that every economy has some "natural" level of unemployment below which inflation will continually accelerate, as scarcities of workers and products trigger an unending wage-price spiral. (Economist Edmund Phelps of Columbia University, an originator of the natural-rate concept, has rightly noted that it is not, strictly speaking, "natural." Rather, it's affected by government policies, social customs, and institutions—a society with generous unemployment benefits, for example, may have a higher natural unemployment rate than one with only meager benefits. The reason is that in a country with generous benefits, the unemployed are less inclined to take new jobs. Therefore, labor market scarcities and the resulting inflationary pressures can occur at higher reported unemployment rates. In the United States, the natural rate of unemployment is now thought to be about 6 percent, though estimates vary; in Europe, with more extensive unemployment insurance and welfare benefits, the rates are typically put a few percentage points higher.)

WITH HINDSIGHT, the sixties' long economic expansion—106 months, from early 1961 to late 1969—was no triumph of advanced thinking. It was simply an inflationary boom. Government cut taxes, loosened credit, and increased spending (mainly, though not exclusively, to pay for the Vietnam War). The result was a surge in jobs and inflation. Between 1961 and 1969, inflation went from less than 1 to more than 6 percent.[5] What happened had happened many times before, usually during wars, when governments unleashed torrents of new spending financed with increasingly worthless money. In this case, the initial rationale for loose credit and deficit spending stemmed from a deliberate decision to stimulate the economy and avoid recession; the Vietnam War then compounded inflationary pressures, because it increased military spending without corresponding tax increases. The Keynesians' blind spot was their inability to admit that recessions are sometimes necessary. Gluts of goods and workers suppress inflation. Businesses—seeing profits decline or disappear—hold down labor costs. Subsiding prices and higher unemployment make workers more accepting of lower wage increases. Without such correctives, inflation can gain a toehold in behavior and expectations. If companies always expect to produce at full capacity, why limit price increases? If workers always expect to have jobs, why limit wage demands?

For Keynesian economists to concede these realities would have destroyed the very appeal of the "new economics." That appeal was about abolishing recessions, not praising their hidden virtues. That seemed a throwback to the crusty world of "classical" economics, which held that business cycles occur largely through spontaneous and self-regulating mechanisms. The Keynesians minimized the economy's self-regulating nature and magnified the government's powers. In turn, their error ultimately reflected a misreading of the Depression. The Depression, of course, was the pivotal event in the evolution of modern economic thought, mainly because it gave rise to Keynesianism. Oddly, it was not much studied by Keynes's American disciples. Rather, they simply assumed that his theory explained it. Keynes's masterpiece, *The General Theory of Employment, Interest and Money*, published in 1936, sought to show why an economy could slip into a deep slump from which it might never spontaneously recover. Business and consumer confidence might be so shattered that no possible drop in interest rates would stimulate new spending; the economy would be caught in a "liquidity trap." Likewise, wages might be rigid. Workers might resist cuts even if prices were falling. Companies would remain unprofitable and wouldn't be induced to hire more workers. The implication seemed plain: if these traditional mechanisms (flexible wages and interest rates) had been disarmed, governments had to act to ensure economic recovery.

Although this seemed a plausible explanation of the Depression, it doesn't fit the facts. Put another way, Keynes seems to have misunderstood the Depression. What is remarkable about his *General Theory* is that it contains few references to the Depression itself. There is virtually no discussion of the specific conditions that might have led to the collapse, and there is no sense that the Depression might have been an exceptional event. Instead, Keynes was looking for a general theory to understand the economy at all times and in all places. But as it happens, the Depression is best explained by precisely the peculiar circumstances of the time that he ignored. Specifically, the central cause of the Depression was the futile effort by major governments (those in the United States, Britain, France, and most other European countries) to preserve the gold standard. This converted what would have been a normal, if severe, business slump into a crushing calamity. In some ways, the conclusions that might be drawn from the 1930s are the exact opposites of those that Keynes and his followers drew. The central problem was not that the economy's self-correcting mechanisms had spontaneously gone dead, requiring governmental intervention to generate economic expansion. Rather, the problem was that the self-correcting mechanisms had been overridden by deliberate government policies intended to preserve the nineteenth-century gold standard.

It was not that governments consciously pursued economic suicide. But their actions were conditioned by the prevailing wisdom (embraced by the public as well as national leaders) that the value of money could be protected only if it were ultimately backed by something—gold, in this case—that governments could not create at will. By itself, paper money was considered unreliable, because governments could print as much of it as they wished. Governments somehow had to be policed. Gold did that. Governments kept gold stocks to back their paper currency; individuals, businesses, or other governments could exchange paper money for gold at a fixed price. (In the United States, that price was one ounce of gold for $20.68 between 1879 and 1933.) Governments would go to great lengths to protect their gold stocks, because without them, the foundations of public trust in money and government would, it was thought, disintegrate. But this mentality drove governments around the world to take actions that clearly worsened the Depression.

In the United States, for example, the Federal Reserve failed in its original mission: to prevent banking panics that would ravage the economy. Between 1929 and 1933, banks failed at a terrifying rate, and the number of banks declined from nearly 25,000 to about 14,000. There were at least four waves of panic from late 1930 until early 1933. The economy's initial downturn was probably a reaction to the consumer spending boom of the 1920s, when Americans bought millions of new cars, radios, and other appliances; the stock market crash of 1929 then aggravated the effect by making people uncertain and fearful. But the banking collapse (the worst in U.S. history) prevented the economy from recovering. Between 1929 and 1933, the money supply (cash plus checking accounts) dropped by about one third. Depositors and share-holders in failed banks lost the equivalent of nearly 2.5 percent of national income. Desperate to have cash to meet withdrawals, banks called old loans and resisted making new ones. In 1929, banks had loans equal to 85 percent of their deposits; by January 1933, this figure had dropped to 58 percent, and in addition, borrowers at failed banks often lost credit altogether. The Depression fed on itself. Prices collapsed; between mid-1929 and mid-1932, wholesale prices dropped 40 percent. Many borrowers couldn't repay their debts. Farms were repossessed; businesses went bankrupt. Rising unemployment reduced spending.[6]

The Federal Reserve's failure to mitigate the banking crisis highlighted the contradictions in its original charter. The Fed couldn't succeed as a "lender of last resort" unless it was eager to lend, and often it wasn't. By law, the Fed was committed to holding gold stocks equal to 40 percent of outstanding Federal Reserve notes (paper money). Providing more funds to banks would have reassured depositors, who feared their banks would run out of cash. But that might also have undermined confidence in the gold standard by increasing the amount of cash that could have been exchanged for gold. Comparable considerations often led the Fed to raise interest rates when it should have lowered them (or at least kept them low). For example, after Britain left the gold standard in September 1931, the Federal Reserve raised its discount rate from 1.5 to 3.5 percent, a huge increase for an economy that was in collapse. The reason for doing so was to protect U.S. gold stocks. Once Britain left gold (that is, refused to exchange gold for paper currency), fears that America would do likewise naturally increased. Investors were tempted to cash in dollars for gold. Higher interest rates aimed to thwart these pressures. Gold earns no interest. To buy it, investors either had to use interest-bearing assets, such as bank deposits, or had to borrow. Higher interest rates made both alternatives less attractive.

The best proof that the defense of gold was at the core of the Depression is the fact that once governments abandoned gold—the United States effectively did so in 1933—their economies began to recover. Between 1933 and 1936, the U.S. unemployment rate dropped from 25 to 17 percent. Freed from defending gold, the Fed could follow policies that encouraged recovery.[7] The argument about how the Fed might have cushioned the Depression is, of course, highly simplified. The Fed would not simply have given cash to strapped banks. It could have "discounted"—that is, lent against—some of banks' own assets. Or it could have engaged in more aggressive "open market" operations by buying U.S. Treasury securities on the open market. This, too, would have had the effect of providing banks with extra cash without requiring them to raise cash by calling in loans. The complaint against the Federal Reserve (and other government central banks) is not that they failed to allow interest rates to fall during the Depression. For example, the Federal Reserve lowered its discount rate from 6 to 2.5 percent between October 1929 and June 1930. The complaint is that the Fed—and other central banks—sometimes reversed themselves in the midst of the crisis, thus tightening policy when they should have continued easing or not supporting banks sufficiently with cash during bank runs.

The crucial point is that the Depression's severity resulted from specific government decisions—not, as Keynes contended, from the economy's inherent tendency to drop into a ditch from which it couldn't escape. In turn, this misinterpretation had a profound historic effect. It encouraged active government economic management rather than illuminating the mistakes of government economic management. Any historic understanding of the Depression was lost after the Second World War because Keynes's theory was so ascendant. There was scattered skepticism, but the first major intellectual challenge to it did not occur until 1963, with the publication of *A Monetary History of the United States, 1867–1960* by Milton Friedman and Anna Schwartz. This massive work presented the first detailed argument that the Depression resulted from the Federal Reserve's failure to prevent bank failures and the resulting huge drop in the money supply. But Friedman and Schwartz attributed the Fed's policy simply to incompetence. Moreover, their assault came after Keynesianism had achieved political influence and intellectual dominance. Only in the late 1980s did economic historians Peter Temin and Barry Eichengreen convincingly demonstrate the critical role played by the gold standard in the Depression.[8]

BUT THESE AND OTHER intellectual assaults on Keynesianism (at least that brand popularized and practiced in the 1960s and 1970s) were not decisive in its undoing. What was decisive was bitter experience. For the initial Keynesian failure in the Kennedy-Johnson years, though discouraging, did not breed defeatism. Instead, it inspired a frantic search (in both academic journals and government policies) for new ways to redeem the Keynesian promise of reconciling "full employment" with low inflation. The most obvious approach was wage-price controls, and so they were, perhaps inevitably, tried. Displeased with the slow recovery from the 1969–1970 recession, President Richard M. Nixon—facing reelection in 1972—imposed temporary controls in August 1971. (The controls were part of a package to end the dollar's international convertibility—that is, the U.S. commitment to convert dollars held by other governments into gold at $35 an ounce. This differed from the general gold standard, because only governments could ask for gold. Ordinary citizens or private companies, whether American or foreign, could not.) The decision was heavily political. Nixon "would explain that . . . if he didn't do it the Democrats would win the presidency and they would impose permanent controls," Herbert Stein, a member of Nixon's Council of Economic Advisers, later wrote. This justification, though self-serving and exaggerated, was not entirely illogical. The main advocates of controls were some Keynesian and mainly Democratic economists, who saw controls as the only way to reach "full employment." The Democratic Congress authorized the controls on the assumption that Nixon, who opposed the measure, would never use the authority. The Democrats then expected to embarrass him by arguing that he hadn't done everything in his power to halt inflation and cut unemployment.[9]

The trouble with controls is that they can work for a while—and then they break down from complexity, public resentment, or both. This is precisely what happened. Nixon's controls were initially popular. With inflation suppressed, the recovery quickened. The unemployment rate, 6.1 percent in August 1971, dropped to 5.5 percent by the next September, just before the election.[10] By seeming to stop inflation, the controls had created the illusion that economic growth could easily increase. Government spending was raised; interest rates stayed low. These policies intensified inflationary pressures, which were disguised by the controls. Once the controls were removed, however, inflation zoomed to 11 percent in 1974, more than triple the 1973 level (3.2 percent) and double the 1970 level (5.7 percent). The collapse of the controls was predictable. The longer controls remain, the more they have to be modified. Exceptions proliferate, because not all prices can be controlled; some companies will inevitably experience increases in their costs and, if they can't raise their own prices, will go bankrupt. In other cases, scarcities require prices or wages to increase both to blunt demand and to encourage supply. What particularly doomed Nixon's controls was the impossibility of suppressing prices set in international markets, especially for oil and grain. The Yom Kippur War in 1973 aggravated oil price increases, and poor harvests had increased grain prices, which raised American retail meat prices (feed grain is a major cost for meat producers). Nixon tried, against his economists' advice, a second wage-price freeze in June 1973. It was a debacle, as Stein later wrote:

> Cattle were being withheld from the market, chickens were being drowned, and the foodstore shelves were being emptied. The freeze was then lifted in steps, beginning within a little more than a month after it had been imposed. From then on, everyone knew that the system could not last much longer. The controls ended on April 30, 1974, when authority for them expired, and the President did not ask for their renewal.*[11]

The lesson did not take. In many ways, President Jimmy Carter and his advisers repeated Nixon's mistakes. They pushed hard to lower unemployment after the 1973–1975 recession. They underestimated inflation and the impact on inflationary expectations of their commitment to "full employment." (A sign of the times: in 1978, Congress passed the Humphrey-Hawkins legislation, named after its cosponsors, Senator Hubert Humphrey and Representative Augustus Hawkins. It committed the government to achieving 4 percent unemployment and zero inflation by 1983.) Carter then dabbled with informal wage and price guidelines (the standards issued in late 1978 called

---

*The reason chickens were drowned and cattle were withheld from market is that, with high feed prices, they could not be sold profitably under controlled prices. While arguing that the controls were bound to collapse, I would add that there are circumstances when they can "work"—in the sense that they will be tolerated by the public, which will allow for necessary exceptions—for long periods. Mainly, the circumstances occur during a crisis of some sort, when the inconveniences and inconsistencies of controls seem unimportant compared with some larger social objective. War is the obvious example.

for a limit on wage increases of 7 percent and on price increases of 5.75 percent in the next year). These were ineffective. By 1979, double-digit inflation had returned.

With hindsight, the Keynesian episode was surely the most fateful and damaging of the postwar economy. What had occurred was a two-decade experiment about our ability to reach and maintain "full employment." All during these years, "full employment" was the basic standard by which economic policy was judged. Three times (in the 1960s and after the recessions of 1969–1970 and 1973–1975), government policies tried to reach and sustain it. Three times, they failed. Unemployment could be reduced to low levels; but it could not be perpetually held at some fixed, low level without spawning high inflation. The mechanisms by which this occurred were easy money and credit policies. It is hard to judge this experiment kindly. It surely intensified the severity of the two harshest postwar recessions (those of 1973–1975 and 1981–1982) and left a legacy of lingering inflation that—even in the mid-1990s—is only gradually being eliminated. Probably most important of all, it created an entirely new set of public expectations. It whetted the popular appetite for economic salvation. It forged the explicit alliance between economics and politics. And its failure left a void that other economists rushed to fill. None could or did.

THE FAILURE OF the monetarist episode was also, in many ways, predictable. Monetarism's central insight is indisputably correct: inflation—a general increase in prices, as opposed to the rise of a few prices—is always a monetary phenomenon. That is, it results from "too much money chasing too few goods"; moreover, government can prevent this by controlling the growth of money. But modern monetarism goes beyond this basic idea and recommends that government central banks (the Federal Reserve in the United States) strictly limit money growth to a fixed annual rate of increase. For example, if the economy were deemed capable of growing 3 percent a year, the Federal Reserve might increase the money supply only 3 percent a year. This would provide (the argument runs) enough money to allow the economy to expand—but not so much that inflation will occur. In the monetarist view, the economy's instability often stems from the instability of money and credit policy. When the Federal Reserve creates too much money, it fosters inflation. But when the Fed slows down money growth too much, it triggers a recession. The obvious solution is to keep money growth steady; the unstated assumption is that the private economy, on its own, tends toward stable growth.*

This sounds too good to be true, because it is. There are two problems: first, we don't know what "money" is; and second, the public's demand for money—however defined—constantly fluctuates in relation to the economy's output. Although simple in concept, money isn't in practice. In theory, it's used to buy and sell things (a "medium of exchange") or to preserve wealth (a "store of value"). The trouble is that the ways societies meet these needs are always changing. Until the nineteenth century, checks were rarely used; now they are considered "money," because they are a common means of payment. In recent decades, the explosion of credit cards (1 billion of them in 1991) has also minimized the use of cash.[12] So have electronic fund transfers and automatic deposit of paychecks. In practice, what we call "money" is merely a statistic reflecting the best guesses of what actually serves as money. The Federal Reserve periodically alters its statistics to incorporate changing customs. Even without this uncertainty, the public's fluctuating demand for money confounds the mechanical operation of a money rule. In the Depression, when people were terrified and prices were falling, the public demand for gold and cash soared; the Federal Reserve's failure to accommodate this shift in demand made the Depression worse. At other times, the public may want to hold less money. In these circumstances, if the Federal Reserve maintains a steady growth of money, it may incite inflation.

Between October 1979 and October 1982, the Federal Reserve actually tried to control one definition of the money supply. The effort was abandoned, in part because the advent of NOW accounts

---

*The way in which the Federal Reserve actually creates money mystifies many people. It needn't. The process is fairly simple. When the Fed wants to increase the money supply, it buys U.S. Treasury securities (such as bonds, notes, and bills) from banks and other investors. The Fed's payments for these securities then add to the money on deposit or in circulation. This creates more funds for banks to lend, which tends to depress short-term interest rates. If the Fed wants to reduce the money supply or raise interest rates, it does just the opposite: it sells Treasury securities. The money used to pay for these securities then goes on deposit at the Fed and out of circulation, and short-term rates tend to rise.

(interest-bearing checking accounts) made the statistic for the basic money supply (cash plus checking accounts) less useful. Before, checking deposits had been used mainly to pay bills; after NOW accounts, checking deposits were also useful as savings accounts. Naturally, the new "money" did not behave exactly as had the old. Such shifts compel the Federal Reserve to exercise judgment as to when to loosen or tighten its policies. It does not have the luxury of relying on a simple and static statistic. But this is not monetarism's fatal flaw, which is that money and credit constitute only one influence—although an important one—on the economy. Therefore, controlling money rigidly will not automatically stabilize the economy's performance. In professional journals and conferences, monetarist economists admit as much. But popularized monetarism has implied otherwise; it has fingered erratic monetary policy as a major source of economic instability. Many monetarists, for instance, blame most recessions on declines in money growth. The idea seems to be that all or most recessions might otherwise have been avoided. This is certainly not true, and any attempt to have done so would have resulted in higher inflation.[13]

THE FIXATION ON a single explanation of the economy's performance was also the hallmark of supply-side economics—and also, not surprisingly, its failing. In contrast to Keynesianism and monetarism, which were academic ideas that were popularized, supply-side economics was a popular concept that then influenced academic thinking. Promoted initially by Robert L. Bartley, editor of the editorial pages of the *Wall Street Journal*, and a handful of economists, the central idea was (and is) sound: government taxes and regulations can, at some point, become punitive and self-defeating. They can discourage so much risk taking, work, or investment that they sharply reduce economic growth. Supply-side economists advocated cuts in tax rates and regulations. The impression became widespread that, through faster economic growth, these would pay for themselves. That is, economic growth would increase so much that additional taxes, reflecting higher personal incomes and profits, would offset any loss of tax revenue from lower tax rates. The extravagance of these promises has itself become a subject of controversy. Some supply-side economists claimed they never said tax cuts would pay for themselves; these views (the supply-siders complain) were parodies created by critics to make supply-side policies look silly. In truth, some extravagant claims were made; but the claims were also parodied (even as supply-siders were becoming more restrained) to discredit them.

No matter. The general idea was given a test run. Strictly speaking, President Ronald Reagan's economic policies (dubbed "Reaganomics") were not the supply-side manifesto. Reagan blended "supply-side economics, monetarism, and traditional Republican budget-balancing" in his rhetoric and policies, as economist Paul Craig Roberts, an adviser, once put it. Reagan was no one's tool. He used the slogans and ideas that suited him. Still, Congress did cut top tax rates substantially (from 70 percent in 1980 to a low of 28 percent in 1988); and new regulations were slowed, if not stopped.* Yet, the economy's underlying growth rate edged up only slightly in the 1980s. The experience "refuted the irresponsible conjectures of some supply-side polemicists that a general reduction in tax rates would substantially increase economic growth and might increase tax revenues," as William Niskanen, a member of Reagan's Council of Economic Advisers (and not a supply-side zealot), later wrote. Taxes and regulations clearly matter for the economy, but they are only some of the many things that matter. What also counts (to mention just a few other things) is technology, corporate management, workers' skills, interest rates, savings and investment, popular tastes, and foreign exchange rates.[14]

OURS IS, TO REPEAT, a market economy. It does not operate strictly according to the rhythms prescribed by election rhetoric or desired by government policies. Government influences the economy, but it is only one of many important influences. It is surely in our interest to learn how government can best exercise its influence—what to do, when, and what not to do—but this is quite different from pretending that government can fully control the process. Economists in the public arena have tended to fudge or deny this distinction. At academic conferences and in professional journals, they may acknowledge lim-

---

*The top personal income tax rate was subsequently raised to 31 percent in 1990 and 39.6 percent in 1993.

its, uncertainty, ignorance, or self-doubt. But in popular and political settings, humility recedes. The power of public policy (where economists' talents can be brought to bear) assumes awesome proportions. What everyone has wanted to hear is that, by and large, the instruments of constructive change lie within the government's grasp, if only they can be discovered and deployed. And economists pursuing public power have pandered to this, whether by arguing that government could directly manage the economy or—as with the supply-siders—that the repeal of undesirable policies would miraculously improve economic performance.

It is in this sense that economics has sought to project a cheery face and is heavily implicated in the emergence of the psychology of entitlement. By aspiring to play a larger role in political life, economists (at least those actively engaged in public debate) have overstated what they know, what they can do, and how quickly they can do it. Of course, some simplification of thinking is inevitable. To be useful, as opposed to merely informative, knowledge must be organized and ordered. To focus on every conceivable adverse contingency is to become paralyzed. It is to miss the forest for the trees or even the twigs. But the simplification of economic ideas has gone much further than that. The drive for political relevance smothers hedged statements and promotes sweeping generalizations. And these grand pronouncements are taken seriously, because economists have been preaching to an eager and sometimes almost willfully gullible audience. Political leaders have enthusiastically used economic arguments to promote themselves and attack their opponents. There is now an almost seamless process through which economists and political leaders use and misuse each other. Economists supply the live ammunition for political combat and are rewarded with high rank. Those who find the combat distasteful or dishonest are, as a practical matter, increasingly excluded, because they are unwilling—or unable—to conform their ideas and statements to political necessity. The process continues, because the public has been thirsty for assurances that widely desired economic goals are attainable or that widely deplored economic problems are someone's fault.

The result is perpetuation of a misleading picture of the economy and the illusion that its shortcomings are easily susceptible to solution. Some policies are clearly better than others, and political debate sometimes constructively rewards them. But all too often, the process is skewed. The trouble is that the time horizons for politics and economics can differ substantially. Some sensible economic ideas may be distasteful politically. They may not show results until well after the next election, or even later than that. And some foolish economic ideas may have huge political appeal. They may have immediately pleasurable consequences, even if they ultimately prove disastrous (Nixon's wage-price controls are an obvious example). But politicians, concerned with the election cycle, tend to focus on immediate gains, and economists who wish to satisfy them do the same. So the marriage of politics and economics, sensible in the abstract (why, after all, shouldn't government promote a stronger economy?), has not worked well in practice. It began, though, in the spirit of the times, which is the belief in organized and open-ended progress, and it is hardly surprising that the same spirit animated modern managers, who were the other great advocates of the new capitalism.

7

The Myth of Management

MANAGEMENT IS ONE of our most overused, least understood, and most expedient concepts. We visualize it as the means by which companies mold themselves into our desired Good Corporations, combining economic efficiency and social enlightenment. Management signifies, in this sense, a body of knowledge or set of skills that enables enterprises to attain this higher level of economic and social competence. Companies cease to be heartless masses of workers and machines, dedicated only to production and profits, and become agents of well-being for their workers, customers, and shareholders. As instruments of this transformation, modern managers (or, at any rate, good managers) portray themselves—and are portrayed—as a new class of business leader. They are less rapacious and more responsible than the old capitalists, say, the Rockefellers and Morgans, who single-mindedly pursued power and domination with little thought for others. Modern business leaders have become professionals; they are no longer predators. "Management . . . expresses basic beliefs of modern Western society," Peter Drucker, a popular postwar management thinker, wrote in

1954. "It expresses the belief in the possibility of controlling man's livelihood through systematic organization of economic resources. It expresses the belief that economic change can be made into the most powerful engine for human betterment and social justice."[1]

This idea of management is a myth: a figment of our collective imaginations. It projects business (especially big business) as we would like to see it, not as it actually is. It converts our major corporations into vehicles for social progress, because they fulfill our individual wants for security and material well-being, while also satisfying society's need for ever greater national wealth. In popular consciousness, good management involves the realization of these obviously desirable goals, which are elevated into informal (but expected) entitlements. Otherwise, it's hard to say what management actually is and what it does. It is certainly not a precise set of skills, a body of knowledge, or a bundle of business techniques that apply to all companies. To "manage" is to run something. Beyond that, the word does not mean much. It does not describe what the people who actually run enterprises do from day to day.

The once common notion that a good manager can manage almost anything now seems patently absurd. In few other realms of activity do we assume that professionals are like so many interchangeable parts. People have different talents, temperaments, training, interests, and experiences. They specialize. A good professional football coach is not a good baseball coach. A good surgeon is not a good pediatrician. Why should a good bank manager be a good store manager? Some executives may effectively cross industry lines; most do not. The same truism applies to many managerial tasks. What works in one company, in one industry, or at one time may not work at another company, in another industry, or at another time. All this seems plain, and yet the postwar faith in management exerted (and continues to exert) a powerful stranglehold on the American psyche. That faith spanned the political spectrum. Liberal Harvard economist John Kenneth Galbraith called management the "technostructure" and argued that it had largely replaced the market economy with a new era of "planning."*

---

*Indeed, Galbraith predicted that the rise of "planning" signaled a convergence of capitalism and communism. Economic progress, he argued, depended on new technology and industrial organization. Both could flourish under either system, because both required "planning" by the "technostructure." Needless to say, the convergence did not occur as Galbraith anticipated.

For their part, the leaders of U.S. corporations devoutly believed, at least through the early 1970s, in the theology of management. They could craft increasingly compassionate and productive organizations, because they had pioneered the world's best business practices and were, therefore, in a class by themselves.

It was an article of faith that most large corporations were essentially immortal. From time to time, an exceptionally mismanaged firm might experience problems (or even go bankrupt), but the overwhelming majority of companies could reasonably expect to exist forever, providing permanent employment for their workers and permanent profits for their shareholders. Ordinary Americans generally shared this self-confidence, and, because it was so widespread, the fact that many of our largest and most prestigious companies—General Motors, IBM, Sears, Ford, Xerox, and Citicorp, to name but a few—fell on hard times in the 1970s, 1980s, and 1990s came as a genuine shock. Even now, the belief in good management is so strong that corporate failures are almost routinely attributed to "bad" management, as if all business errors ought to be preventable and that corporate eclipse, when it occurs, reflects human shortcomings and mistakes. Big companies should rise but, if they are well managed, they should not fall.

This firm faith in management was premised on the belief that modern economies are fundamentally different from their preindustrial predecessors. The dominance of large, apparently immortal corporations meant that managerial competence (so it was thought) had replaced erratic markets as the decisive force in determining national economic success or failure. Only big companies, Galbraith and others contended, had the money and know-how to develop and deploy complex new technologies. These new technologies would generate new products and better efficiency. Because this process is the key to commercial success and because size is essential, most major industries would have only a handful of big companies. This changed the nature of the market system. Adam Smith's atomized markets presumed that multitudes of powerless sellers (farmers, small merchants, and local factories) faced multitudes of powerless buyers; both were at the whim of devastating price swings, ruled by unpredictable forces of supply and demand. By contrast, the modern economy spawned industries dominated by a few large companies, which had far more control over their costs, prices, and (therefore) profits. They were not made by the market; they made the market.

The upshot was (the argument continued) that big companies had transformed economic life. They attracted the most talented people by offering better pay and job security than smaller firms. The superior organization of the large firm meant that the entrepreneur, a romantic character who created new enterprises, was dead or dying. "The real accomplishment of modern science and technology consists in taking quite ordinary men, informing them narrowly and deeply and then, through appropriate organization, arranging to have their knowledge combined with that of other specialized but equally ordinary men," Galbraith wrote in 1967. "This dispenses the need for genius."[2] Moreover, corporations had become so stable and profitable that their very character had changed. Gone was an obsessive focus on survival and profit maximization. Instead, managers could afford to emphasize other personal, professional, and political goals: the corporation's prestige, the well-being and satisfaction of its managers and other employees, and—by being "responsible"—its social respectability.

These ideas are, in fact, all partially true. Big companies do dominate modern economies; markets are a far cry from Adam Smith's ideal; management is important in determining corporate (or national) economic success or failure; and executives do worry about much more than profits (by the late 1960s, social responsibility had become a byword of corporate America). The trouble is that all these plausible-sounding ideas are not wholly true. They have never fully described how business actually operates. The seductive theorizing about management was done mainly by two classes of people: those who had never run or worked in any business,* or those (often corporate executives) who had an interest in portraying business in the most favorable light. Each underestimated the personality, drama, immense diversity, and uncertainty of real-life business. Everything became a matter of calculation and technique. Methods could be generalized; management was a universal discipline. There are indeed many useful techniques, from accounting practices to produc-

---

*Needless to say, this author is no different. I have worked for several large companies and, as a writer and reporter, have also been self-employed. Otherwise, I am an observer of—and not a participant in—business.

tion methods, that can be adopted by many companies. But it is often the human element, combined with chance and timing, that determines how companies arise, thrive, or founder.

The idea that the entrepreneur was dead, for instance, was spectacularly wrong. In the past half century, some of the largest and most influential businesses have been created by single-minded individuals, who pursued their own visions obsessively. Consider McDonald's, the story of both an immense company and a cultural phenomenon, fast food. It started with Richard and Maurice McDonald, two brothers who owned a successful drive-in restaurant in San Bernardino, California. In 1948, they converted their drive-in (where customers drove up and placed orders, which were then cooked) into the nation's first fast-food restaurant (where customers placed orders for precooked food). The menu was reduced, food standardized. Each hamburger had ketchup, onions, and two pickles. Prices were cut, from thirty to fifteen cents. As Richard McDonald later recalled:

> Our whole concept was based on speed, lower prices and volume. We were going after big, big volumes by lowering prices and by having the customer serve himself. My God, the carhops were slow. We'd say to ourselves that there had to be a faster way. The cars were jamming up the lot. Customers weren't demanding it, but our intuition told us that they would like speed. Everything was moving faster. The supermarkets and dime stores had already converted to self-service, and it was obvious the future of drive-ins was self-service.

But the McDonald brothers did not create McDonald's, the chain. That feat belonged to Ray Kroc, a frustrated salesman who first visited the McDonalds' restaurant as the owner (and main salesman) of a small company that sold milk-shake mixers. He quickly saw the potential. Kroc bought the rights to copy the McDonalds' formula and opened his first restaurant in Des Plaines, Illinois, in 1955. Kroc's success stemmed from the strong concept and his compulsive attention to detail. He decreed standardized menus and low prices. People should know exactly what they would get at McDonald's. To attract families, he demanded cleanliness and made regular inspections. For the same reason, he imposed strict quality standards on suppliers. And he created a franchise and supplier system that would adhere to these principles by creating a generous profit-sharing formula by which franchise operators had "an opportunity—unheard of in franchising—to become rich before he became rich," as John Love observed in a superb history of McDonald's. Kroc's own ambition was more to construct a huge company than to become wealthy.[3]

With details changed, the McDonald's story has been repeated thousands of times since the Second World War. Strong-willed and ambitious owner-managers have built vast enterprises, often starting with modest amounts of money. Consider a skimpy list: Wal-Mart, the late Sam Walton; Microsoft, Bill Gates; MCI, the late William McGowan; Digital Equipment, Ken Olsen; Apple Computer, Steven Jobs; Toys "R" Us, Charles Lazarus; Intel, Gordon Moore and the late Robert Noyce. Almost every story of a new business is different and highly personal. Federal Express, although a phenomenal success now, almost failed five or six times in its first two years. On its first day of flying, it carried six packages; after more than two years of operating, it had accumulated losses of $29 million and owed lenders $49 million. Founder Fred Smith and a small group of executives sustained the company through energy, faith in the concept, and bravado. At one point, Smith needed a good day at the casino tables in Las Vegas to generate the cash for the weekly payroll. Not all new ventures involve such extreme melodrama. But most require dedication and drudgery, with no assurance of success. The same is true of most commercial projects, whether creating new products or opening new markets. Management is methodical; real-life business is messy.[4]

Not only did the cult of management underestimate the power of personal ambition and vision, it exaggerated the efficiency and stability of the large organization. Just because big companies do not face Adam Smith's markets does not mean they are protected from market pressures. The market is more than a horde of buyers and sellers haggling over price. It is also an arena in which new products, methods, and ideas are constantly approved or rejected. Big Business's reputed strengths provide no permanent sanctuary. It is true, for example, that firms with more than 10,000 workers perform nearly 80 percent of all commercial R&D. But this is misleading.[5] Most corporate R&D involves the improvements of existing products or processes: developing new cars; making paint more durable; reducing the defects in computer chips. These gains, through critical, do not constitute the breakthroughs that can create new industries and undermine old ones. Big companies often lack the patience for such breakthroughs: the return on investment is not fast enough or safe enough to satisfy the organization's requirements or to suit the ambitions of risk-averse career managers.* Or sometimes, companies cannot genuinely fathom new possibilities, which confound existing technologies or business methods. Consider the modern copying machine. The basic technology was discovered in 1938 by Chester Carlson. The technology was offered to no less than twenty-one major companies, including IBM, RCA, and GE. All rejected it. Only a small Rochester firm, Haloid, took the gamble. It acquired Carlson's idea in 1947 but needed thirteen years to perfect a commercial machine. In 1960, it introduced the model 914, which made seven virtually identical copies a minute—a phenomenal rate at the time. Haloid became Xerox.[6]

It is precisely these sorts of breakthroughs—in technology, products, services, and business methods—that can wound corporate giants by altering competitive conditions. Examples abound. IBM defended its mainframe computer against large, well-financed rivals (among them: General Electric, RCA, and Fujitsu) but was undermined by the advent of the personal computer, which spawned new computer uses and appealed to new customers. For years, General Motors kept Ford and Chrysler at bay. But it couldn't resist Japanese automakers that had pioneered new production methods that cut costs and reduced defects. Likewise, Sears was undercut by Wal-Mart, which developed new techniques of buying and inventory control that, along with greater reliance on self-service, permitted much lower prices. American, United, and Delta Airlines suffered from low-cost competition from Southwest

---

*Corporate executives often contend that their short-term focus results from pressures from the financial markets to show quarter-to-quarter profit increases. The argument is that large institutional investors—pension funds, mutual funds, insurance companies—will drive down a company's stock if profits don't regularly rise. This supposedly discourages managers from taking the long-term risks that might reduce short-term profits. I omit this as a major cause of corporate failure, because I doubt its importance. Mostly, it rationalizes top executives' own mistakes. Anyone who examines large companies that have gotten in serious trouble over the past fifteen years (Chrysler, General Motors, IBM, Digital Equipment, to name a few) will be hard-pressed to blame institutional investors for their misfortunes.

Airlines, whose operating practices permitted much lower ticket prices. Turner Broadcasting (CNN) and other cable TV operations assaulted the three traditional television networks.

The Peter Principle afflicts many big companies: they expand to their level of incompetence. Success sows the seeds of failure. It fosters overconfidence, waste, and insularity. Corporate bureaucracies expand, and executive privileges increase. In the mid-1970s, Bethlehem Steel had seven corporate jets and subsidized golf courses used by executives. Meanwhile, General Electric had begun to "strangle" on its own rules, as Noel Tichy and Stratford Sherman concluded in a study of the company. "For executives, mastery of arduous procedures had become an art form . . . [and] an unspoken requirement for advancement." GE's plight especially reflected blind faith in management as a universal discipline. In 1951, Ralph Cordiner, GE's chairman, created a team to codify the company's best ideas. Two years later, it produced the Blue Books, a five-volume (3,464-page) encyclopedia. In succeeding years, the books got fatter. "A manager is a manager is a manager," Cordiner liked to say.[7]

It is not just top executives who succumb to sloppiness, laziness, or luxury. Workers often expect success to be shared in the form of higher wages, better benefits, and less demanding work schedules. Up to a point, this is normal and desirable. But the line between reasonable reward and self-defeating excess is easily crossed. In the 1960s and 1970s, heavily unionized industries (steel and autos, for example) pressed for huge wage settlements while resisting changes in wasteful work practices. Labor peace was often purchased with lavish wage agreements that ultimately made companies uncompetitive. At nonunion companies, similar impulses operated. Companies often provided automatic across-the-board salary increases and routine promotions. Workers felt entitled to their jobs and paychecks, and by and large, companies agreed. "Under the double influence of their corporate compassion and their rich treasuries," management consultant Judith Bardwick has noted of the 1960s and 1970s, "organizations . . . stopped evaluating employees and discharging those who were not productive; they failed to hold people accountable for their performance."[8]

Finally, corporate eclipse flows from financial forces. Every thriving enterprise has what business historian Alfred Chandler, Jr., calls an "organizational capability": it knows how to do some things exceptionally well.[9] When it can reinvest its profits to do those things, its prospects are good. This does not mean that the company must always do the same thing. It can branch into related fields by building on its strengths. For example, Du Pont moved from making explosives into making commercial chemicals. However, the time usually comes when this sort of evolution is hard. The company's basic markets have matured. Executives are then caught between the desire to grow and the paucity of good investment choices. Facing this situation, the company might resign itself to slow growth and concentrate on remaining profitable and paying out its profits to shareholders. But such stagnation violates our culture of growth, our concept of "making it." Executives often believe (sometime correctly) that a failure to grow is fatal. A company, in this view, that stands still is likely to fall behind, because it will be too cautious and backward-looking.

Unfortunately, the other investment alternatives are all risky and unappealing, too. Basically, the company has three choices. It can:

1. *Continue to invest in its existing businesses.* The hope is that markets aren't truly saturated or that new investments will somehow expand sales (by driving other companies from the market, making products more appealing, or lowering costs to consumers). The risk is that the investments will simply be made out of habit and that, ultimately, there will be overinvestment. The surplus investments would then be inefficient and generate low (or no) profits.

2. *Try to develop new products or services.* The dangers are obvious. These new products may take the company well beyond its competence. It has to learn new technologies, new markets, and (often) new business methods. If the company is trying to enter an already existing market (for example, a telephone company trying to make computers), it will face entrenched competitors. If it is trying to create genuinely new products, it faces the possibility that those products can't be developed or won't become commercially viable.

3. *Avoid these problems by acquiring already existing businesses.* The telephone company that wants to get into computers can buy a computer company. (This is what the American Telephone & Telegraph Co. did after its own efforts to enter the computer market foundered; it bought NCR.) But this approach to diversification also carries big risks. The purchase price for other companies may be too high; the

firms may not want to sell except at a premium. In plain language, the acquisition may be a waste of money.* Moreover, the buying company may (again) venture beyond its competence or have trouble motivating workers in its new acquisition. If it buys too many companies, its own management structure may become top-heavy.

Now, it is not inevitable that big, successful companies—whose markets have matured—will make mediocre investments. But the odds seem to favor it, and indeed, that has been the recent experience. A study by economists Dennis C. Mueller of the University of Maryland and Elizabeth Reardon of the Department of Justice examined the profitability of corporate investments by 641 firms between 1970 and 1988. The study found that about four fifths of the companies had below-average returns; essentially, the profitability of these firms was a mix of high returns on old investments and mediocre or low returns on new.[11] It is not true, as many commentators have wrongly concluded, that big is bad. In business, big is often inevitable, because good products create large markets and markets themselves have, as a result of lower communications and transportation costs, expanded. Big companies have inherent strengths: the economies of scale of mass markets; the ability to serve customers as they move; the opportunity to transfer lessons from one market or product to others (something learned in Germany may work in the United States, or vice versa); ample capital to finance new products and research; and staying power to see new products to market. But what is true is that big is not invincible.

THE OBVIOUS QUESTION ARISES: Why did corporate America, which seemed so successful and stable in the 1950s and 1960s, become so con-

---

*A simple example shows why this may be so. Suppose a company is making a $15 per share profit and its stock is selling for $100. In this case, it is making a 15 percent annual return. Why would it want to sell if another company offered $100 for its shares? A higher price may make the sale attractive. Suppose the buyout occurs at $120 a share—a 20 percent premium. But the buying company now has a higher investment. The $15 of annual profits represent only a 12.5 percent return on its $120 investment. The acquisition makes financial sense only if the buying company can improve the profits above $18 a share (a 15 percent return on $120). In fact, the premium for corporate buyouts has averaged about one third in recent years. It was 32 percent between 1982 and 1991.[10] (Incidentally, AT&T's purchase of NCR failed; the computer operation is to be spun off.)

vulsed in the late 1970s and 1980s? Part of the answer is that the picture
of earlier success is exaggerated. Even then, there were corporate failures and setbacks. The best known were the Edsel and Penn Central:
the first was Ford's ill-fated new car of 1957 (it was discontinued after
poor sales) and the second was the bankruptcy of the nation's largest
railroad in 1970 (it had diversified into nonrailroad businesses and over-
borrowed to do so). But in the prevailing optimism, such examples of
corporate fallibility were dismissed as aberrations. In 1963, *Fortune* magazine published an anthology of stories about corporate troubles called
Corporations in Crisis, which noted in passing: "A search of the libraries
discloses no book, indeed no article, devoted to a discussion of corporate crises *in general*" (emphasis in original).[12] The idea of generalized
failure simply didn't occur to people. That said, many companies did
get into trouble more or less simultaneously. Why?

What happened is that corporate profit margins slowly declined
between the 1950s and the early 1970s—and then collapsed. By the
mid-1970s, companies didn't have the flexibility they had had two
decades earlier. Profit margins were narrower, debts higher. With
higher margins, corporate executives felt confident that they were
both discharging their traditional economic duties (that is, earning
profits for their owners) while also fulfilling the newer obligations of
being a responsible corporate citizen. As margins narrowed, goals
seemed more in conflict. Managers paid more attention to costs and
efficiency, even if that meant paying less attention to "being responsible." The following table shows just how dramatic was the change in
gross profit margins—that is, the difference between a firm's costs
and its revenues. Commerce Department data provide an approxi-
mation of this for all nonfinancial corporations (all corporations excluding banks, insurance companies, securities houses, and other
financial firms). Pretax profits as a percentage of nonfinancial corporations' total output (roughly speaking, their total sales) were:

Slipping Profit Margins

1950s	16.9%
1960s	15.7%
1970s	10.7%
1980s	8.7%[13]

The reasons for the collapse in profit margins are not entirely clear. To some extent, the expansionary (and ultimately inflationary) economic policies of the 1960s and 1970s temporarily hid problems and encouraged inefficiencies. The subsequent recessions ruthlessly exposed weakness, depressed profits, or created losses. Beyond this, many companies encountered new competitive pressures from now familiar sources: more foreign rivals (affected industries—autos, steel, machine tools, office copiers, semiconductors), domestic deregulation and the breakup of the American Telephone & Telegraph Co. (affected industries—airlines, railroads, phone companies), and new technologies (affected industries—computers, television). The adverse effects of excessive corporate diversification—the explosion of conglomerates and multidivisional firms—also have hurt many firms. Finally, companies relied more heavily on borrowing (bank loans, bonds) to finance new investment as opposed to using retained profits or selling new stock. Between the late 1960s and the mid-1980s, the share of corporate cash flow needed to pay interest on loans roughly doubled.[14] (While profit margins—profits as a share of sales— dropped dramatically, other measures of corporate profitability, such as profits in relation to stockholders' equity, did not suffer equivalent declines. The shift in financing either caused or compensated for lower margins.)

The collapse of profit margins, the growing reliance on debt, and intensified competition undermined the power, moral authority, and independence of corporate managers. Modern management techniques did not protect them. Management is what management does. It consists of the prevailing practices, attitudes, and approaches that business leaders take toward their needs. In this sense, it is always self-serving. If those needs are misperceived or evoke ill-conceived responses, then management will be inept. In part, this is what happened. In a now famous article in the *Harvard Business Review* in 1980, Robert Hayes and the late William Abernathy argued that postwar American managers had progressively developed a new style that emphasized "analytic detachment rather than the insight that comes from 'hands on' experience."[15] Top executives imagined themselves as commanding generals who could deploy armies without concerning themselves with how the troops were trained or whether the weapons worked. Top managers devised "strategy"—decided the company's overall direction—and dealt with outside constituencies, from government regulators to local communities. The less glorious jobs of ensuring reliable products, competitive costs, and customer satisfaction fell to those in lower echelons.

In this fashion, postwar management theories mostly justified what managers were already doing or were inclined to do. In the 1950s and 1960s, one pervasive need was to justify the growing size and diversity of their companies. By 1968, for example, General Electric had 190 departments (ranging in size from $1.7 million in sales up to $391 million in sales). These reported to 46 divisions, which reported to 10 "groups" that, in turn, reported to GE's top executive. Sure enough, a rationale for diversification was found. Corporate managers (it was argued) could make better investments than others—whether individuals, pension funds, or mutual funds. Executives were said to know more about products and technologies. If companies reinvested wisely, their stock prices would rise; shareholders would benefit more than if they had invested themselves. The argument for management power was also helped by the tax system, which encouraged companies to retain profits by imposing a double tax on dividends.*

New management techniques aimed to help managers exercise their expanded power. For example, the Boston Consulting Group (BCG), a major consulting firm, advised clients to classify their products or businesses into one of four categories based on growth and market share (the proportion of total product sales enjoyed by the company): "cash cows"—mature businesses with slow growth and

---

*Dividends are taxed once when earned as corporate profits (through the corporate income tax) and again when received by individuals (through the personal income tax). In theory, stockholders might be better off if a company paid no dividends. Consider a company that earns $10 per share. Assume (for simplicity's sake) that the corporate and personal tax rates are 40 percent. The company has 40 percent of its profits taxed away through the corporate tax rate—$4 in this case. Now suppose it pays the rest ($6, in this case) as dividends to individuals; another 40 percent will be taxed away, or $2.40. The total tax is $6.40. But if the company doesn't pay the money as dividends, it will keep the entire $6. If this were reflected in the company's stock price, the stock would rise $6, and shareholders who needed the cash could sell. Their profit ($6 in this case) would be taxed at the rate for capital gains, which for most of the postwar period has been below the tax on personal income. Thus, the incentive for companies to retain profits in the name of the shareholders; however, the theoretical gain would be lost to shareholders if the company used its money poorly. So would society as a whole.

high market share (typically, these businesses generated more profits than they needed for new investment); "dogs"—businesses with low market share, low growth, and poor profits; "problem children"— rapidly growing businesses that had low market shares and, therefore, weren't highly profitable; and "stars" with high growth rates and high market shares, which promised huge future profits (however, "stars" required large new investments to sustain their growth). The task of managers was to milk the cows, ditch the dogs, discipline the problem children, and catch the stars. The trouble, of course, is that no one said how the stars were created or how the cows could stay productive if milked perpetually. The management theories were grandiose; tedious details were swept aside.[16]

By the 1980s, the theories' soundness—and executives' autonomy—were under siege. As managerial reputation and authority eroded, the challenges to it multiplied. These played out in various ways, some traditional (superior cars displaced inferior cars) and some less so. One untraditional way was the eighties' wave of hostile corporate takeovers and so-called leveraged buyouts. Investors bought entire companies, usually with borrowed money (the "leverage") from bank loans or low-grade ("junk") bonds. The idea was to profit by dismantling excessively diversified companies or tapping misinvested earnings. In turn, the new pressures—from takeovers, foreign competition, deregulated markets, new technologies—inspired new management concepts, including "restructuring," "downsizing," "reengineering," and "total quality management." (Restructuring and downsizing usually refer to making a company smaller by firing people or selling businesses. Reengineering involves wholly new ways of doing distinct jobs, such as designing components.) And rather than retaining profits, companies increasingly disgorged them to keep investors happy. In 1994, for instance, companies repurchased $65 billion of their own shares. By reducing the shares outstanding, such stock buybacks theoretically raise profits per share and the company's stock price.[17]

In practice, then, management methods are malleable and constantly shift to achieve actions that managers—for whatever reason— desire. Capitalism hasn't changed that much after all. As an economic system, it is given to cycles of experimentation and excess that are not just an unfortunate side effect. They are the way capitalism generates new ideas, products, methods, and technologies. But they are also how productive investments become unproductive, how markets (for everything from toys to buildings) become saturated, and how sensible business decisions degenerate into suicidal speculation. Good ideas become bad ideas because they are overdone. The earliest conglomerates may, for instance, have made sense, in that poorly managed companies were taken over by managers with superior skills or management techniques (for example, better budget or personnel practices). Similarly, the early wave of hostile takeovers and leveraged buyouts in the 1980s seems to have made economic sense, often resulting in increases in operating profits from 20 to 30 percent.[18] But by the late 1980s, the takeover boom had turned speculative, involving too much debt and too little potential for savings. When the economy went into a recession, many overindebted companies went bankrupt, and investors lost huge sums.

WHAT WE HAVE is a system of bureaucratic capitalism that mixes the pressures of bureaucracy and the market. Companies are creatures of both. On the one hand, executives are captains of industry, supposedly dedicated to maximizing profits and efficiency. On the other, they are custodians of organizations where they have often spent most of their professional lives. Their personal power, prestige, sense of identity, and well-being are often bound up with their company and their place in it. These dual roles frequently collide. Michael Jensen, a corporate finance expert at the Harvard Business School, has put it this way:

> Corporate managers are the agents of shareholders, a relationship fraught with conflicting interests. . . . Managers have incentives to cause their firms to grow beyond optimal size. Growth increases managers' power by increasing the resources under their control. It is also associated with increases in managers' compensation, because changes in compensation are positively related to the growth in sales. The tendency of firms to reward middle managers through promotion [i.e., jobs with greater responsibilities and salaries] rather than year-to-year bonuses also creates a strong organization bias towards growth to supply the new positions that such promotion-based reward systems require.[19]

In the early postwar decades, the tensions were muffled, because the economy was strong and because the stock market—where capitalists, whoever they might be, earn their returns—boomed. Managers enjoyed autonomy; they could, generally speaking, make choices as they saw fit. As conditions changed, managers lost flexibility. Power shifted from the executive suite to the market, and the change fed on itself. None of this dooms large companies to irreversible decline or extinction. The metaphor of the big company as dinosaur is misleading. Many have recovered from major setbacks, having achieved dramatic gains in efficiency and quality. In 1979, Ford required nearly five workers in its assembly plants to produce one auto a day; by 1993, that figure had been reduced to three.[20] Other companies whose fortunes also revived spectacularly include Caterpillar, Xerox, Chrysler, Texas Instruments, and Citicorp. But the improvement typically had been prompted by outside pressures, and this involved sweeping social implications.

The immortality of the large corporations can no longer be presumed, and the consequence is that the "good corporation" can't always be good—or at least as good as it was expected to be. It can no longer automatically fulfill all its preferred social commitments. Sometime in the 1980s, this became intuitively obvious. Until then, it was possible to think that corporate blunders reflected only isolated mistakes of individual executives or companies. Some companies—those that, by conventional wisdom, were well managed—still seemed immune to setbacks. These firms seemed to be oases of permanent competence and security. Even in the early 1980s, workers at IBM were reassured in a short book (*About Your Company*—an explanation of the firm's beliefs and its benefits) of the firm's commitment to full employment:

> In nearly 40 years, no person employed on a regular basis by IBM has lost as much as one hour of working time because of a layoff. When recessions come or there is a major product shift, some companies handle the work-force imbalances that result by letting people go. IBM hasn't done that, hopes never to have to. People are a treasured resource. They are treated like one. . . . It's hardly a surprise that one of the main reasons people like to work for IBM is the company's all-out effort to maintain full employment.[21]

But by mid-decade, or thereabouts, such promises had evaporated. Nor was it still plausible to believe that corporate missteps reflected only individual errors. Too many companies were affected. Between 1986 and 1994, for example, IBM cut its workforce from 407,000 to 215,000. Many other companies that once had formal or informal policies of full employment engaged in similar reductions, though some losses occurred through early retirements, normal job turnover, or selling entire divisions. After 1990, Sears reduced its workforce of 500,000 by 137,000 (51,000 involved sales of divisions).[22] Companies changed because conditions changed; if IBM hadn't become less paternalistic, it might have gone bankrupt. "What has happened," writes one executive, "is that 'good' has been redefined in the face of economic reality." Once undesirable behavior is condoned or even encouraged. Managers are quicker to cut jobs, fringe benefits, and wages than they were fifteen or twenty years ago. Surveys by the American Management Association of major companies between 1990 and 1994 found that roughly half resorted to major layoffs and that these continued even after the 1990–1991 recession. Likewise, companies have moved away from automatic wage increases to "merit" increases ("pay for performance" in management jargon). One 1994 survey of 317 major companies found that 90 percent used "pay for performance."[23]

The face of American capitalism has changed. It is no longer so calm, composed, or compassionate. It is less protective and more predatory. It no longer promises ultimate security or endless entitlement. Instead, it preaches the inevitability of change, implying that change is often cruel. American business has been cast in a harsher light. In some ways, this new imagery distorts, just as the old did. The transformation of the corporate spirit of the past fifteen or twenty years is undeniable. But the shift in corporate practice has been less stark. There was always more turbulence and less security than the old, self-serving image of modern management acknowledged. And there are still plenty of companies that offer career jobs, generous fringe benefits, and substantial security. They have to. Social norms have altered. Most companies cannot afford to treat workers with the arbitrariness of the 1890s or even the 1930s, because if they did, they would lose their best workers to other firms with more appealing practices.

Still, the aura that American business was marching inexorably toward a future in which most workers would be guaranteed security, job satisfaction, and ample private welfare has been shattered, and with that has come heightened anxiety. Turmoil in corporate America may be less than headlines imply, but no one can be certain of being spared it. The myth of management was (and is) that some sort of quasi-science could put capitalism's jarring process of experimentation, exertion, and excess behind us. In our mind's eye, modern management would remake corporate America into a giant Good Corporation. But what we call corporate America is not a monolith. It is an immensely fluid system that is always being depleted of and replenished with companies. Even its biggest, best-known, and most prestigious firms do not have a right to permanence. The myth of management allowed us to imagine corporate America as rising above the market. In reality, the market is stronger, more erratic, more complicated, and more enduring than any corporation. Companies may try to predict, shape, or exploit it. But they cannot defeat it.

8

The Real Economy

❧ ❧ ❧ ❧

THERE IS NO "NEW CAPITALISM," only an evolution of the old. Compared with a half century ago—or, more aptly, the end of the 1920s—the evolution has been enormous. Ours is truly a "mixed" economy in the sense that government and private enterprise share economic power. Government's influence is far larger than hardly anyone would have imagined in 1929. Taxes are higher, regulations are more pervasive, and business has become an explicit instrument of public policies, from pollution control to product labeling. Still, the system's essential private features survive. Most consumption, investment, and production decisions are privately made, and the profit motive remains legitimate. Despite its imperfections, the system continues to generate impressive gains. For most Americans, it has dramatically improved living standards and economic security. It has made life longer and less physically punishing. There will always be timeless questions about whether all our material abundance satisfies our spiritual needs or makes us happier. But few Americans would, if given the chance, choose to revert to a poorer era when most people worked harder, received less, and suffered more. Almost none of us would consider that to be a happier or more appealing time. And we would be right.[1]

The trouble is that, in capitalism, gain and pain are often inter-twined—something we have difficulty admitting. The postwar image of the economy as a giant machine is the wrong image. If a machine breaks, it can be fixed. The parts can be cleaned, repaired, or re-placed. But as we have seen, our economic mechanics consistently fail, because they are not dealing with a machine. A better image for the economy is that of a vast river. Although its waters usually seem calm, change abounds as countless varieties of fish, other animals, and plants flourish and perish; and there are occasional floods or droughts that cannot be prevented by man-made improvements (dams, levees). Our economy moves by similar rhythms of growth, decay, and renewal. Many industries and technologies thrive, while others decline. Business cycles endure. We can influence, through government policies and business practices, these rhythms and cycles for good or ill. But in the end, we cannot abolish them without crip-pling the economy. The rise and fall of companies, products, and technologies—though obviously disruptive—is the way the economy increases incomes and creates jobs. And recessions—though obvi-ously unpleasant—do provide benefits by dampening inflation and forcing firms to be more efficient. The economy is chronically unsta-ble; the only solace is that it also seems to have self-correcting mech-anisms that generally limit its instability.

There is, in short, an unavoidable conflict between the economy's essential nature and our postwar ambitions: creating security and suppressing instability. This does not mean that we are helpless or are condemned to "laissez-faire"—a reviled but irrelevant phrase. In modern societies, laissez-faire (literally, "to let happen") does not exist. By their nature, governments influence economies. Govern-ments make laws, impose taxes, grant privileges, and regulate trade. A state of nature—no government—means anarchy in practice; long-term business relations are difficult, if not impossible. But gov-ernments, though essential, are imperfect. Once they exist, they be-come instruments for competing ideas and interests. Our own history is strewn with controversies over government's proper economic role. In the nineteenth century, debates recurred over bank regulation, tariffs, and sound money. By the twentieth century, government was trying to curb big business and improve social conditions through, for example, child labor laws. Our own era is distinctive only in that our ambitions became so sweeping. The real choice, then, is not between laissez-faire and government intervention. It is between constructive and destructive intervention. What ought to guide us are general principles that seem to have worked over time. Ideally, we can learn from the past half century something about what we can usefully influence and what we can't.

One lesson is that sustained inflation (anything above a 2 percent annual increase in recorded prices) is immensely destructive. It encourages speculation, deters productive investment, and saps public confidence. But inflation can be prevented by government through its money and credit policies. There are two reasons for tolerating 0 to 2 percent price changes. First, our price statistics simply aren't good enough to determine pure price stability. For example, they only imperfectly adjust for quality changes. If new computers or shoes are better than the old and have higher prices, then part or all of the price increase represents quality improvements, not inflation. The Bureau of Labor Statistics, which calculates the major price indexes, makes quality adjustments for a few items, such as cars. But mainly, the job is just too big. Second, we have rarely achieved total price stability. Even in the nineteenth century, there were often long periods of slowly rising or falling prices. Crude stability was maintained over decades, because declines offset increases. But forcing absolute declines now—as a way of maintaining long-term stability—strikes me as a mistake that would depress production by creating new uncertainties. It is probably true (as many economists in the 1960s argued) that a "little bit" of inflation is not especially damaging. The difference between 2 and 3 percent inflation or 3 and 4 percent is not huge. Wages and interest rates adjust. There are losses to some groups and gains to others. But these are probably no greater than the random gains and losses that occur in any economy as vast as ours. The trouble with treating a "bit more" inflation as harmless is that government has no anchor for its policies and, at some point, a bit more becomes harmful. A 3 percent rate becomes 4, then slides toward 5 or 6. People and businesses don't know how high it will go, and when that happens, they try to exploit it and protect themselves against it. It takes on a momentum of its own.

Unfortunately, only periodic recessions seem capable of quelling inflation. Wage-price controls may succeed temporarily, especially when a crisis (such as a war) creates a public tolerance for the arbitrariness and anomalies that controls involve. But such occasions are rare and, by their very nature, momentary. To see every recession, then, as a "failure"—an attitude common today among the public and some economists—is wrong. Recessions are merely a feature of our system. They have vices and virtues. Recognizing only the vices (lost production, greater unemployment, more insecurity) may mean sacrificing the virtues. If government is too eager to prevent slumps—or reverse them once they've started—it may squander its best chance of containing inflation. Put another way, the public must be willing to tolerate occasional slumps. Informally, the brush with double-digit inflation in the late 1970s seems to have created this tolerance. Paul Volcker, chairman of the Federal Reserve between 1979 and 1987 and the man whose policies suffocated double-digit inflation, later put it this way: "What we [discovered] . . . is that at a certain point in the inflationary process, public opinion will support strong policies to restore stability even though those policies seem to entail harsh short-term costs." ("Seem to"? In late 1982, unemployment rose to nearly 11 percent.) As a result, price stability is now discussed as an important goal, unlike twenty years ago, and inflation's long-term direction has been down. In 1980, it was 13.5 percent; in 1994, it was 2.6 percent.[2]

But the consensus is crude. It could crumble under public pressure. Recessions are always denounced, and arguments are still made that government can permanently hold unemployment close to its "natural rate." (Recall that this is the rate that supposedly prevents higher inflation; it is now estimated at about 6 percent, though on this, too, economists disagree.[3]) This is a chimera. Even most economists doubt it can be done with fiscal policy (changes in taxes and spending). It takes too long for Congress to act, and the bias toward budget deficits (cutting taxes or increasing spending, but not the opposite) is too strong. Abstractly, monetary policy—changes in interest rates and money growth—seems more promising. To promote economic expansion, the Federal Reserve would lower interest rates. Spending and borrowing would increase. To stem inflationary pressures, the Fed would raise rates. A judicious balancing should succeed. Unfortunately, in practice, the connections between changes in interest rates and total borrowing and spending are loose and inexact.

Long and uncertain lags occur between rate changes and their effects. Once the dangers of a recession or inflation become apparent, it may be too late to avert either. Judgments have to be made; mistakes will happen. If the Federal Reserve always strives to lower unemployment, its mistakes will likely be inflationary ones.[4]

A second lesson of the past half century is that the market is the basic source of rising living standards. By "market," what is meant (again) is an open, competitive process that encourages and allows people and companies to advance new ideas, products, technologies, and business techniques. It is not just raw investment or new technology that enhances economic growth; rather, it is the murky and intricate process by which these are put to good use. The market's great virtue is that it enables the new to displace the old, while maintaining constant pressure for efficiency. We cannot expect to reap all its rewards if we try to suppress all its costs, uncertainties, and inconveniences. These can be easily identified—whether job insecurity, income inequality, pollution, or episodes of overinvestment—and labeled "market failures." Politically and psychologically, we rebel against them. We do not want unfettered free markets if they exalt economic growth over all other values and interests. Americans are almost certainly willing to sacrifice some economic growth in return for making our society seem fairer and less tumultuous. But we are not willing to sacrifice *all* growth, and there's the rub. The dilemma (one shared by most advanced societies) is how to reconcile this deep desire for security with equally unrelenting demands for higher living standards.

The eclipse of the Good Corporation aggravates the dilemma. Our social safety net now has more gaps than people wanted or anticipated, precisely because corporations are providing less than expected job security and fringe benefits. One alternative is to have government provide more, but this might harm the economy and also triggers Americans' distrust of government. The supply-siders of the 1980s may have erred in their extravagant predictions of how much lower tax rates and fewer regulations would stimulate faster economic growth. Still, their general point was correct. Government spending, taxes, and regulations can—at some point—become so oppressive that they significantly damage economic growth. Indeed, bigger government may be one cause of the slowdown that has already occurred. But without bigger government, the safety net may grow more tattered and perforated. There are unavoidable choices, made harder by the cumulative effects of government actions. One tax or regulation, in isolation, may have little adverse impact on economic growth. But the combined impact of many regulations and taxes may have a much larger effect.

The experience of Europe is both instructive and disturbing. More than the United States, European societies have striven to mitigate the adverse effects of the market process through generous welfare programs and protective regulations limiting, for example, companies' rights to fire workers. The result has been been perverse: a steady rise of joblessness over the past two decades that was only temporarily relieved by periods of economic expansion. Between 1974 and 1994, the European Union's unemployment rate rose from 3 to 11 percent. Private jobs (as opposed to government jobs) barely increased over the entire period. High taxes and tough regulations discouraged new companies from forming by raising costs and lowering the rewards of success; strict layoff regulations deterred hiring, because firing became so hard. And generous unemployment benefits meant that the jobless felt less pressure to find new work, especially if it involved lower wages or moving. The process was insidious because it occurred so slowly and imperceptibly. There was no obvious flash point making clear the connection between the protections and benefits that people wanted and the feeble job creation that they did not want. European societies now generally recognize the connection, but they are hard-pressed to do much about it. Protections and benefits have become heavily embedded in the political system and popular expectations. There is no guarantee that we will not fall into the same trap[5] because the temptation to tinker is permanent.

WE WILL ALWAYS be able to imagine ways to improve the economy—to increase growth, soften slumps, or reduce glaring inequalities. Some of these improvements may materialize, but many won't. The economy is indeed an immense system in which isolated changes don't usually have isolated consequences. Doing x may result in y (desired) and z (not) and also maybe m, n, and q (all unanticipated). Consequences are collective and cumulative. They interact and occur over extended periods. Our political debates typically assume, understandably but often incorrectly, that all the ramifications can be foretold and judged. They can't. We cannot control what we do not understand, and that is a great deal. Anyone who thinks otherwise should reflect on recent history. Every economy poses basic questions about its stability, growth potential, and income (and wealth) distribution. To ask these questions about the U.S. economy in the past half century is to illuminate the limits of our knowledge.

1. *What determines economic stability?* As we have seen, the economy has become more stable since the Second World War. Economic expansions last longer, and slumps are milder.* But there is no real consensus about why. My belief (argued earlier) is that today's greater stability stems from a series of historic changes: the lesser roles for farming and manufacturing, given to wild swings in production and income; the end of the gold standard and changes in the banking system that improved financial stability; and government programs (such as Social Security and unemployment insurance) that stabilize people's incomes. But this explanation is only an informed hunch, and surprisingly, economists and historians have not devoted much effort to explaining the differences between pre- and postwar business cycles. What they have tried to explain, without much success, is why business cycles occur at all. In truth, their understanding has not advanced much since Wesley C. Mitchell (1874–1948), the preeminent American business cycle economist.

To Mitchell, business cycles were largely self-generating and self-destructing. Expansions self-destructed, because spending went to excess. Overoptimistic consumers or companies spent too much on new housing, factories, or inventories. Heavy spending bid up prices and wages; higher inflation increased uncertainty and squeezed profit margins. Slumps occurred; overextended borrowers cut back; companies couldn't sell all their output; or lower profits depressed new investment. But the declines ultimately generated recoveries. Excess inventories were sold, and lower prices stimulated buying; falling interest rates spurred borrowing, and lower wages encouraged hiring. The intricate process never worked instantaneously or precisely the same way twice. But it worked. Our system seemed condemned to

*For a fuller discussion, see pages 79–80 and note 17, p. 255.

both miscalculation and recuperation. So it still seems. The one major element of modern business cycles absent in Mitchell's time is explicit shifts in government policy: mainly, interest rate changes by the Federal Reserve. These obviously influence spending patterns and have been incorporated into economists' models.[6]

2. *Why has the economy's growth slowed?* No one disagrees that it has, mainly because the annual growth of productivity—output per hour worked—has slowed, from about 3 percent between the late 1940s and early 1970s to an average of about 1 percent since then. But no one has convincingly explained the productivity slump. It may be a case of historic myopia. Since the early nineteenth century, productivity gains have averaged only about 1.5 percent annually, which is not too different from recent increases. (These averaged slightly less than 1 percent in the late 1970s and slightly more than 1 percent since the mid-1980s.) By this theory, the early postwar productivity burst was exceptional. The Depression left huge backlogs in the demand for housing, cars, appliances, and industrial machinery. Similarly, new technologies (synthetic fibers, plastics, television, improved commercial aircraft) had been delayed. The United States was also the only major economy unscathed by the war; Europe, Japan, and other nations had a huge appetite for U.S. exports. Taken together, it is argued, all these favorable forces created huge onetime gains in production and efficiency.

Maybe. The trouble is that we really don't know what "normal" productivity gains should be. Is 1 or 1.5 percent a year all that can be expected? Perhaps not. The productivity slump might reflect more passing problems: inflation, poorer management, the spread of conglomerates, and the growing burden of taxes and regulations on business innovation. It's also possible that some of the slowdown is a statistical mirage. We devote some economic resources (business investment, worker time) to a cleaner environment and safer working conditions. These activities improve our well-being but don't create tangible products (like cars) and, therefore, aren't counted in productivity statistics. All these theories are plausible and are consistent with a gradual improvement in productivity in the past two decades. (Between 1973 and 1979, when inflation was high and rising, productivity grew only 0.7 percent annually. Between 1980 and 1989, the average increase was 1.2 percent; between 1990 and 1994, it was 2.1 percent.[7])

3. *Why has income inequality increased?* We understand fairly well what's happened to the very rich and the very poor. For the wealthy, new technologies—television, jet travel, satellites—have raised their pay. Stars and athletes play to larger audiences; executives run bigger, global companies. All profit from what economists Robert Frank of Cornell and Philip Cook of Duke term "winner-take-all markets." Although luck or tiny talent differences may decide who's a CEO or an NBA starter, the winners reap disproportionate rewards. Meanwhile, more single-parent families and immigrants have swelled the ranks of the poor. Between 1970 and 1990, immigrants rose from 4.8 to 7.9 percent of Americans; in the same period, the number of single-parent families doubled to about 15 million. Both groups have low average incomes.[8] The real puzzle is the widening income gap among most other workers: between the skilled and unskilled; older and younger workers (allowing, of course, for education); and even workers with similar educations (say, college graduates). Some common theories aren't convincing. Inexpensive imports are blamed for destroying well-paid factory jobs. But the impact is modest, because trade affects only some manufacturing jobs, which are only about a sixth of all jobs. Computers are said to have helped the skilled (who are adept) and hurt the unskilled (who aren't). Maybe—but this can't explain more inequality among those with similar educations or between older workers and younger—the latter, being more familiar with computers, should have benefitted from new technology.

Greater inequality may simply be another fallout of more economic turbulence and less economic optimism. In the heyday of the Good Corporation—when recessions were becoming obsolete—companies hired eagerly and resisted firing. They adopted compensation practices emphasizing "internal equity" (fairness within the firm); there were across-the-board pay increases to compensate for inflation and reflect improved productivity. Younger and less skilled workers, usually the last hired, benefited; so did the least productive workers. These practices had an economic logic. Companies expected to be operating near peak capacity. Overhead costs would always be covered. A larger workforce could mean higher corporate sales and profits. By the 1980s, this optimism had wilted. Companies became obsessed with cost cutting—as opposed to sales growth—to improve profits. Where possible, wages for new workers were cut.

"Downsizing" meant more layoffs. Now the young and unskilled (the last hired and first fired) suffered; so did anyone who lost a job and was thrust into a harsher labor market. Companies decreased automatic wage increases and relied more on "merit" raises. All these changes increased inequality. But this theory is just that; among economists, there is no consensus to explain rising inequality.[9]

Our ignorance on all these critical matters underlines how faulty the scientific and engineering metaphors have been when applied to the economy. It is not that greater economic understanding is impossible. Some of today's unanswered questions (slower growth, rising inequality, etc.) may be settled by further study. We understand the Depression much better now than in the 1930s or even in the 1960s. But this sort of understanding is historic, not scientific. It illuminates specific events or trends. It does not establish enduring scientific truths that hold at all times and enable us to predict or manipulate the future. Great economic changes often proceed by indirection. They crystallize from a multitude of smaller changes—often apparently unrelated to one another—that may occur over many years or decades. The full consequences of today's events, actions, and policies may not emerge for many years. Everything relates to everything else, and the consequences of changes (planned or unplanned) flow from the mixing of many isolated events and trends. These collective effects—again, for good or ill—are ultimately what count: the way that high inflation led to the savings-and-loan crisis is a perfect illustration of this haphazard process in action. The implication of our ignorance is simple. Those who claim they can cure business cycles, dramatically accelerate economic growth, or sharply reduce inequality are usually exaggerating.

IT IS NOT JUST ignorance that frustrates economic management. It is also rhetoric. The modern, mixed economy is more than an economic process. It is also a political and social process. Government is constantly solicited and enlisted to promote or safeguard the well-being of particular social groups, industries, workers, or favored ways of life. There is no convenient separation of economic argument from social policy or political preference. The result is an unavoidable tendency to depict the economy in terms that support avowed (or assumed) goals. There is nothing necessarily dishonest in this. It is simply part of the system, dating back to the earliest days of the republic and becoming more prominent in the past century. (In the 1790s, Alexander Hamilton favored a stronger national government and constructed an economic theory to justify it. In the 1890s, agrarian populists deplored Big Business and constructed an economic theory to justify their hostility.) But it does mean that economic analysis and argument are often subordinated to political or social purposes and cannot always be taken as expressions of disinterested truth. Practical judgments are routinely clouded and complicated by self-serving rhetoric that spans the political and ideological spectrum.

Just because the market is a formidable force for economic growth, for example, does not mean that everything done in its name will succeed or even accurately describe a given policy. Businesses constantly strive to use government to secure commercial advantage or protection, often casting their efforts as pro-market when they aren't. Government is used to frustrate the market or, at any rate, to give it a particular twist. Some policies (subsidies, tax preferences) are self-interested; others are merely dubious. For example, one oft repeated suggestion holds that economic growth could be raised by inducing greater corporate investment through business tax breaks or some other means. The idea is that declining investment has depressed economic growth and living standards. The trouble is that investment hasn't been declining, as the table below indicates. It shows business investment as a share of national income (GDP) over the past four decades.

Business Investment as a Share of Gross Domestic Product[10]

1950s	9.7%
1960s	10.0%
1970s	11.2%
1980s	12.1%

Poor investment, rather than low investment, may have undermined growth. In the 1980s, there was huge overinvestment in office buildings, hotels, and shopping centers. The amount of shopping center space increased by nearly 50 percent.[11] Vacancy rates soared. Interestingly, the overinvestment stemmed in part from excessively generous tax breaks enacted in 1981 (and largely repealed in 1986). Ordinary corporate investment is also often wasteful. In the 1980s, IBM and General Motors, to take two examples, invested vast amounts in what turned out to be unneeded factories. Between 1981 and 1990, GM's investment alone totaled $76 billion. How well we invest matters as much as how much.

Glorification of the market can conceal parasitic activity. In a wealthy society, people and companies can enrich themselves not only by becoming more productive (that is, raising society's output of goods and services) but also by redistributing some of the existing income and wealth (that is, moving it from those who have it to themselves). There are many ways to do this. Government policies are manipulated through subsidies, tax breaks, or regulatory preferences. Corporate executives devise generous pay packages for themselves; less exalted managers and workers pad expense accounts. Some corporate takeovers merely shift wealth away from one group of investors to another. Litigation moves huge amounts among competing claimants. Though often "private" and of "the market," these activities usually aren't productive. Labels mislead.

On the other hand, the condemnation of the market—inspired by the desire for more security or greater equality—often exaggerates the dangers of change. We have repeatedly been told, for example, that the rise of the "service economy" threatens lower living standards. High-value manufacturing (the argument goes) is receding before low-value services, and we'll become a nation of hamburger flippers. Not so. As previously noted, industrial production has steadily risen. In 1994, it was 40 percent higher than in 1980 and almost four times higher than in 1950.[12] The plateauing of manufacturing jobs merely signifies higher productivity: more things are being made with relatively fewer people. This is the path to higher, not lower, living standards. It means we can enjoy more services: more health care, more recreation (cable TV, Disney World), or more schooling. Indeed, the distinction between manufacturing and services is often artificial, because the two are intertwined. Most services require manufactured products, and most manufactured goods supply services. Communications and entertainment—services—need telephones, satellites, and cameras. Cars and planes—goods—provide transportation services.

The main reason services are stigmatized is to justify trade protection or government subsidies (tax breaks, grants) for industrial workers and companies. The same motive spawns criticism of globalization—the growing importance of international trade and investment. Its visibility is undeniable. We drive cars made in Japan, wear shoes made in Taiwan, and drink beer brewed in Mexico. Our mutual funds invest in Hong Kong; our hotels and office buildings are sometimes owned by Japanese or Germans. We are warned that we are being "taken over" or that a flood of cheap imports is depressing American living standards. None of this is true. Imports equal only about 11 percent of our economy's production (GDP), and exports equal about 10 percent.[13] Our living standards depend mainly on how efficiently we produce at home, not our trade balance. Global competition does affect more U.S. workers, often adversely. But all competition threatens someone; in this sense, foreign competition is no different.

Whether by imports or new investment in the United States, greater global competition generally raises Americans' living standards—and not the reverse. It compels U.S. companies to improve their efficiency and product quality. Global specialization also raises incomes. So-called cheap imports substitute for more expensive products, and U.S. exports generally support high-wage industries (commercial aircraft, computers, industrial machinery). We are not being "taken over"; despite higher foreign investment, Americans own more than 90 percent of U.S. industrial and financial assets. In the end, globalization is probably inevitable, because it stems from new communication and transportation technologies that have cut the cost of doing business across borders. The first transatlantic telephone cable in 1956 could carry 36 simultaneous calls (before that, transatlantic calls occurred only by radio); a fiber optic cable laid in the early 1990s could carry 80,000. In this period, the cost of a three-minute call between New York and London dropped from $12 to $2 (and the drop would have been greater if inflation were taken into account). None of this will be repealed.*[14]

---

*I don't mean that the growth of the global economy carries no dangers or uncertainties. Conceivably, the growing interaction of so many nations—each with its own culture and national interests—and the expansion of multinational business is altering the way that national economies and financial markets operate, in potentially unstable ways similar to those of the gold standard in the 1930s. Although there is little evidence of this, it's possible. But this is a much different danger than the commonly expressed fear that we are being overwhelmed by imports or foreign investment.

ALMOST ALL PARTICIPANTS in our economic debates have an interest in exaggerating their understanding of the economy and their ability to control it. The perverse result of this self-serving optimism is to give economic commentary and analysis a pessimistic bias. That is, we are forever discovering what's "wrong" with the economy so we can set it "right." The routine framework for analysis is to define a "problem" so the proferred "solution" will seem necessary and compelling. These debating conventions obscure the considerable success of the mixed economy, especially its recuperation since the late 1970s. Indeed, it seems sounder in the mid-1990s than it has in years. Workers—though clearly more anxious—have near-record incomes. Inflation has subsided, and productivity growth has modestly improved. Chastened companies are more competitive and less given to inflationary wage and price behavior. But this sort of gradual, spontaneous, and flawed improvement offends the purposefulness of modern economics and management, which assumed an almost infinite capacity to overhaul and perfect the economy. The contemporary consciousness finds it hard to admit that the economy is mostly self-regulating and that, although we may act on it, our efforts may be inconsequential or even harmful.

Our understanding of the forces that have produced America's success are highly general, and to the extent that they are understood, they do not seem to permit anything more than loose control. By the best economic statistics—admittedly crude—the United States surpassed Britain as the world's richest nation about 1870 and still remains so, though the gap has dramatically narrowed since the Second World War. The initial American advantages seem to have been our rich natural resources (iron ore, coal, oil, and fertile farmlands) and the vast size of our market. These fostered investment in resource-dependent industries (steel, railroads, electric utilities) and allowed long production runs that created economies of scale and low unit costs. Since 1945, other countries have adopted known technologies and increasingly shared traditional U.S. advantages: lower transportation costs gave them access to cheap raw materials, and declining trade barriers expanded markets. But superimposed on America's natural advantages has been the general nature of our economic system, which emphasizes and rewards risk taking and flexibility. This may explain why other advanced countries haven't yet completely attained U.S. income levels.*[15]

The broad lesson of this history is that a market-based economic system requires a tolerance for change, even if change is sometimes unsettling. If government is overused to construct security or protect favored industries, then it will compromise capitalism's vitality. Capitalism, whether new or old, depends on a connection between risk and reward, and if the connection is severed or drastically altered, then the system won't work as intended or expected. On the other hand, the market is not all-knowing. It makes mistakes. Its very essence is the discovery process that occurs through trial and error. The abrupt jolts of this ongoing exploration are what offend many Americans and lead them to appeal to government for protection. But in an economy like ours, it is impossible to prevent all economic insecurity and instability. The best antidote against sudden and wrenching instability may be continual, modest instability. Looking back over the past half century, it would have been better to suppress the incipient inflation of the 1960s sooner, even if that meant more frequent recessions. And it would have been better if companies had been less compassionate and more competitive sooner. A society that accepts some insecurity may suffer less of it than one that avidly pursues absolute security.

Coping with this dilemma is the permanent predicament of the mixed economy. Government and business need each other. The political curbs on the raw power of business have made corporations more acceptable to the public. Government can tap the economy's productive base for national purposes. But there are contradictions inherent in the process. Government is held responsible for delivering economic benefits that it can only crudely influence, while business is burdened with taxes and regulations that barely relate to its central economic missions (production and profits). What this means is that our mixed economy cannot mix forever if it is to remain vibrant.

---

*One basic indicator of relative income is the average amount for each citizen. In 1993, gross domestic product per person was 84 percent of the U.S. level in Japan, 77 percent in France, 76 percent in Germany (the German figure has been reduced by the unification of East and West Germany), and 70 percent in Great Britain, according to estimates of the Organization of Economic Cooperation and Development.[16]

Government and business have different roles, even if they overlap. If boundaries aren't maintained, neither may be able to perform. Business may not be able to expand incomes and jobs. Government may not be able to set reasonable rules of conduct and help the needy. The new capitalism unsuccessfully sought to suppress the dilemma. Economists and managers held themselves out as the guarantors of utopian affluence and, in the process, of benevolent government built on prosperity. In that sense, the new capitalism led directly to the politics of overpromise.

III

The Politics of Overpromise

9

Colliding Ideals

※ ※ ※ ※

THE POLITICS OF OVERPROMISE is not just a random exaggeration or an occasionally unmet obligation. It is rather the
systematic and routine tendency of government to make more
commitments than can reasonably be fulfilled. The politics of overpromise naturally flowed from the faith that an ever expanding economy would provide all the extra income needed for government to
satisfy its new commitments. By the time this optimism collapsed,
the pattern had been set. Politics had become both sensitive to and
contemptuous of public opinion. On the one hand, it caters faith-
fully to public demands, even when these are obviously in conflict.
On the other, it implicitly assumes that the public is so dim-witted
that the inconsistencies will never be discovered. Sooner or later,
though, they are. Government and politicians then become scapegoats—and tempting ones, because their policies fall so far short of
their promises.

Although understandable, this sort of vilification is ultimately
self-deceptive. It presumes that government and politics are somehow

manipulated by sinister forces—whether "special interests," "entrenched bureaucrats," "career politicians," or "policy elites"—that ignore what Americans want. Just the opposite is more often true. Government is so responsive to popular demands that it has lost much of its capacity to distinguish between what's desirable (a great deal) and what's doable (much less). The overuse of government reflects an enduring dilemma of democracy, argues political scientist Edward Banfield.[1] Democratic government is supposed to respond to popular wishes. But government that responds too willingly falls into disrepute. The reason is that popular demands are often contradictory or impractical. Acceding to too many of them, therefore, triggers disillusion. Government pledges to solve many insoluble problems. When this becomes obvious, the public scorns government.

Not surprisingly, popular esteem for government has fallen as government has grown. By the 1990s, roughly 70 percent of Americans found the federal government wasteful. In the past, there was, despite a traditional suspicion of government, less resentment. A 1941 survey asked whether there was "too much power in Washington"; 56 percent of the respondents said no and 32 percent said yes. In 1965, a poll asked whether the federal government "does too much for the people"; 32 percent said no, and only 26 percent said yes (34 percent thought things were "about right"). Government now does so much for so many that almost everyone can find something to fault. People resent government precisely because they depend on it. What it gives, it can take away, modify, or threaten. Nevertheless, the present disenchantment has not radically reduced demands for government to do more. In 1992, a poll found that 42 percent of Americans thought government "should use its power more vigorously to promote the well-being of all segments of the population" (39 percent disagreed). By wide margins, Americans think government should spend more on education (68 percent), aid to the poor (61 percent), and health care (66 percent).[2]

Government's transformation is by now a familiar story. In 1929, government spending accounted for about 11 percent of the nation's economic output (3 percent for the federal government, the rest for states, counties, and municipalities). By 1990, this share had risen to about 38 percent (nearly two thirds of it federal). Even more telling has been the shift in spending. In 1954, defense spending accounted for 70 percent of the federal budget. By 1993, it was only 20 percent—

and declining. Older Americans are now the chief beneficiaries of federal money, receiving about a third of federal outlays. Social Security and Medicare dominate. But the government also provides grants and loans to roughly half of all college students, subsidizes farmers and artists, supports research and development, and distributes food stamps to almost one of ten Americans.[3] Beyond its spending, the federal government also insures bank deposits and pensions. It regulates pollution emissions, employment practices, and food labels. It provides tax breaks for health insurance and home mortgages. It sets safety standards for cars, airlines, coal mines, factories, and drinking water.

Less well understood is why government has burgeoned. Superficially, traditional ideas of limited government have simply receded before a flood tide of new social and political demands. The concept of the "public interest" as a rationale for government action has become plastic. All manner of groups have argued that their ideas and interests involve the public interest and deserve, in one way or another, governmental support. Government is expected to organize progress and eliminate society's imperfections. With such a broad mandate, few areas of national life escape its influence. "We have strayed from the expectations of our founding fathers . . . not because we have found alternative justifications for a government role but as a result of the inevitable tug-of-war of politics," writes political scientist Richard Zeckhauser. "Few outside the academy [i.e., universities] are concerned with what our founding fathers wrote on this issue."[4]

This is accurate as far as it goes, but it does not go far enough. The politics of overpromise reveals a fundamental contradiction in our political culture. Colliding ideas—the one of limited government, the other of open-ended government—contest with each other. The doctrine of limited government was, as one scholar has put it, "the great principle of the revolution." As colonies, we broke with England because we felt that the mother country had abused her power. Early Americans adopted a skeptical view of human nature. People coveted power and, if given the opportunity, would misuse it to exploit others for their own advantage.[5] Wise government would anticipate and prevent such abuse. The trouble is that, from the beginning, we have also embraced another idea, which announces itself at the start of the Declaration of Independence. It says that "all Men are created equal, that they are endowed by the Creator with certain unalienable Rights, that among these are Life, Liberty, and the Pursuit of Happiness—That to secure these rights, Governments are instituted among Men."

The whole focus is on the individual's well-being. Advancing happiness, preserving liberty, and promoting equality are not just objectives. They are "rights." Government exists to advance and protect these rights. Nothing could be more hostile to limited government. Happiness and equality are hard to define and harder to attain. They are not specific tasks such as defending the country or collecting the garbage. They are deeply subjective and infinitely elastic. A government expected to make its citizens happy and equal faces an impossible mission. It can succeed at many of its appointed roles and still fail at its overarching purpose. Such a government is utterly open-ended, because the obstacles to happiness and equality are unending.

There has always been a tension between the two views: government as threat and government as benefactor. In colonial America, people were obsessed with the evils of power. "[They] dwelt on it endlessly, almost compulsively; it is referred to, discussed . . . at length and in similar terms by writers of almost all backgrounds and positions in the Anglo-American controversy," writes historian Bernard Bailyn. By its nature, power had an aggressive "tendency to expand itself beyond legitimate boundaries." For the colonists, liberty was not the "concern of all, governors and governed alike, but only of the governed," said Bailyn. "The wielders of power did not speak for it [liberty], nor did they naturally serve it. Their interest was to use and develop power."[6] Therefore, government had to be checked. But government should also advance happiness—Thomas Jefferson's phrase in the Declaration of Independence was not just clever rhetoric. It reflected prevailing views. Indeed, Jefferson was more cautious (and also more libertarian, in modern terms) than many of his contemporaries. While he spoke of "the pursuit of happiness," others believed government existed to achieve happiness. "We ought to consider what is the end of government, before we determine which is the best form," John Adams wrote in 1776. "Upon this point all speculative politicians will agree, that the happiness of society is the end of government, as all divines and and moral philosophers will agree that the happiness of the individual is the end of man."[7]

In the context of Adams's time, his sweeping vision did not necessarily imply a large national government. For Adams, representative government itself involved inherent benefits that would make society civil, prosperous, and happy. In 1776, most governments ruled by "fear," he wrote. By contrast, representative government "introduces knowledge among the people, and inspires them with a conscious dignity becoming freemen. . . . You will find among them some elegance, perhaps, but more solidity; a little pleasure, but a great deal of business; some politeness, but more civility."[8] Still, Adams's rhetoric (and the thinking that it reflected) created latent obligations for government, and the central conflict—between government as threat and government as benefactor—animated the debate over the Constitution. The fact that there was a Constitutional Convention in 1787 merely affirmed that the problem could not be evaded. As rebels, Americans could indulge an unlimited disgust for English power, but as citizens of a new nation, they discovered the pain of powerless government. The Articles of Confederation had proven disastrous. National government was a skeleton. It could not tax (it could ask the states for contributions but could not enforce its demands). It could not effectively negotiate foreign trade treaties, because states were free to impose their own tariffs. It could not coin money. The 1780s were a period of economic collapse. States printed inflationary amounts of paper money and engaged (by tariffs) in commercial wars. The national government was virtually incapable of having a foreign policy or of compelling the withdrawal of the remaining British troops.

The basic dilemma was that government was untrustworthy (because it would be corrupted by ordinary ambition) but weak government was worse (because it led to anarchy). Government was necessary to restrain men, but in turn government had to be restrained. The Constitution could not—and did not—repeal the dilemma. By and large, the delegates to the Convention were men of property. They wanted a country that would enable them to enjoy property's benefits. But as leaders of the Revolution, they also shared its consciousness. They dealt with the dilemma on many levels. The new Constitution was itself a series of compromises. To quiet fears of excessive power, it fragmented government's powers. The legislature had two houses, each with a separate system of representation. Power was further spread among the presidency, Congress, the courts, and the states. Indeed, the central practical issue of the Constitutional Convention was how much power to cede to the central government and how much to leave with the states.

Still, the Constitution's ratification (nine of the thirteen states had to approve before it could take effect in those states) provoked a bitter struggle. The anti-Federalists argued that the new national government was too powerful. The Federalists claimed that its powers were necessary and sufficiently restrained. The whole debate highlighted the tension between the dislike of government and an underlying optimism that good government might improve the national condition (that is, promote happiness). Ratification was not preordained. In three critical states—Massachusetts, Virginia, and New York—it was approved by only narrow margins: 19 votes out of 355 in Massachusetts, 10 out of 168 in Virginia, and 3 out of 57 in New York. Moreover, some who voted for it did so only on the assumption (which did not come to pass) that the first Congress would endorse constitutional amendments reducing the power of "the Congress over elections, taxation, commerce, and the military," as constitutional scholar Robert Goldwin has noted.[9]

After ratification, the basic tension persisted. Alexander Hamilton (the first secretary of the treasury) championed centralized and powerful government, while Jefferson (the first secretary of state) favored more limited government. Hamilton aimed to advance a cohesive and self-sufficient nation, while Jefferson focused more on the independence and well-being of the individual citizen. Neither prevailed completely. There never was a time that the national government was totally disconnected from what we would today call economic or social policy. From the start, land policy—who could get land in new territories and under what conditions—was a crucial part of national politics. It obviously affected economic development. In 1862, Congress enacted the Homestead Act, which enabled settlers to claim 160 acres as long as they improved their land for five years. There were also huge land distributions to railroads and state colleges. Throughout the nineteenth century, tariffs (which were the government's main source of revenue) were an enormously contentious issue; manufacturers liked them, farmers (buyers of manufactured goods) did not. Congress also spent some money on "internal improvements"—what we now call public works. Harbors and rivers were the main areas of investment, with the work done by the Army Corps of Engineers.[10]

In the late nineteenth century, the British writer James Bryce noted the underlying contradiction in his *The American Commonwealth*, which was published in 1888 and is something of a successor to Tocqueville's *Democracy in America*, published fifty years earlier. Americans, he found, believed that the "less of government the better; that is to say, the fewer occasions for interfering with individual citizens are allowed to officials, and the less time citizens have to spend looking after their officials, so much the more will the citizens and the community prosper." This was dogma, but American democracy imposed upon it a pragmatic willingness to use government. "Having lived longer under a democratic government," Bryce wrote, "the American masses have realized more perfectly than those of Europe that they are themselves the government. Their absolute command of its organization . . . makes them turn more quickly to it for the accomplishment of their purposes." He cited many examples, mostly by states: Massachusetts, Rhode Island, and Illinois compelled corporations to pay workers weekly; Alabama barred banks from charging more than 8 percent for loans; New York prohibited hotels from barring guests on the basis of "race, creed . . . or colour." States provided widespread aids to farmers, from analyzing soils to supplying seed. "The farmer of Kansas or Iowa is more palpably the object of the paternal solicitude of his legislature than the farmer of any European country," wrote Bryce.[11]

Perhaps more important than all these examples was the explosion of pensions for Union Civil War veterans and their dependents. This was the first widespread federal income transfer program, and its existence belies "the usual presumption of an absence of federal involvement in social welfare before the New Deal," as social historian Theda Skocpol has written. The program was not small. By 1910, about 28 percent of men over sixty-five—more than half a million—received pensions. In addition, benefits went to more than 300,000 widows, orphans, and other dependents of veterans. Between 1880 and 1910, the program accounted for roughly a quarter of all federal spending. In part, the generous pensions were justified on moral grounds. Veterans were deemed to be deserving. But the pensions were also expedient political handouts; they cemented loyalty to the Republican Party, which was identified with the Civil War. The initial pension law, passed in 1862, had restricted benefits to those who had suffered disabilities "incurred as a direct consequence of . . . military duty" or "from causes which can be directly traced" to military duty. But the law was regularly liberalized. For example, the 1890 Dependent Pension Act cut the link between pension and war injuries and opened pensions to any Union veteran who had served ninety days, regardless of whether he had been in combat.[12]

More generally, political parties in the late nineteenth and early twentieth centuries informally fulfilled some of the social welfare functions that governments provided elsewhere. Parties supplied jobs through patronage, and for immigrants they aided (in return for votes) in the process of assimilation in a strange and often menacing new country. The population of New York City, for example, nearly doubled during the first three decades of the twentieth century, rising to 6.9 million. The growth was fueled by hundreds of thousands of Slavic, Jewish, and Italian immigrants from eastern and southern Europe. Between 1910 and 1930, the population of the Bronx alone jumped from 430,000 to 1.3 million. Tammany Hall, the Democratic party machine, enlisted these new Americans into its ranks. "Tammany captains ran steamboat excursions to clambakes in College Point, Queens, staged torchlight parades complete with fireworks, provided food baskets and coal to the needy, and knitted together masses of people in a huge and threatening city," as political writer Michael Barone has written.[13]

STILL, JEFFERSONIAN RHETORIC about limited government was not hollow. Although optimistic Americans always used government to improve the "general welfare" and to advance national betterment, these uses were exceptions. Through the late nineteenth century, the national government confined itself mainly to military matters, foreign affairs, and international commerce. Most internal improvements (canals, roads, and railroads) were financed and organized by states, local governments, and private interests. Hamilton, striving to create a coherent national economy, had hoped that the government would establish a strong central bank (akin to today's Federal Reserve) and issue reliable currency. Congress did neither. It twice chartered national banks designed to play the role that Hamilton had envisioned; but the banks became controversial, and their charters lapsed. Circulating money consisted of gold and silver coin (minted by the government) and paper banknotes (issued by private banks) that fluctuated in value. Not until 1863 did Congress create national paper money, as a way of financing the Civil War, and even then it was not regulated by a central bank until 1914. Government might have been more ambitious. At the time, England had a central bank (the Bank of England). The French had an active program of national road building. These models were known and ignored.

What we now call activism—especially at the national level—was usually seen as unconstitutional and undesirable. Government, it was thought, couldn't solve most everyday problems; excessively powerful government would threaten liberty. In 1887, Congress passed the Texas Seed Bill, which would have sent seed to farmers devastated by drought. The money involved ($10,000) was "a trifling amount, even in those days . . . and the beneficiaries seemed deserving enough," as Robert Higgs has noted. Yet, President Grover Cleveland vetoed the bill, saying he could "find no warrant for such an appropriation in the Constitution." Then he sternly added: "Though the people support the Government, the Government should not support the people." That attitude was common. In 1894, nearly a fifth of the workforce was unemployed. Nevertheless, Congress rejected proposals for relief work. Said one senator: "My idea is that each individual citizen should look to himself. . . . It is not the purpose of this Government to give work to individuals throughout the United States by appropriating money that belongs to other people."[14]

At the national level, government leaders did not consider themselves indifferent, only prudent. They might practice limited government, but they still saw American government as a source of salvation for humanity. In his first extended message to Congress justifying the Union position in the Civil War, Lincoln echoed the same theme. What was at stake, he argued, was the survival of government dedicated to the betterment of the human condition:

> This is essentially a people's contest. On the side of the Union is
> a struggle for maintaining in the world that form and substance
> of government whose leading object is to elevate the condition

of men—to lift artificial weights from all shoulders; to clear the paths of laudable pursuit for all; to afford all an unfettered start, and a fair chance in the race of life . . . that is the leading object of the government for whose existence we contend.[15]

Lincoln's words emphasize the continuity in American political rhetoric. What he said then could be said today. But the meaning would be different. Today, his words would justify expansive government programs. But to Lincoln's contemporaries, they did not. Lincoln, as Richard Hofstadter has noted, "spoke for those millions of Americans who had begun their lives as hired workers—as farm hands, clerks, teachers, mechanics, flatboat men, and rail-splitters— and had passed into the ranks of landed farmers, prosperous grocers, lawyers, mechanics, physicians, and politicians. Theirs were the traditional ideals of the Protestant ethic: hard work, frugality, temperance, and a touch of ability applied long and hard enough would lift a man into the propertied or professional class and give him independence and respect if not wealth and prestige. Failure to rise in the economic scale was generally viewed as a fault in the individual, not in society. It was the outward sign of an inward lack of grace—of idleness, indulgence, waste or incapacity." In short, government free of tyranny would generally allow people to better themselves.[16]

Everyone had a chance. People succeeded, because they strived. It was the faith in individual opportunity that married the rhetoric of helpful government with the reality of limited government. But the marriage began to dissolve once rising industrialization and urbanization weakened the faith. Between 1870 and 1910, the urban population in cities of more than 100,000 roughly quintupled, growing from 4.1 million to 20.3 million. The portion of Americans living in rural areas (those with less than 2,500 people) dropped from three quarters to one half.[17] These were the outward signs of a truly national economy—connected initially by railroads and telegraph and later by telephone and roads—and of the growth of huge companies that ran railroads, made steel, refined oil, packaged beef, refined sugar, and sold consumer goods through the mails. All this undermined confidence that individuals, with hard work and self-discipline, could control their destinies. On the contrary, they seemed increasingly at the whim of massive enterprises that they could not influence as individuals. Workers could be hired or fired at a moment's notice. They could be mangled by machinery or burned in metal making. Farmers felt victimized by discriminatory railroad rates. Small merchants and wholesalers feared being overwhelmed by huge firms.

As the late historian Christopher Lasch has noted, these economic changes had a profound political and psychological effect, because they upset the prevailing belief in self-sufficiency and virtue, of the sort championed by Jefferson, Jackson, and Lincoln. The faith was that, with time, almost anyone could achieve economic independence as a farmer, craftsman, artisan, or professional. Economic and social conditions were drubbing the faith and fueling populism, as farmers and craftsmen felt overwhelmed by larger forces. Properly understood, Lasch argues, populism was a yearning to recapture earlier freedoms. "Nineteenth-century populism meant something quite specific: producerism; a defense of endangered crafts (including the craft of farming); opposition to the new class of public creditors and to the whole machinery of modern finance; opposition to wage labor," Lasch wrote. "Populists inherited from earlier political traditions . . . the principle that property ownership and the personal independence it confers are absolutely essential preconditions to citizenship. In the nineteenth century, the validity of this principle was still widely acknowledged. . . . What was not widely acknowledged was that it no longer corresponded to social practice."[18]

But the response to these developments reaffirmed, in many ways, traditional national values. Americans had always distrusted concentrated power, which is exactly what the new creditors and corporations seemed to embody. To many Americans, they jeopardized individual liberties. It was natural to resort to government to resist this new power, even though government had itself once seemed the major source of concentrated power. There was an obvious contradiction here, and it was resolved—almost reflexively—by using government sparingly. Government was enlisted to check corporate power. But it was not used aggressively to engineer social improvement. In 1887, Congress created the Interstate Commerce Commission to regulate railroad rates. In 1890, it enacted the Sherman Act, the first antitrust law, to prevent monopoly. In 1906, the predecessor agency of the Food and Drug Administration was created to police food processing plants. By 1920, forty-three states had adopted workers' compensation laws, which required companies to insure their workers against industrial accidents.[19] All these measures aimed at the perceived flaws of large companies. Still, government's size and spending remained modest until the 1930s by today's standards. Most Americans did not pay the federal income tax, which had been adopted in 1913 (the threshold for taxes was set quite high). Regulatory agencies were still few. Old presumptions against government involvement remained.

What shattered them were the Great Depression and the Second World War. As I argued earlier, these twin traumas spawned the politics of problem solving. Americans did not rush head-on into new government programs. But they did abandon long-standing inhibitions against government. "Many people who had previously harbored nineteenth-century ideas changed their minds," Robert Higgs has observed. "People came to look to government as an agency to protect themselves."[20] The Depression overwhelmed private charity. Wartime victory buttressed faith in government. What reinforced these lessons was Americans' pragmatic streak: the impulse to do what "worked," which—as Bryce had noted—was an impulse that abided contradiction. Although people still called themselves liberals and conservatives, politics (aside from contesting elections) increasingly focused on deciding what issues were "problems" and what the appropriate responses ought to be. Thus, the environment, employment discrimination, health care, and crime moved onto the national agenda. In general, these were not issues even in the 1950s. "A consensus had developed around a reasonable set of social goals: education, housing, health care, environmental protection," wrote one commentator. "Americans agreed that we weren't going to throw people out in the snow, but we also agreed we weren't going to build socialism. [The debate shifted] to technique—the practical question of making things work."[21]

Something remains a private responsibility as long as it is not defined as an obstacle to collective happiness. Once that happens, it is neither a public nor a private responsibility. It becomes subject to the shifting tides of politics, public opinion, and intellectual fashion. The rub, of course, is that Americans' newfound willingness to use government has not reduced their suspicion of government. This is less puzzling than it seems. The explanation comes in two parts. The first is that Americans do not distrust government as government. They distrust concentrated power—wherever it exists—because that

threatens individuals' autonomy and freedom. So government becomes acceptable when it is counteracting some other form of concentrated power (say, business), even though ever bigger government
also arouses Americans' suspicion of power. The second explanation
is Americans' tendency to compartmentalize their perception of government, viewing the discrete programs that provide them benefits as
individuals (whether Social Security or farm subsidies) separately
from the government's larger operations. The first are judged favorably, while the second are deplored.

These clashing views—our huge dependence on government and
distrust of it—are obviously connected: if people expected government to do less, they could have lower taxes, less regulation, and fewer
disappointments; or, if they were more appreciative of government's
benefits, they might be more tolerant of its taxes, regulations, and
shortcomings. Politics has acquired a schizoid quality. Practical politicians, who instinctively reflect public opinion, will behave inconsis-
tently if public opinion is inconsistent. It is, and they are. (This is
especially true now, because politicians have become so independent
of party control and protection: they have to fend for themselves and,
therefore, are hypersensitive to any threat to their political survival.)
A workable public philosophy might help us deal with our predicament. A public philosophy is a set of ideas that distinguishes between
public (i.e., governmental) and private (i.e., nongovernmental) responsibilities. It is a group of beliefs about what government ought to
accomplish (that is, the limits of its public purpose) and what it might
accomplish (that is, the limits of its competence). Both are necessary,
for there are many things that we might like government to do that it
cannot practically do. But Americans lack any real public philosophy
and do not regret its absence.

Quite the opposite. Seeing ourselves as pragmatic, we have traditionally disdained abstract concepts like "philosophies," "theories,"
and "ideologies." As Bryce remarked on the states' inclination to regulate in the nineteenth century: "Economic theory did not stop them,
for practical men are proud of getting on without theory."[22] Our political rhetoric still echoes Jefferson and Hamilton, the one preaching
republican self-reliance and the other rational government. But actual practice has diverged from both. Government has become an all-
purpose agency for improvement and redemption, unbounded by

any clear limits on its uses or a tradition of self-restraint. But the origins of the contradiction—the distrust of government and the desire
for it—date to at least the early nineteenth century. In a typically in-
sightful passage, Tocqueville noted it in the late 1830s:

> An American attends to his private concerns as if he were alone
> in the world, and the next minute he gives himself up to the com-
> mon welfare as if he had forgotten them. At one time he seems
> animated by the most selfish cupidity; at another, by the most
> lively patriotism. The human heart cannot be thus divided. The
> inhabitants of the United States display so strong and so similar
> a passion for their own welfare and for their freedom that it may
> be supposed that these passions are united and mingled in some
> part of their character. And indeed, the Americans believe their
> freedom to be the best instrument and surest safeguard of their
> welfare; they are attached to the one by the other. They by no
> means think they are not called upon to take a part in public af-
> fairs; they believe, on the contrary, that *their chief business is to secure*
> *for themselves a government which allows them to acquire the things they covet*
> *and which will not debar them from the peaceful enjoyment of those posses-*
> *sions which they have already acquired*[23] [emphasis added].

Put simply, Americans didn't like government and believed that
freedom was the best guarantor of their well-being. But government
also existed to "allow them to acquire the things they covet," and
once freedom itself ceased to be the best way "to acquire the things
they covet," government was used more aggressively as a substitute.
Thus has the original contradiction in our political culture grown to
mammoth proportions with the multiplication of the public's needs
and wants. Government bends under the weight of the contradiction.
No government can ensure happiness, and even "the pursuit of happiness" is now incompatible with limited government because "happiness" has assumed so many public meanings. Government and
politics have been cast into a difficult and perhaps impossible position. They are imagined as both protectors and assailants of our individualism. Little wonder that a government dedicated to happiness
now breeds much unhappiness.

10

Borrow and Spend

✍ ✍ ✍ ✍

HUGE FEDERAL BUDGET DEFICITS are the most visible evidence of overcommitted government. Since 1961, the federal budget has been in deficit in all but one year (1969). Deficits have occurred when unemployment was high (for example, in 1983, when it was 9.6 percent) or low (for example, in 1966, when it was 3.8 percent). As a political event, deficits are precisely what they seem to be: a reflection of the persisting gap between Americans' high demand for governmental services and their lower tolerance for taxes. The absence of a widely accepted public philosophy has made it hard for presidents and Congress to withdraw benefits (whether spending programs or tax breaks) once granted, because there are few grounds for deciding that one group's benefits are more or less deserving than another's. Politically, every program has enjoyed squatters' rights; possession is nine tenths of the law. It is hard to pose the pivotal question—Does spending on program XYZ serve a genuine national need (that is, something that can and ought to be done by the federal government)?—because the very concept of a national need has lost most practical meaning.

It would, of course, be impossible to subject every proposal for government spending to a grand philosophical debate about government's role in society. No successful democracy—and America's is history's most successful—could function in this way. Every small dispute might mushroom into a nasty and irreconcilable conflict if differences of opinion always threatened to become collisions of principle. But it is not too much to expect that a successful society will create generally shared norms—beliefs that don't have to be debated constantly—about the limits and purposes of government. Within these boundaries, then, the political process could maneuver from day to day. Proposals for new government spending would either fit within the existing boundaries or provoke a debate over whether changed circumstances justified altering the boundaries. Government cannot easily be controlled or command public respect unless there are some limits on its activities that are intuitively grasped and widely supported. These are the limits that have been lost, and budget deficits attest to their absence.*

Until the 1960s, the informal belief in the virtue of a balanced budget created a discipline that, if not fostering an explicit public philosophy, at least compelled a crude calibration of the costs and benefits of new government spending. Was the potential gain worth the pain of extra taxes? Once budget deficits became routine, even this discipline vanished. The budget expresses the public's preferences, and unfortunately, these have been inconsistent. In the main, Americans have wanted: (1) generous spending programs, especially for older Americans; (2) stable—or lower—tax burdens; (3) an adequate national defense; and (4) a balanced budget. Budget deficits have not been a conscious choice. But Americans have disdained the alternatives, and deficits have occurred by default. They have been the path of least resistance, and it is easy to see why. Despite constant complaints about high taxes, the federal tax burden has remained remarkably stable in the postwar period. Since 1952, it has essentially fluctuated between 18 and 19 percent of our national income (gross

---

*In November 1994, voters elected the first Republican Congress in forty years. It pledged to balance the budget by 2002 and, in the spring of 1995, presented plans to do so. Even if these plans pass—unclear as this book goes to press—it will be some years before we know whether Congress can follow through on the year-to-year spending and tax decisions that would actually achieve a balanced budget. The budget plan, if approved, would merely prescribe a path by which a balanced budget might be attained.

domestic product).* In some years, it dropped below that; it was 16.5 percent in 1959, for example. And in a few years, it exceeded that; in 1969 and 1980, for instance, it hit 20.2 percent. But the overall stability of the tax burden suggests that, once it moves beyond 19 or 20 percent of GDP, popular discontent escalates. So raising taxes isn't easy.[1]

Neither is cutting spending. Vast segments of society now depend on federal programs, as the table on the next page shows. In 1992, roughly half of all families received some type of federal income transfer. In budget jargon, these are "entitlements": payments that automatically go to beneficiaries if they satisfy certain requirements. For example, people over sixty-two generally qualify for Social Security retirement benefits if they have worked for ten years. All entitlement programs—everything from Social Security to food stamps—represented 61 percent of non-interest federal spending in 1995. That is, they were nearly two thirds of all federal spending excluding interest payments on the national debt, which, as a practical matter, must be paid. (In 1995, interest payments were 15 percent of spending.) Three decades earlier, such entitlements were only 31 percent of non-interest spending.[2] Essentially, defense spending has declined, and entitlements have risen. Entitlements are in turn dominated by spending on older Americans through Social Security, Medicare (providing health insurance for the over-sixty-five population), and Medicaid (covering nursing-home care for many indigent elderly). Traditional welfare programs such as Aid to Families with Dependent Children (which provides monthly payments to poor, single mothers), public housing, and food stamps are a much smaller part of the total.[†] (Because many families received more than one benefit, the total of all the individual programs exceeds 50 percent. For instance, most families on Medicare also collected Social Security.)[3]

---

*I have used "national income" to refer to gross domestic product—total national production in a year—which is not what economists mean, strictly speaking, by the term. Broadly speaking, our national income is what's available for us to consume. In technical terms, national income is statistically derived by reducing total production (GDP) by the amount of depreciation, which is the obsolescence of buildings and machinery. This is, however, a fairly obscure point, and for clarity's sake, I have adopted the commonsense terminology that GDP measures annual national income.

[†]As this goes to press, Congress was considering transforming some entitlement programs—those for the poor, such as AFDC—into "block" grants to states. That is, the states would receive only a fixed amount of money for the programs. People wouldn't automatically qualify for benefits; each state would decide who qualifies for what benefits. Even if this occurred, the major entitlements (Social Security, Medicare) would remain.

Families Receiving Federal Payments, 1992[4]

Program	Number of Families (millions)	Share of Families (percent)
At least one benefit	54.5	51.7
Social Security	27.2	25.7
Medicare	25.3	24.0
Medicaid	12.8	12.1
Food stamps	9.8	9.2
Unemployment compensation	9.0	8.5
Subsidized school lunch	7.9	7.5
Government retirement	4.7	4.5
Aid to Families with Dependent Children	4.1	3.9
Supplemental Security Income	4.1	3.8
Energy assistance	3.8	3.6
Educational aid	3.6	3.4

Indeed, the table actually understates the reach of government programs. The survey on which it is based, for example, did not ask about agricultural subsidies. In 1992, about 676,000 farm households received $9.2 billion in such subsidies. And the survey question was so general that it missed many families that received educational benefits. In 1992, the Education Department estimated that 6.2 million students received federally aided college loans or grants and that another 622,000 children participated in the Head Start program; even assuming that some recipients were in the same family, these numbers imply a participation rate of 5 to 6 percent. Still, huge numbers of Americans now receive—or expect to receive—government benefits, and the dependence stretches across income lines. Among the richest fifth of families in 1992, 30 percent received at least one benefit, as did 37 percent in the second richest fifth. Any effort to reduce federal spending substantially (say, by a fifth or a sixth) must inevitably affect large numbers of voters.[5]

It is widely, but mistakenly, believed that big deficits originated with Presidents Ronald Reagan and George Bush. True, annual deficits and the resulting federal debt ballooned during the Reagan-Bush years. In the 1970s, the deficits averaged $35 billion a year. In the

Reagan-Bush years (1981–1993), they averaged $189 billion annually. The federal debt went from $785 billion in 1981 to $3 trillion in 1992.* But these figures obscure as much as they reveal. (It's important to grasp the distinction between the deficit and the debt. The deficit is the annual gap between spending and revenues; the debt is the government's accumulated borrowings to cover these annual deficits.) One reason is that defense spending stopped declining. Between 1968 and 1980, defense had dropped from 46 to 23 percent of federal outlays; this reflected the end of the Vietnam War and a hiatus in new weapons programs.[6] These declines helped finance higher domestic spending. But by the early 1980s, there was a consensus that the cutbacks had gone too far. This was not just Reagan's view; it was a general reaction to the Iranian hostage crisis of 1979–1980. Once the defense slide stopped, the basic cause of big deficits became clearer: Americans' inconsistent demands. In addition, inflation and economic growth exploded the dollar amounts of the deficits in the 1980s; almost everything (measured in dollars) was costlier.

The next table reveals what actually happened: the 1980s deficits simply extended a process started in the 1960s. The table gives what economists call the "structural deficit" as a share of gross domestic product (national income). The structural budget balance—surplus or deficit—is sometimes referred to as the "full employment" balance. It assumes that unemployment rates remain constant at a low level (usually between 5 and 6 percent). This erases the effects of recessions, which reduce taxes and raise government spending for unemployment benefits and other welfare payments. The budget is estimated as if the economy were operating at peak capacity. Measuring the resulting deficit as a share of national income indicates the basic gap between our demand for government and our willingness to be taxed. As the table shows, the gap rose from 1.5 percent of our in-

---

*These debt figures refer to debt "held by the public." A large amount of government debt is also held by federal trust funds, such as the Social Security trust fund. I have not used these larger figures, because the government really cannot owe money to itself. If one part of government owes money to another—say, the general treasury owes money to the Social Security trust fund—the debts can be managed by cutting spending. For example, if future Social Security benefits were cut, the Social Security trust fund would present fewer of its bonds for redemption to the Treasury. Likewise, Congress could cut other spending and redeem the Social Security fund's bonds without a general tax increase.

come in the 1960s to 3 percent in the 1980s. By contrast, the structural deficit was zero at the end of the 1950s.

Structural Deficit as a Percentage of GDP[7]

1960s	1.5%
1970s	2.2%
1980s	3.2%

This gap is the crux of the political impasse. In the mid-1990s, the gap has narrowed slightly, because the end of the Cold War has resulted in a further fall in defense spending. The Congressional Budget Office projects "structural deficits" of 2.7 to 3 percent of GDP for the years 1995 to 2000. But the essential collision remains between the desire for low taxes and high government services. In the 1980s, the inconsistencies simply became more glaring and less manageable. By 1981, the federal tax burden was at its highest level since the Second World War, 20.2 percent of GDP. Reagan exploited the intense anti-tax mood. His tax "cuts" merely reduced the tax burden to levels that had prevailed in the 1970s. The first Reagan tax bill lowered taxes to about 18 percent of GDP, but after subsequent increases, taxes in the Reagan years averaged 18.9 percent of GDP compared with 18.5 percent in the 1970s. In the 1960s and 1970s, rising domestic spending had been cushioned by falling defense spending and low interest payments on the federal debt. By the 1980s, the interest burden was rising, and defense spending was no longer falling. Avoiding deficits required either higher taxes or lower domestic spending. There was no consensus for either.[8]

CONCERNING THE BUDGET, overcommitted government does not mean we have too much or too little government. It means—in this instance—that we have more government than people are willing to pay for with taxes. Budgetary politics were pleasant enough in the 1960s and early 1970s, because optimistic assumptions about economic growth created the illusion that future tax revenues would always overtake spending. Congress created new programs and benefits; new constituencies were pleased and made dependent on government. But going in the opposite direction has been almost impossible. In the 1980s, Congress killed only two major nondefense programs: general revenue sharing (unrestricted federal grants to state and local governments) and urban development action grants (a form of urban renewal).[9] Once benefits are conferred, recipients feel entitled. Without any public philosophy—delineating what is and isn't government's responsibility—every group considers itself as equally entitled as every other group, and as more groups become beneficiaries, more feel entitled. Distinctions between public and private responsibilities, already blurred, become more so.

The result is that programs outlive the circumstances that inspired them or survive despite proven ineffectiveness. They endure because they create their own constituencies, protective congressional committees, and rationales. Farm subsidies are perhaps the most vivid example. They date to the 1930s, when they were justified as a way of sustaining agricultural incomes and preserving the family farm. Since then, the number of farms has fallen by more than two thirds. (In 1935, there were 6.8 million farms; by 1991, the number was 2.1 million.) Growing mechanization and the use of improved seed varieties and agricultural chemicals have fostered a broad farming consolidation. Fewer and bigger farms produce more food than ever. Some family farms have survived; many have not. No one can pretend that the subsidy programs have altered the general trends or are necessary to ensure food production. Nevertheless, farm subsidies endure and are still justified as aid to family farms. The same rationale supports other farm programs, despite obvious waste. The Farmers Home Administration continues to make low-interest loans to farmers even though delinquency rates from borrowers have been as high as 70 percent.[10]

Having become dependent on government, Americans are loathe to abandon their dependency or even curb it. This is certainly true of the largest category of federal spending: aid to older Americans, accounting for one third of all outlays. On average, the federal government now spends about $13,000 annually on every person over sixty-five, mainly through Social Security, Medicare, and Medicaid. When these programs were enacted, most older Americans were considered "needy" by virtue of age. Private pensions were scarce; health insurance was skimpy. But postwar prosperity severed the connection between age and "neediness." Americans saved more, and pensions spread. As a group, older Americans are as prosperous as other Americans. Yet, it has proven hard to trim benefits for the well-to-do. A "contract," it's said, was made by government and shouldn't be broken. In fact, no contract was ever made. Congress simply enriched Social Security on a regular basis. Between 1952 and 1971, Congress raised benefit levels seven times; in 1972, it passed a 20 percent increase and "indexed" benefits to inflation (that is, future benefits would increase automatically with prices). In 1965, it created Medicare. Many retirees enjoy benefits that they could not conceivably have expected as young or even middle-aged workers, because the benefits did not exist.*[11]

IT IS NOT TRUE, of course, that the government never before ran budget deficits. There have almost always been deficits during wars. Between 1940 and 1946, the federal debt increased by a factor of six, and at the end of the war, it stood at 114 percent of GDP. Proportionally, this is about twice as high as it is today (52 percent of GDP in 1995). Likewise, budgets also shifted toward deficits during severe economic downturns, even in the nineteenth century. In emergencies, it was simply too difficult to raise taxes or cut spending sufficiently to sustain a stable budget balance. During the Second World War, taxes would have had to have been raised more than sixfold. In fact, they were only tripled. (They went from 7 to 21 percent of national income; they would have had to go to 45 percent.) During economic slumps, normal revenue sources shriveled (in the nineteenth century, tariffs were the largest source of revenue and dropped when the economy weakened). Making up for losses was hard. What has distinguished our own era is not the existence of deficits but their size and persistence. They have been tolerated in a way that is entirely disconnected from previous American experience.[12]

The critical event in this transformation was the conversion of the budget from a primarily political document into an instrument of economic policy. This occurred in the 1960s. Until then, federal bud-

*Again, proposals made by Republicans as this book goes to press would reduce future growth of some spending for older Americans, especially Medicare. But even if these go into effect, spending on older Americans will remain the largest category of federal spending.

gets were treated mainly as an expression of political and even moral values and interests. A balanced budget was seen as a practical way of disciplining government and checking threats to liberty. In this sense, the balanced budget idea merely represented another expression of popular resistance to strong, centralized government. Political scientist James Savage, after a meticulous review of the history of the balanced budget, put it this way:

> The balanced budget idea, embodied in the concept of "corruption," guided public policy not only on budgetary matters but also on such related issues as administrative growth, "internal improvements" [such as roads and harbors], the nature of currency, banking, tariffs, national defense, and especially federal-state relations. Borrowed from classical and English political thought, the concept of corruption became uniquely American. . . . In the American context, balanced budgets originally assumed their symbolic characteristics in the years of Jeffersonian and Jacksonian democracy. A balanced national budget signified a popular willingness and ability to limit the purpose and size of the federal government, to restrain its influence in the economy, to protect states' rights, to maintain the Constitution's balance of powers and to promote Republican virtue.[13]

Not everyone was fanatical about this. Alexander Hamilton actually saw the debt incurred during the American Revolution as a boon, because it justified a stronger national government with broader taxing powers—something that Hamilton favored—to repay the debt. "A national debt if it is not excessive," he wrote in 1781, "will be to us a national blessing; it will be a powerful cement to our union." Hamilton believed that it would foster a common purpose and, beyond that, establish the government's creditworthiness: its ability to repay past debts. This was necessary, he argued, because "in times of public dangers, especially from foreign war," it would be necessary to borrow.[14] Unless government was a good credit risk, it would have to resort to inflationary tides of paper money. By contrast, Jefferson championed balanced budgets. Whereas Hamilton cared about the nation, Jefferson cared about liberty.[15] He distrusted government and

yearned to keep it small. His writings brim with antigovernment out-
bursts. "If we can prevent the Government from wasting the labor of
the people, under the pretense of caring for them, they will be
happy," he once said. Or: "I regard economy [in government] among
the first and most important virtues." Without it, "we must be taxed
in our meat and our drink, in our necessities and comforts, in our
labor and our amusements."[16]

The government that Americans got mixed both Jefferson's and
Hamilton's visions. Government went beyond Jefferson's minimalist
ideal, but it did not incorporate many of Hamilton's proposals for
central control. And its early budget practices were decidedly cautious and restrained. After Jefferson's election in 1800, the government ran an almost continuous budget surplus—with a major
exception for the War of 1812—until the Panic of 1837, one of the
worst economic collapses in the nation's history. Before the Civil War,
the national debt (the accumulation of all past borrowing) reached a
peak of $127 million in 1815; by 1836, it had been reduced to a mere
$38,000. The Civil War resulted in an explosion of borrowing; in
1867, the federal debt hit the then unimaginable level of $2.8 billion.
But after the war, there was widespread agreement to reduce the
debt. Every budget for three decades (from 1866 to 1895) was in surplus; by 1893, the debt dipped below $1 billion.* Considering that the
economy had more than doubled in size, this meant that the debt
burden had been reduced enormously. One foreign diplomat summarized the prevailing opinion in America as a "strong and controlling sense that debt was always and everywhere an evil; that it was a
good thing to 'work off' the mortgage, even if it involved working
very hard."[17]

What is remarkable about these traditional attitudes is that they
survived the Great Depression and the Second World War, which resulted in continuous and immense deficits between 1931 and 1946.
"Roosevelt never felt comfortable with deficit spending," writes Sav-

---

*These surpluses would seem to contradict my earlier statement (see page 162) that nine-
teenth-century governments permitted the budget to adjust according to the business
cycle. Not so. True, there were no deficits for three decades after the Civil War. But surpluses dropped dramatically during economic slumps. For example, between 1871 and
1873, the surplus declined from $96.6 million to $2.3 million. Likewise, it decreased from
$40.1 million to $6.9 million between 1877 and 1879.[18]

age.[19] In 1932, he criticized Hoover for running deficits and pledged to restore a balanced budget if elected. In 1938, he actually attempted to do so. Truman also advocated a balanced budget, and although he also favored higher domestic spending, he balanced four of seven budgets from 1946 to 1952. President Eisenhower was an even more outspoken supporter of balanced budgets. At various times, he resisted calls from fellow Republicans to cut taxes—though he agreed they were too high—and from Democrats to lower taxes and to raise spending. Eisenhower didn't insist on a balanced budget all the time. He recognized that trying to balance the budget in a recession might be self-defeating. But he did not see the budget primarily as a tool to manage the economy. It was mostly a vehicle for expressing governmental responsibilities. Budget balancing was a prudent discipline. In a 1960 message to Congress, he said,

> This truth we must take to heart: in good times, we must at the very least pay our way. . . . This simply means that we must adhere to necessary programs and sensible priorities. . . . If the Congress prefers other priorities at greater cost, responsibility dictates that it accompany them with additional taxes to pay the bill.[20]

It was precisely this view of the budget that was lost in the 1960s. The Kennedy-Johnson economists changed the popular perception of both the budget and deficits. Henceforth, the budget balance (surplus or deficit) was to be debated and analyzed mostly for its impact on the economy. The effect was to legitimize deficits and to distract governmental leaders and the public from political questions about the worth of particular spending programs and taxes. A relatively simple rule governing budget behavior (government programs worth having are worth supporting through taxes) was replaced by a constantly shifting set of economic considerations. Transforming the budget debate into an economic debate was thus an invitation to confusion and paralysis, precisely because there is no consensus—nor is there likely to be—on the budget deficit's economic effects. In this vacuum, economic arguments could be (and regularly have been by presidents and congressional leaders of both parties) advanced to justify political expediency: spending more and taxing less.

This does not mean that the budget and large deficits have no economic consequences. It does mean that no one knows precisely what those consequences are, in part because they may vary according to circumstances. Except for extraordinary events—mainly wars—annual changes in the budget aren't likely to have more than a modest impact on the economy's growth rate. The main reason is that plausible tax and spending changes are small in the context of what is today roughly a $7 trillion economy. Tax or spending changes of $70 billion represent only 1 percent of GDP; and the effects could easily be neutralized. For example, larger budget deficits might spur spending. But the effect could easily be offset by an adverse shift in inflation, the trade balance, or interest rates. And, arguably, the long-run effects of persistent deficits could be either good or bad. They might "crowd out" private investment, undermining future living standards. Likewise, wasteful government spending might substitute for productive private spending. On the other hand, productive government spending (on, say, education or research and development) might conceivably raise the economy's long-term growth. Claims and counterclaims of all sorts can be made, and none can easily be judged, because the consequences—whatever they might be—are usually lodged in the hazy future. Budget politics has thus become a debaters' delight, pitting one self-serving speculation against another.

Economic ignorance has also favored deficits in another respect: because large, continuous deficits clearly didn't lead to an immediate calamity—as some had said they would—they were made much less fearsome. Seeds of doubt were planted about the folk wisdom, and the longer the deficits continued, the more the folk wisdom decayed. People became accustomed to big deficits, which, though they might be deplored, did not truly seem to matter. If deficits weren't bad, maybe they were good. Perhaps Americans could have their cake and eat it, too. Using the budget as a tool to remake the economy rather than one to define governmental responsibilities had obvious political appeal. It promised a stronger economy without the pain of higher taxes or lower spending. Public opinion had shifted. The virtue of the balanced budget wasn't repudiated. But it was rejected as a routine and rigid standard. Instead, it became an ignored ideal. It might be obtained sometime in the future, even if there were always plausible reasons for not obtaining it in the present.

BUDGET POLITICS in recent decades have accurately reflected these popular inconsistencies. Congress and presidents have paid verbal homage to balanced budgets without actually balancing the budget. Nevertheless, through a series of laws, Congress has tried to discipline itself. In 1985, for example, it enacted the Gramm-Rudman-Hollings law. The law was named after its authors, Senators Phil Gramm of Texas, Warren Rudman of New Hampshire, and Ernest Hollings of South Carolina. The first two are Republicans—Rudman has since retired—and Hollings is a Democrat. On paper, the plan required Congress to eliminate the deficit gradually by meeting a series of legislated targets. The deficit would be cut to $172 billion in fiscal 1986, $144 billion in fiscal 1987, and zero by 1991. If Congress missed the targets, then the law would trigger automatic across-the-board spending cuts (called "sequestrations") to meet the targets. One way or another, Congress would take the needed, if unpopular, actions. The plan seemed doomed to work. But of course, it didn't. Sequestration—the automatic spending cuts—was a fairly porous process, because it excluded many popular entitlement programs, starting with Social Security. And when the targets threatened distasteful spending cuts, the targets themselves were altered in 1987. Three years later, they were abandoned altogether, when President Bush and Congress agreed upon a major "deficit reduction" plan. Another program was enacted in 1993 by Congress and President Clinton.[21]

These plans were portrayed as being bigger than they were. Both were described as involving about $500 billion in deficit reduction over five years. When evaluated, the amounts proved somewhat less, significantly so in the case of the Clinton package. (The Congressional Budget Office judged the reductions in the 1990 plan at $496 billion and those in the 1993 plan at $433 billion.)[22] More important, these reductions paled against actual federal spending. For example, spending over the five years covered by the Clinton plan was projected to be nearly $8 trillion. These packages prevented the deficit from getting much worse, but did not do much more. This does not mean that balancing the budget—at least in the immediate future—would involve draconian changes. In 1996, for example, the deficit is estimated by the Congressional Budget Office to be about $200 billion on spending of $1.6 trillion and taxes of $1.4 trillion. If deficits were ended by a plan consisting of two-thirds spending cuts ($132 billion) and one-third tax increases ($68 billion), the respective spending cuts and tax increases would average 8 and 5 percent, respectively. Even these changes are overstated; they ignore the interest rate savings of lower government debt.

Budget deficits have persisted for so long because they reflect a powerful political logic. The appeal of a balanced budget has been weak, because it pits visible and identifiable losses against invisible and speculative gains. The immediate economic advantages of lower deficits are not obvious, just as the immediate drawbacks aren't. (Budget deficits are often said, for example, to raise long-term interest rates on bonds and mortgages, implying that lower deficits would reduce those rates. Maybe. But so far the impact has been small. Interest rates are formed in financial markets, based on the judgments of thousands of investors. Until now, factors other than budget deficits—for example, expectations of future inflation—have had more influence on their decisions.) Moreover, confronting the deficits might provoke a wrenching debate about basic governmental principles—what should government do, and for whom?—that political leaders have instinctively avoided. For example, how much should government provide collective benefits (say, defense) and how much should it redistribute income (through, say, Social Security)? Tolerating deficits has enabled Americans to avoid such questions, which will become more insistent as the population ages.

But just because the system has operated according to a discernible logic does not mean people are pleased with the results. Not only are deficits seen as irresponsible but they are also upsetting on a personal level, because they imply that existing benefits may some day be cut or existing taxes may some day be raised. But whose benefits or whose taxes? By how much? When? Because there are no answers to these questions, people are anxious about them; and because government's benefits and burdens are spread so widely, the anxiety—though perhaps subconscious—is widespread. Deficits also generate disappointment in another way. They have made it harder for government to embark on new programs. In the physics of politics, existing programs and constituencies are more powerful than unborn programs and phantom constituencies. Government becomes backward-looking, tied to established commitments and interest groups,

ulation (who would appreciate them), while the costs might be dispersed over a relatively large population (who would, therefore, be unaware that there was any cost at all). But as government has grown, it has been harder to disguise costs. The totality of government spending and regulation is now so large that the costs are increasingly visible and, therefore, vulnerable to political scrutiny and attack.

This poses a fundamental problem of political accountability and responsibility. In a democracy, the virtues and vices of added government somehow need to be balanced. Otherwise, government may unwisely extend its power in ways that prove ineffectual or unpopular. Or it may impose costs on the economy that cannot easily be borne. The tradition of balanced budgets provided an informal method of compelling consideration of competing claims. Once this tradition was lost, it has been impossible (as yet) to restore it through an act of political will. Whatever the costs of budget deficits, they are highly subjective and mainly invisible. They are dispersed throughout society and probably extended over time. It is hard to fit them into political deliberations and popular thinking. They are not desired, but politically, they possess great inertia. And as noted, the problems of dealing with regulations are, if anything, even more difficult.

The irony is that the discipline to limit government—whether through spending or regulation—has been eroded in part by the very fragmented nature of American government. The Founders wanted it to be hard to change. It is. But government acquires power during emergencies (wars) or good times (when extra government seems relatively cheap), and when these pass, the very political inertia that was intended to limit government's growth makes it difficult to reverse its growth. There are many power centers, and the convergence of interests required to sanction change gives an enormous advantage to the status quo. Those who already have a stake in government have a common interest in preserving their stake. Groups and their associated congressional committees often exercise effective vetoes over changes in their programs except those that, somehow, seem demanded by overwhelming public pressure. Government that was supposed to keep itself small through the fragmentation of power has become a captive of its own sprawling size and fragmentation. In the process, it has assumed more burdens than it can discharge, because its leaders have been determined to keep the costs and benefits of government as highly separate in the public mind as possible.

11

Elusive Equality

☙ ☙ ☙ ☙

B UDGET DEFICITS, though the clearest expression of overcommitted government, are not the most important. They could be ended fairly quickly, as we have seen. By contrast, government has made many other more sweeping commitments that are virtually unattainable. It has said it would end poverty, erase racial injustice, and eliminate ethnic and sexual discrimination. Progress has been made on each, but none is achievable, because what constitutes "ending poverty" or "erasing racial injustice" is a subjective and constantly shifting target. Each of these commitments reflects a broader reality: government has become the chosen instrument for advancing equality in America. This is not new, but what is new is the increasingly expansive concept of equality. Many groups (or their self-appointed representatives)—women, gay people, Hispanics, welfare recipients, the disabled, prisoners—have all demanded some form of "equality," often insisting on new "rights" akin to those in the Bill of Rights. In addition, many Americans believe that some public or quasi-public services ought to be provided "equally," health care and education being the best examples.

This aggressive pursuit of so much equality for so many is futile. It is doomed not because equality is a bad thing but because it is too ambiguous, ambitious, and emotional an ideal to impose practical limits on worthwhile goals. The concept is cheapened by overuse. Many new "rights" are illusory, and the parallels drawn with the Bill of Rights are false. The right to free speech belongs to everyone equally; so does the right to religion or a jury trial. These rights can be enjoyed by almost everyone on comparable terms: almost every-one can practice a personal religion. But many modern "rights" in-volve social problems or conditions that, by their nature, deny equal outcomes. What does creating "equal rights" for women mean? Does it merely mean eliminating job discrimination? But if that hap-pens and women still feel disadvantaged, must they then face some other inequality: perhaps inadequate child care (mothers cannot easily hold jobs unless someone cares for their children) or sexual harassment? Or, what does "educational equality" mean? It is im-possible to provide an equal education to all, if that means everyone must have an equal ability to read, write and compute. Huge differ-ences are inevitable.

The creation of so many new synthetic rights—another form of entitlement—further feeds popular discontent with government. On the one hand, intended beneficiaries are constantly disappointed. Be-cause equality is an unrealistic goal, its attainment remains perma-nently elusive. Successive remedies seem fraudulent, as new forms of inequality are discovered. If poverty persists, despite the govern-ment's efforts and pledges to end it, then the poor must be victims of unequal schools, or health care or housing, that perpetuates their poverty. But it is not just the intended beneficiaries who are embit-tered. There is an inevitable backlash. By its very nature, the quest for equality is a drive to redistribute social, political, and economic power that not only raises some people up but also pushes—relatively speak-ing, at least—some people down. Naturally, those who feel or fear they may be pushed down object.

If blacks, women, Hispanics, or other minorities receive an ad-vantage in hiring or college admissions, then others (whites, men) may suffer a disadvantage. If schools spend more for disabled stu-dents or those with "special" needs, then there may be less to spend on others. If government subsidizes health care for the poor, then the nonpoor may feel (correctly) that they are being made poorer. In this sense, there is always a constituency against equality. Opponents object that something is being taken away. Moreover, there is often another source of hostility. Preferential policies are often justified as a response to bad behavior: racism, sexism, ageism or some other "ism." Recipients are elevated to a high moral plane, and everyone else is presumed somehow responsible for their plight. But those blamed or burdened often feel innocent and, therefore, wronged. The paradox is that the quest for equality, usually intended to promote social harmony by bringing America closer to its ideals, can have the opposite effect. It can create new sources of conflict and contention.

ALL THESE POSSIBLE PROBLEMS have materialized in practice. Education is a good example. In postwar America, popular enthusiasm for it increased. The aim has been to democratize schooling—to make more of it available to more people. If more people had more schooling, the thinking went, Americans would become richer and more equal. Everyone should graduate from high school, and more Americans should graduate from college. As early as 1948, President Truman's Commission on Higher Education deplored the fact that mostly the well-to-do went beyond high school. Colleges and universities should become "the means by which every citizen, youth, and adult is enabled and encouraged to carry his education . . . as far as his native capacities permit," it said.[1] The egalitarian spirit has largely triumphed. In 1990, nearly 80 percent of the adult population (twenty-five years and older) had a high school diploma compared with 25 percent in 1940; the proportion of those with a college degree (four years or more) had risen from 5 to 21 percent.[2] Schooling at all levels has expanded enormously. State university systems heavily subsidize tuitions, and federal grants and loans provide additional college subsidies.

Up to a point, this embrace of education has succeeded. Educational opportunity has broadened. Our system's very messiness (its many institutions, programs, and admissions requirements) affords people first, second, and third chances. In recent decades, test scores of low-income students have modestly improved. But expanded education has not fully paid its expected dividends. The striving to send

more students further in school—in the name of greater equality—
has spawned waste and mediocrity. For most students, test scores
have stagnated or declined. For example, average scores (as reported
by the National Assessment of Educational Progress) on science and
civics for high school seniors were unchanged between the late 1970s
and late 1980s. Meanwhile, average spending per student (adjusted
for inflation) rose about 25 percent. The same is true at colleges. In
1966, entering college freshmen averaged 466 on their verbal college
board test; by 1990, the average was 422. With so many colleges, getting in is easy, except at 100 to 200 elite institutions. Among high
school seniors, only one in eight does more than two hours of daily
homework. "Coast and get into college and have the same opportunities as someone who works hard," as one put it. "That is the system." But of course, many students aren't ready for college. Dropout
rates are huge; roughly half of freshmen at four-year institutions
never graduate.[3]

Similar confusions and conflicts plague health care—another
area where equal treatment is considered socially just. Health care is
not yet legally classified as a right, but many Americans think of it
that way. President Bill Clinton's proposal in 1993 for national health
insurance would officially have made comprehensive medical care a
right, and although the plan failed in Congress, the promise of universal coverage was one of its most popular features. Polls found, for
example, that about 80 percent of the population favored universal
coverage. Indeed, surveys as far back as the 1930s show similar beliefs.[4] The prevailing view has been that people should have the best
available health care when they "need" it. The postwar health insurance system sought to do precisely that. The assumption was that
most Americans would get insurance at work and that, with the en-
actment of Medicare and Medicaid in 1965, most of the old and the
poor would be covered by government. Gradually, most Americans
would become insured. The right would arise informally without
being formally legislated. No one would be condemned to die or suffer curable illness simply because he or she was poor. In this view, the
need for medical care was fixed; all people lacked was the means to
pay for it.

The rub is that medical "needs" are not fixed and some needs are
more compelling than others. Equality of care, an appealing ideal,

becomes less so in practice. Paradoxically, health care was the most equal when there was less of it—say in the nineteenth century—because it couldn't do much for anyone, regardless of income. Ethical and economic dilemmas have emerged only as better and more expensive medicine has created opportunities to cure diseases and repair injuries. Modern medicine is elastic; it constantly identifies new diseases, disorders, and treatments, as medical ethicist Willard Gaylin has pointed out. "Infertility . . . was not considered a disease until this generation," he writes. "Before then, it was simply a God-given condition. With advances in modern medicine—including artificial insemination, *in vitro* fertilization and surrogate mothers—new cures were discovered for 'illnesses' that now had to be invented."[5] Much of modern medicine does not deal with threats to patients' lives. As with in vitro fertilization, the aim is to improve the quality of their lives. Other procedures (say, organ transplants) are expensive and have low success rates. Somehow, limits have to be set; otherwise, unlimited insurance will mean unlimited spending. "Equality" is unattainable in the sense that all "needs" can be met.

Finally, consider affirmative action—another instrument for "equality." Aside from overt discrimination, it was said, other barriers obstructed blacks' progress. They did not belong to the informal networks by which people were hired and promoted. Or white managers did not know how to recruit blacks. Something more was needed. Courts outlawed hiring practices that, though otherwise reasonable, might have a disparate impact on blacks. In 1971, the Supreme Court, in *Griggs* v. *Duke Power Co.*, banned employment tests and educational requirements (say, a high school diploma) unless they could be shown to be required by a particular job. Meanwhile, the Nixon administration pioneered "goals and timetables" for hiring and promoting blacks. The idea was to compensate for centuries of discrimination even if specific firms or colleges hadn't discriminated themselves. In 1970, the Labor Department required construction companies in Philadelphia to meet hiring goals. All major federal contractors subsequently had to adopt similar plans. Colleges changed admissions policies. The aim was to create "gentle pressure to balance the residue of discrimination," one official later wrote.[6]

Today, the benefits are unclear. True, blacks have achieved huge gains in jobs and college enrollment, but these stemmed heavily from the end of overt discrimination and from new social norms. Between 1970 and 1990, for example, the number of black police rose from 23,796 to 63,855; they constituted 41 percent of new hires. The number of black electricians rose from 14,145 to 43,276 and the number of black bank tellers from 10,633 to 46,322; these accounted for 13 and 16 percent of new hires. Studies by economist Jonathan Leonard of the University of California suggest that federal affirmative action contributed little to these gains; black employment grew only slightly faster at companies with federal contracts than at those without.[7] But whatever the benefits, vast job gaps remain between blacks and whites, and affirmative action has stirred intense resentment among many whites and some blacks. Because it has been extended to women and other minorities (Hispanics, Asian-Americans, Native Americans), it seems to many whites to defy fair play and constitute reverse discrimination. In one survey, only 16 percent of whites favored affirmative action compared with 67 percent of blacks. Even a sympathetic observer, political scientist Andrew Hacker, writes that the "whites who lose out are more generally blue-collar workers or persons at lower administrative levels, whose skills are not greatly in demand." In short, more "equality" for some means less for others. Among black managers and professionals, affirmative action is also increasingly resented, because it stigmatizes their success by suggesting it resulted only from preferential treatment.[8]

POLITICS IS ABOUT CHOICES, but those choices cannot be faced if they are denied. The modern concept of equality tends to do precisely that by subsuming the choices under broadly appealing and highly general egalitarian ideals. By casting so much of what government does as a matter of essential equality or absolute rights, unavoidable imperfections and conflicts are obscured or trivialized. It is sometimes said that the modern American idea of equality has gone astray, because it has abandoned a traditional concern for "equality of opportunity"—people should get an equal chance to do well in life—and favored "equality of results"—people are guaranteed certain outcomes. The argument is plausible, because the earliest American concern with equality was essentially a reaction to the inherited inequalities of European societies. In those societies, the feudal legacy often meant that some people were born into aristocracy and privilege. Americans rejected this sort of predeterminism, though they tolerated inequalities based on differences in talent, hard work, risk taking, or even luck. In Federalist Paper No. 10, for example, James Madison talks about "the diversity in the faculties of men," meaning their different skills and abilities.[9] Americans have long believed that effort and reward ought to be connected: those who exert more deserve more.

Despite this, the imagined historic distinction between equality of opportunity and of results may be more fancied than real. Tocqueville—an early commentator on our obsession with equality—did not make a point of it. Rather, he was impressed by the "equality of condition" in the United States. To Tocqueville, Americans lived more alike than did people in Europe and, just as important, felt themselves to be of equal worth. It wasn't merely that Americans believed that no one should automatically be held back by the accident of birth. (Slaves, of course, were the glaring exception.) What was also true, he said, was that Americans had already achieved an astonishing degree of equality in their social relations, and this equality was a powerful influence on popular opinion, politics, and institutions. At the very start of *Democracy in America*, he makes this clear:

Among the novel objects that attracted my attention during my stay in the United States, nothing struck me more forcibly than the general equality of condition among the people. I readily discovered the prodigious influence this primary fact exercises on the whole course of society; it gives a peculiar direction to public opinion and a peculiar tenor to the laws; it imparts new maxims to the governing authorities and peculiar habits to the governed.

I soon perceived that the influence of this fact extends far beyond the political character and the laws of the country, and that it has no less effect on civil society than on the government; it creates opinions, gives birth to new sentiments, founds novel customs, and modifies whatever it does not produce.[10]

Government was not created to impose equality, but it responded to the prejudice against inequality. It might feel impelled to attack in-

stitutions that generated inequality. As Tocqueville noted, the states
struck down English inheritance laws requiring that all land go to the
firstborn son. These laws tended to perpetuate family fortunes,
whereas the new American laws (requiring or permitting estates to be
split among all heirs) did the opposite. The family fortune (the land)
was increasingly subdivided with each passing generation. This might
be said to reflect both a concern for equality of opportunity and
equality of results. It surely fostered opportunity. Everyone might
earn a fortune; those who already had one enjoyed only a fleeting advantage, which would (unless the fortune were replenished) dwindle
with time. Thus, the rejection of English inheritance laws indicated
that Americans were always uneasy with institutions and customs that
seemed to sustain both unequal opportunities and results.

There are other examples of the blurred boundary between
equality of opportunity and of results. In the 1850s, Republicans
preached "free labor, free soil," meaning that government would provide settlers with free land in new territories. Equal opportunity
rhetoric abounded. "Advancement, improvement in condition . . . is
the order of things in a society of equals," Lincoln once declared. In
1857, the *Cincinnati Gazette* opined in an editorial: "Of all the multitude of young men engaged in various employments of this city, there
is not one who does not desire, and even confidently expect, to become rich, and that at an early date." Yet, Republicans also felt that
government should promote what they thought would occur spontaneously. "In the free labor outlook," as historian Eric Foner has
noted, "the objective of social mobility was not great wealth, but the
middle-class goal of economic independence." By providing free
land, government not only would promote that independence among
landowners but would also raise the wages of laborers left in cities.
Nothing in this scheme—enacted as the Homestead Act of 1862—
struck its supporters as un-American. "It does not bring down the
high," said one, "but it raises the low." Homesteading, said another,
"will greatly increase the number of those who belong to what is
called the middle class."[11]

Americans' concept of equality, in short, has always been muddled. It has promoted opportunity but also rebelled at practices that
seemed to produce unjustifiable inequality. Still, no one visiting
America in the nineteenth or early twentieth centuries could have

misread the country's capacity to tolerate huge inequalities. The individualistic temper of American culture and politics might resist rigid social and economic distinctions—conditions that held individuals back and were beyond their power to change—but it also accepted that some people would do much better than others. The very poor were often held in contempt, blamed for their own plight, and not offered much in the way of communal support. "In the land of opportunity," as social historian Michael Katz has noted, "poverty has seemed not only a misfortune but also a moral failure." Most commonly, it was laid to alcoholism. An 1821 report in Massachusetts, for example, contended that "of all the causes of pauperism, intemperance, in the use of spiritous liquors, is the most powerful and universal." In 1834, another commentator was even harsher: "Pauperism is the consequence of willful error, of shameful indolence, of vicious habits. It is a misery of the human condition, the pernicious work of man, the lamentable consequence of bad principles and morals."[12]

If the poor were mainly responsible for their own fate, then they deserved little aid, which came mainly from counties, towns, and churches. Until the early nineteenth century, some poor were auctioned off to families who were willing to accept the lowest amounts for caring for them; others were provided modest amounts of food or fuel as "outdoor relief" (meaning that it was given them and didn't require them to be institutionalized); and still others were sent to poorhouses. None of these approaches was especially humane. The auctioned poor were often treated "more like brutes than human beings." In 1856, New York's poorhouses were described as "badly constructed, ill-arranged, ill-warmed and ill-ventilated" by a select committee of the state legislature. "The rooms are crowded with inmates; and the air, particularly in the sleeping apartments, is very noxious, and to casual visitors, almost insufferable." As for outdoor relief, it was typically minimal. In the 1870s, a family in Brooklyn, New York, might receive only a dollar's worth of food and fuel for a week. This was a time when an unskilled laborer—the lowest-paid worker—might receive $1 or $1.25 a day. Food disbursements consisted of staples like flour, potatoes, or rice. These policies were never popular, and their main virtue was seen as preventing starvation.[13]

The main reason that these policies were not popular (aside from their cost) was that the very provision of relief was viewed as corrupting. From the country's earliest years, Americans distinguished between the worthy and unworthy poor (or the deserving and undeserving). The former consisted mainly of widows, children, and those too sick, old, or enfeebled to work. The latter included the able-bodied who were brought down by their own failings. But in practice, distinctions were hard to make, and relief—of any type—was kept meager to deter people from shirking from work. According to Katz, most people who actually got relief would today be classified as the "deserving poor." In New Bedford, Massachusetts, for example, about 280 families were on relief in 1853. About 110 families were headed by women whose husbands had died, gone to sea, or left them; another 80 were headed by someone sick or old. But the danger of relief, Katz writes, arose not from "whom it helped but [from] the lesson it taught. Its very existence [was seen as] a threat to productivity, morality and the tax rate, because the respectable working class just might learn the possibility of life without labor." Poor relief, in short, stayed spare to remain punitive, and in this respect, it reflected widespread popular beliefs.[14]

People were thought to advance mainly through their own efforts, and an excess of collective compassion might weaken those efforts. By and large, Americans have always thought along these lines, and even during the depths of the Depression, when massive government relief became commonplace, President Franklin Roosevelt felt it necessary to denounce the long-term dangers of becoming too dependent on government. In his 1935 State of the Union message, he formally proposed Social Security, unemployment insurance, and aid to families with dependent children—which he described as helping the deserving poor—while also deploring the effects of indiscriminate relief. "The lessons of history, confirmed by evidence immediately before me," Roosevelt said, "show conclusively that continued dependence upon relief induces a spiritual and moral disintegration fundamentally destructive to the national fiber. To dole out relief in this way is to administer a narcotic, a subtle destroyer of the human spirit. It is inimical to the dictates of sound policy. It is in violation of the traditions of America. Work must be found for able-bodied but destitute workers."[15]

WHAT HAPPENED in postwar America is that these traditional beliefs, though not disappearing, weakened and became overlaid with contradictory programs and practices. Always muddled, Americans grew even more muddled about equality. Its meaning shifted, as equality of condition and outcome were increasingly seen as essential for equality of opportunity. There were three main reasons for this.

The first—the precipitating cause—was the civil rights movement of the 1960s. It made equality and inequality a morality tale, because the prevailing racial inequalities were so stark and seemed, on the whole, so susceptible to legislative remedies. Throughout the South, blacks faced overt discrimination in housing, employment, and public accommodations (buses, hotels, restaurants, swimming pools) that was sanctioned by state law and unchallenged by federal law. In many counties, blacks could not vote freely. The obvious solution was to make such discrimination illegal. The Civil Rights Act of 1964 and the Voting Rights Act of 1965 did so. The first outlawed discrimination in employment, housing, and public accommodations; the second outlawed literacy tests and poll taxes, which had been used by many states and localities to discourage blacks from voting. The assumption—incorrect, as it turned out—was that ending discrimination against blacks would result in equality for blacks. But the civil rights model was widely adopted by other groups (women, Hispanics, the disabled) that cast themselves as oppressed minorities who were being treated unequally. In addition, it fostered a general belief that inequality, once identified, could and should be remedied by political and legal action.

The second reason was a growing conviction that equality of opportunity required a leveling of social conditions. Few political leaders openly advocated equality of outcome, which offended Americans' sense of fair play. But since the 1960s, unequal education, housing, or health care has been seen as destroying equal opportunity, just as English inheritance laws did in the eighteenth century. President Johnson made precisely this argument to justify his Great Society programs. "Negroes are trapped—as many whites are trapped—in inherited, gateless poverty," he said in 1965. "They lack training and skills. They are shut in, in slums, without decent medical care. Private and public poverty combine to cripple their capacities." If people were to have equality of opportunity, then they must have equal education, hous-

ing, and health care. There was (and is) a circularity in these arguments: because people had inferior education, housing, and medical
care, they could not achieve the economic advancement that would
assure them of better education, housing, and medical care. Opportunity and results blended and became confused. Although the importance of individual effort was still respected rhetorically, it had been
subtly devalued by the emphasis on social conditions as an explanation
for those who succeeded and those who didn't.[16]

Finally, the nature of equality changed, because courts increasingly acted as arbiters of social policy and, in the process, translated
more and more worthy goals into legal rights. The recourse to courts
reflected both the rising volume of social legislation (all of which
could be challenged or interpreted judicially) and the calculated efforts by advocacy groups to use the courts. As sociologist Paul Starr
has written: "Every society shapes the demands made against it. In
the United States, the two-party system, the absence of a socialist tradition, and the distinctive role of the judiciary in interpreting the
Constitution encourage the dissatisfied to organize in social movements outside the political parties and to present their demands as
claims under the Bill of Rights. . . . [By the 1970s, groups] marched
mainly through the courts. . . . The new movements advocated the
rights of women, children, prisoners, students, tenants, gays, Chi-
canos, native Americans, and welfare clients. The catalogue of rights
and of groups entitled to them was immensely expanded in both variety and detail."[17]

The result has been to make modern welfare politics incompre-
hensible and, to a large extent, unmanageable. The distinction between a right and a benefit has become blurred. Traditionally,
government benefits reflected political acts by legislatures that could,
therefore, be modified—for better or worse—as political conditions
changed. A right implies something far more permanent. In a land-
mark 1970 decision (*Goldberg* v. *Kelly*), the Supreme Court concluded
that it "may be realistic today to regard welfare entitlements more like
'property' than a 'gratuity,' " as Justice William Brennan wrote. In
other words: the right to property also extended to government benefits. With this leap, benefits became entitled to judicial sheltering and
solicitude under the Constitution's due process clause. In the *Goldberg*
v. *Kelly* case, a disabled welfare recipient (one John Kelly) had been cut

off by New York when he had moved out of the welfare hotel to which his caseworker had assigned him. The state could not do that, Brennan ruled, without first giving Kelly proper notice and then the due process of having a hearing before an "impartial decision-maker." The Court, said Brennan, had to protect individuals against the "bureaucratic state." Courts were there to act, as much as or more than legislatures, as individuals' guardians.

Combining this view with a broad reading of the intent of Congress or state legislatures in creating new programs, courts gave themselves a large independent role in fashioning social policy. Affirmative action, in which they played a critical part, is unique only in its high visibility. In a recent study, political scientist R. Shep Melnick of Brandeis University has meticulously shown how courts systematically expanded programs for food stamps, Aid to Families with Dependent Children, and educational aid for handicapped children. Until the 1960s, courts had rarely interfered with the operation of income transfer programs. But in the 1960s and 1970s, courts became more zealous. "Time and time again federal judges would strike down state rules and federal regulations not because they transgressed clear statutory language, but because they failed to take into account the actual needs of potential beneficiaries," writes Melnick. Similarly, courts enlarged disability programs by expanding eligibility requirements and limiting agencies' authority to purge recipients from the rolls. Many judges came to view their roles as adjunct legislators, guaranteeing that "important legislative purposes . . . are not lost or misdirected in the vast hallways of the federal bureaucracy," as one sympathetic judge put it.[18] The trouble, of course, is not that many of the needs were not genuine or even desirable. The trouble is that not all genuine needs can always be met and that courts are often ill equipped to see or make the choices.

THE CRUSADE for ever greater equality founders on two persisting problems. The first is practicality. Government programs and commitments are often overwhelmed by larger social and economic changes. Government cannot do everything for everybody. People (or institutions) must do some things for themselves. Government can increase people's incomes simply by giving them money; but it cannot make them self-respecting or more productive by giving them money. (Indeed, some social policies, if carried too far, may undermine the very goals they purport to advance. For example, people who have become too dependent on modest public benefits might have—in their absence—developed work skills that ultimately led to higher incomes.) In education, the continuing poor performance of many low-income students has encouraged policies to equalize spending among school districts, even though repeated studies cast doubt on spending as a major source of student success. (More important determinants are students' family backgrounds and parental involvement in schools.)[19] In health care, what needs are to be covered by government and private insurance? Not all are equal. Some save lives; some merely improve the quality of life. The questions involve broad issues of public good, because the rapid growth in health care spending has displaced other government and private spending. Would some of that money have been better used elsewhere?*

The second problem is public opinion. In general, Americans favor more fairness and equality in national life, by which most people mean that all Americans should live decently, have a chance to get ahead, and be spared arbitrary treatment, whether by business, government, or anyone else. This is why public opinion polls have long shown support for government aid to end poverty, improve education, and extend health care. In this sense, Americans are generous. But their generosity is diffuse and shrinks when government's efforts to help some individuals are seen—as they increasingly are—as impinging upon other individuals. More than most peoples, Americans are optimistic about their ability to get ahead and, therefore, less willing to use government as an instrument for social solidarity. Asked whether "success in life is pretty much determined by forces outside our control," 57 percent of Americans disagree. In Europe, much smaller percentages dissent: 33 percent in Germany, 31 percent in Italy, and 36 percent in France. Asked whether it is government's re-

---

*In theory, private health insurance isn't involved. But in practice, it is, because private insurance is heavily subsidized—and, therefore, encouraged—by government. The subsidy occurs through the tax code, because employer-paid insurance (which is income to workers) isn't taxed under the income tax. This has favored the expansion of insurance, which has abetted the spiral of health care spending. Between 1965 and 1993, health care spending rose from 6 to nearly 14 percent of GDP.[20]

sponsibility "to take care of very poor people who can't take care of themselves," only 23 percent of Americans say yes. In Europe, support is much higher: 50 percent in Germany, 62 percent in France and Britain, and 71 percent in Spain.[21]

"The United States stands out among industrial countries in the extent to which its citizens stress individual effort over government assistance," writes political scientist Everett Carll Ladd.[22] The cumulative actions of government over the past three decades to help people have aroused this deep suspicion. But there is something more. Words matter when they affect how people think and act. Is the "right" of someone to a disability hearing really as important as the "right" of free speech? Is the "right" to a welfare check as important as the "right" to freedom of religion? The first set of "rights" here involves details of government—who gets what benefits and under what conditions—while the second set involves fundamental principles of social and political conduct that have guided Americans since the eighteenth century. Details of government can (and should) change as circumstances and public opinion shift. By contrast, basic principles should endure unless the nature of government itself alters. Compressing both meanings under the same label subverts the significance of the bedrock rights and exaggerates the significance of what are, ultimately, passing political questions.

A society that is casual in its enthusiasm for rights and is excessively animated by egalitarian ideals ultimately risks becoming engulfed by absurdities. Government is driven by the demands for new and more varied forms of equality and, in the process, risks being overwhelmed by those who feel mistreated for almost any reason. The absolutist nature of a right—when applied to so many issues— "inhibits dialogue that might lead towards consensus, accommodation, or at least the discovery of common ground," as Harvard Law professor Mary Ann Glendon has remarked.[23] Absurdities are not merely theoretical possibilities. The Equal Employment Opportunity Commission has now said that fat people may be victims of discrimination and entitled to federal protection. No less a figure than Vice President Al Gore has suggested communications companies should be taxed to subsidize computer and other advanced communications services for the poor so that there might be "universal service." Otherwise, society might subdivide between "information haves" and "information have-nots." In San Francisco, the city was sued because, although Candlestick Park had moved to make accommodations for the disabled, it had done so in a separate section. "I cried and I cried for three days, because nobody had ever discriminated against me before," said one distraught fan. "You are segregated to a section of seating that is restricted only for the disabled. I came on Mother's Day, and they said I couldn't sit with my son and my husband."[24]

Everyone is ultimately entitled to everything. The great harm— or danger—is to destroy people's faith in government itself, because (quite obviously) everyone cannot have everything. To try to impose equality on a vast panorama of its activities is to overburden government. A sensitivity to important and indefensible inequalities easily slips into the indiscriminate habit of judging most social and political issues in terms of equality. The result is guaranteed failure, because complete equality is a chimera. There has always been inequality and always will be. Individual talent and temperament are too varied; fortune and circumstance are too fickle. Even if this were not so, could we ever agree upon what constitutes equality? Is it equality of income, freedom, or happiness? Is everyone entitled to equal computing power and vacations? To make government the guardian of equality is to ordain overcommitment. The resulting disappointments erode the foundations of public consent and trust that democracy requires. As Benjamin Franklin once said: "Much of the Strength and Efficiency of any Government, in procuring & securing Happiness to the People, depends on . . . the general Opinion of the Goodness of that Government." But that government cannot be good which constantly promises to do what, in the end, cannot be done.

12

Suicidal Government

☙ ☙ ☙ ☙

T HE RESULT OF THESE VARIOUS TRENDS is that, at the close of
the twentieth century, American government and politics seem
almost suicidal. They compulsively generate public distrust. Government has become overcommitted in the sense that it has promised to
do things that can't be done or things that, however desirable in isolation, are incompatible. Government therefore welshes on many
promises and undermines public confidence in itself and in the nation's political leadership. At the same time, the growth of government has seemed to make politics less democratic, because bigger
government seems more remote from public opinion and more difficult to understand. This is not so much the result of deliberate se-
crecy, though that occurs, as of ordinary obscurity. Most people
simply do not have the time or inclination to follow most of what government does because government does so many things and, even if
they did, would find most of it hopelessly boring and technical. The
trouble is that government's obscurity sows suspicion. People constantly discover that government affects and acts upon them in ways

that they never imagined, can't understand, and can't seem (except with a great investment of time, effort, and sometimes money) to influence. Government has become a misunderstood, mistrusted, and unpredictable neighbor, even while it was trying to become almost everyone's friend.

Most Americans now scrutinize government on two levels: as members of distinct groups with discrete interests in specific policies; and as members of the broader public, which views government's performance in a highly generalized way. With resulting pressures often at odds, elected leaders must somehow cater to both. On the one hand, they must struggle to satisfy the demands of the hordes of interest groups that descend incessantly on government. Of course, not all can be satisfied all the time, but if politicians antagonize too many of these groups too often, they may endanger their political careers. Disgruntled groups and their followers may somehow mobilize against them. On the other hand, paying scrupulous attention to these various interest groups may create government that, on a more general level, offends many Americans and operates in ways that sometimes do more harm than good. This is a permanent dilemma of modern government and, more than specific events (the Vietnam War, Watergate, etc.), explains the erosion of popular esteem for the nation's political leadership and institutions.

The irony is that the Founders constructed a system of decentralized government with dispersed powers in the hope that such a system would inhibit the growth of government. Power fragmented would be power frustrated. As we have seen, this has not happened. Government has grown despite the obstacles to its growth, and indeed, the fragmented nature of the system has, in some ways, actually encouraged its growth. As the Founders expected, our system does have a multitude of power centers: the federal government, states, local governments, courts (at all levels), and regulatory agencies (again, at all levels). And as the Founders also expected, this splintering of power can sometimes frustrate the exercise of power. American government was not meant to operate smoothly and swiftly, and it doesn't. Congress can obstruct the president and vice versa; the courts can obstruct both. The various parts of government are constantly bickering with one another over which is responsible for a particular governmental task. But this same splintered system has also abetted the growth of government, because the multitude of power centers creates a multitude of avenues for influence.

Those who have wanted to enlist government on their side have gone wherever they think they have the best chance for success. If national government isn't sympathetic, then maybe the states are. If legislators aren't, maybe judges are. A bias for growth has existed both because the intellectual climate has changed (government is seen as the ultimate problem solver) and because demands for the extension of government power have been made where opposition has been least. It is precisely the decentralized nature of the American system that affords all these opportunities for influence, and once created, governmental power has been hard to reduce for the same reason—the decentralized nature of the system. All levels of government guard the powers they already have. All levels seek to exercise power at the expense of others. Courts impose mandates to be implemented by localities (towns, cities, counties), states, or the federal government. State and local governments strive to exploit federal programs for the most dollars. The federal government seeks to control states and localities through mandates or partially funded programs (i.e., the federal government may pay for 50 percent of the costs but, in so doing, sets conditions that determine how 100 percent of the money is spent). Efforts to reduce government encounter all the constituencies that have stakes in existing programs. The difficulty of getting government to do anything—the inertia that was intended by the Founders—works to sustain the status quo.

THE FRUSTRATION OF this system feeds Americans' historic suspicion of government—of unchecked power—and creates a politics of antipolitics. Americans still disdain politics as a profession, while trying to accommodate their rising and unrelenting needs to influence government. On the one hand, most Americans want nothing to do with government. They want to be left alone; they want to be free; they distrust politicians and always have. In their daily lives, they are not especially political. One recent survey found that only 60 percent of Americans discussed politics even a few times a week (for voters, the proportion was slightly higher; for nonvoters, much lower).[1] On the other hand, Americans are constantly involved with government

and don't want it to withdraw existing benefits or impose new burdens. Or they believe that government should support what is (to
them) some compelling cause. The simultaneous loathing of professional politicians and the desire to shape government coexist through
a political culture of reform and amateur politics that, though it has
long existed, has now evolved into something of a national mania.
"Single-issue" constituencies, "public interest" groups, "citizens' lob-
bies," and advocacy groups of all varieties have proliferated. Their
leaders often sincerely protest that they are "above politics" even
while being immersed in it.

The process is circular: the more groups exploit government for
their own purposes, the more powerful government becomes—and
the more reason to influence it. Political scientist James Q. Wilson recently offered a mundane example of this evolution. Consider, said
Wilson, the interstate highway program. When Congress first passed
it in 1956, the law ran 28 pages. Essentially, it created a new system of
highways and imposed the taxes to build them. When the program
was reauthorized in 1991, the law was ten times as long (293 pages)
and had come to incorporate a long list of new aims. Aside from
building highways and mass transit systems, the new program also required the secretary of transportation to:

> relieve congestion, improve air quality, preserve historic sites,
> encourage the use of auto seat belts and motorcycle helmets,
> control erosion and storm water runoff, monitor traffic and col-
> lect data on speeding, reduce drunk driving, require environ-
> mental impact studies, control outdoor advertising, develop
> standards for high-occupancy vehicles, require metropolitan
> and statewide planning, use recycled rubber in making asphalt,
> set aside 10 percent of construction monies for small businesses
> owned by disadvantaged individuals, buy iron and steel from
> U.S. suppliers, establish new rules for renting equipment, give
> preferential employment to Native Americans if a highway is to
> be built near a reservation, and control the use of calcium mag-
> nesium acetate in performing seismic retrofits on bridges.[2]

This transformation of government has inevitably moved power
away from the elected to the unelected. As early as 1912, Woodrow

Wilson worried about such a shift. Discussing expanded governmental economic regulation—which he favored—he also saw possible drawbacks. "What I fear, therefore, is a government of experts. . . . God forbid that in a democratic country we should resign the task [of governing] and give the government over to experts. What are we if we are to be scientifically taken care of by a small number of gentlemen who are the only men who understand the job? Because if we don't understand the job, then we are not a free people."[3] What Wilson feared has come to pass. The number of senators and representatives has been almost flat since the second decade of the twentieth century (the House of Representatives has been at 435 members since 1911, though it temporarily went to 437 with the admission of Alaska and Hawaii to statehood), while the government's workload has exploded. The extra work had to be absorbed elsewhere. Between the late 1940s and the early 1990s, the size of Congress's staff jumped from 2,400 to about 11,000.[*4] In the 1970s alone, the number of federal regulatory agencies rose from twenty to twenty-eight. The additions included the Environmental Protection Agency, the Occupational Safety and Health Administration, and the Pension Benefit Guaranty Corporation.

In turn, the growth of bureaucratic government has fostered the parallel expansion of what the *National Journal* calls the "influence industry": all the lobbyists, lawyers, consultants, and other "experts" who watch, analyze, and influence government. By one count, more than 100 think tanks—a term first applied to the Rand Corporation after the Second World War—exist in Washington alone. Two thirds of them opened after 1970. A directory of Washington "representatives" (mostly lobbyists, public relations representatives, and lawyers) counted about 7,000 when it was first published in the mid-1970s. By the early 1990s, the figure had doubled. If the directory had existed in the 1950s, the number would probably have been 1,000 or 2,000. Perhaps a third of these representatives are long-standing industry and professional groups, such as the National Farmers Union, the Amer-

*In 1995, the new Republican majority in the House of Representatives pledged to reduce its staff by one third. At this writing (mid-1995), no conclusive figures exist to judge whether that pledge was realized. Even if the House succeeds, total congressional staff—which includes Senate staff and joint agencies, such as the Congressional Budget Office—would not necessarily be cut by a third.

ican Medical Association, and the National Soft Drink Association. Another fifth are advocacy groups for special causes, from the Muscular Dystrophy Association to the Religious Coalition for Abortion Rights. Most of the remaining groups are groups representing the specific interests of large and small popular constituencies: the American Association of Retired Persons (32 million members, founded in 1958), the National Rifle Association (2.7 million members, founded in 1871), the National Gay and Lesbian Task Force (17,000 individual members and 100 organizational members, founded in 1973).[5]

"Special interests" are routinely deplored, but what constitutes a special interest is mainly in the eye of the beholder. The growth of these groups is simply the logical extension of the growth of government and the need to influence its activities. When government is limited, it can be more easily influenced through elections. Voters can get a sense of where their representatives stand on major issues, and legislators can judge their constituents' general feelings. As governmental activities proliferate, this is harder for both voters and legislators. Legislators are called upon to advance the views and interests of their constituents when these are not known, not knowable, or at odds with one another. After all, who can stay abreast of the Superfund, the Social Security disability program, grazing fees, Medicare reimbursement rules, eligibility requirements for food stamps, and the development of a new jet fighter? Inevitably, representatives decide most detailed issues less on the basis of public opinion than on their general beliefs and the realities of legislative politics: the interaction of interested lobbyists, interest groups, bureaucrats, and experts. But the outcomes may surprise voters, who may discover—when they care, that is—that their legislators have taken unexpected or distasteful positions.

OF COURSE, THIS HAS always been true. As a mass, the people could not govern. Everyone cannot vote on everything, and since the earliest days of the republic, there have been striking examples of how the politics of governing—that is, the maneuvering of political interests and actors—has determined the outcome of critical issues. It is doubtful, for instance, that the electors who voted for George Washington foresaw his policies, determined as they were by a struggle for Washington's mind between Hamilton and Jefferson. Nor could these electors have predicted that the nation's capital would be moved from Philadelphia to a new city, Washington, as part of a compromise to pay the Revolutionary debts. (Southern members of Congress disliked the debt policy; moving the capital south was a sop to win their support.) Compromise, logrolling, and horse trading have always been a pervasive part of governing. It is the nature of representative government. But it is truer today than ever, and the declining importance of elective politics feeds public disillusion, precisely because the American ideology attaches so much importance to popular will. Americans of all political views still cling ferociously to the Revolution's central idea, which is that government belongs to "the people." After all, the opening words of the Constitution are "We the People."

What aggravates popular frustration with politics—the sense of powerlessness to affect government—is the appearance that elected officials have become more, not less, important. The main reason for this is television and other new technologies. Our political leaders have never been more exposed than now. The president is on national TV news almost daily. Live sessions of Congress, committee hearings, and important speeches are broadcast on C-Span. News coverage runs around the clock on CNN. Technology has made politics more visible and vocal; political leaders routinely pronounce themselves on a vast array of issues. And new technologies (constant opinion polls, focus groups, and call-in shows) provide more ways to gauge public opinion, or what passes for public opinion. Thus, technology creates the impression that our elected leaders have gained in power and can better represent the "people's views," when the opposite is true. Politicians' power has been diluted, and the explosion of various public opinions (often inconsistent) makes representing them more difficult. But the contrast between what political leaders regularly promise and what they can deliver reinforces the popular perception that politics and government must have grown increasingly unresponsive and corrupt.

Conceivably, strong political parties or ideologies might mute popular discontent. Voting is always an act of faith, because no one can predict all the issues that elected officials will face. But if candidates or parties have strong ideologies—a clear set of values that will inform their decisions—the uncertainty diminishes. Well-known ideologies will shape officials' responses to many unpredicted contingencies. Likewise, strong parties can determine their legislators' priorities. Voters can then judge on a party's past performance. But the United States does not have (and never has had) strong and highly ideological parties, at least compared with Europe's parliamentary democracies. Moreover, the power of political parties has waned in recent decades. Until the 1950s, the parties—meaning local and state party chiefs—controlled presidential nominations, as political scientist Edward Banfield has described:

> In the days of the "old" party system—from Andrew Jackson's time to about the mid-1950s—both national parties were loose confederations of state parties that came alive every four years to nominate presidential and vice-presidential candidates and then to wage campaigns for them. Some state parties existed in name only, but most were loose alliances of city machines, state and local officeholders, labor unions and other interest groups, and some wealthy individuals. To be taken seriously as a contender for the presidential nomination, one had to be a leading figure in a major state party organization or have the backing of someone who was. The state leaders, many of whom were governors or senators, were political professionals who typically had worked themselves into positions of power by faithful service to the party. A few party leaders in each state, usually in some sort of convention—a "smoke-filled room"—chose the state's delegates to the national party convention.[6]

Aside from controlling presidential nominations—their most visible role—parties also decided who did and didn't go into politics. Harry Truman, for example, didn't spontaneously enter politics but was approached by Kansas City political boss Tom Pendergast. "They are trying to run me for [county office] . . . , and I guess they'll do it before they are through," Truman wrote to a friend in 1922. Parties "got out the vote" and rewarded supporters with patronage jobs. Pendergast was once asked if jobholders were asked to donate at election time. "Why shouldn't they be?" he responded incredulously. "That's how they got their jobs."[7] Today, parties are mostly political labels; but party organizations have generally lost their roles in picking presidential candidates or budding politicians. If Truman were alive now, he wouldn't be apprenticed by his local party chief. To enter politics, he would try to raise money among family and sympathizers; he would then find a political consultant to organize his campaign. Likewise, party leaders are largely excluded from presidential selection, which occurs mainly through primaries. The parties' loss of power has stemmed partly from explicit reforms and partly from broad societal trends. The expansion of primaries aimed to give more power to rank-and-file members and to remove the taint of party corruption by a few unelected leaders. (In practice, the increasing importance of primaries seems to have empowered fringe elements of both parties, whose members are more motivated and organized to vote in primaries than average voters.) Meanwhile, television and other new technologies, such as direct mail, have made it easier for candidates to raise money and appeal independently to voters.

Compounding the parties' decline is the fact that the party faithful have become a lot less so. Even in the 1950s, party loyalties were strong. The Depression and the Second World War created large Democratic majorities, and these allegiances—apart from how people felt on specific issues—were passed from parents to children. Being a Democrat or a Republican was one way people defined themselves. It still is but much less so. President Eisenhower inspired ticket splitting on a massive scale; otherwise, he could not have won. The war in Vietnam and rising inflation in the 1960s undermined Democratic allegiances without strengthening Republican ones. In 1960, nearly two thirds of the electorate voted a straight party ticket; by 1972, the proportion was only one third.[8] (It is possible that the Republican congressional victory of 1994 will alter these patterns. Specifically, congressional party leadership played an important role in the victories of many new House Republican members. As a result, it is conceivable that the party—or at least party leadership in the House—will have more power and influence over its members than either the Democratic or Republican party has had in the recent past. It is also conceivable that new and stronger party loyalties are forming. But it is too early to make final judgments.)

Party allegiances eroded not only because the rules and institutions that sustained the parties weakened but also because social conditions changed. As the Depression receded into history—and as the generation shaped by it became a smaller part of the electorate—so did its political magnetism. In the Depression, middle-class poverty and insecurity galvanized millions of voters to become Democrats. Postwar affluence dimmed these fears. As more voters completed high school and college, straight party-line voting lost respectability. It implied that voters weren't independent minded. Finally, the mushrooming of issues—a cause and consequence of government's growth—made it harder for either party to maintain a permanent band of faithful. Too many potential voters might be offended by the party's performance or position on various issues.[9]

AS A RESULT, elected officials are more independent than ever. "Who sent us the political leaders we have? There is a simple answer to that question. They sent themselves," writes political analyst Alan Ehrenhalt in a recent book. "And they got where they are through a combination of ambition, talent, and the willingness to devote whatever time was necessary to seek and hold office." Officials are mostly beholden to themselves and the political bases—of voters, financial supporters, and interest groups—they have created. Superficially, this may seem an advance. Senators and representatives can vote their consciences and don't have to submit to party bosses. Campaigns can be run on the "issues." Democracy (it might be argued) is enhanced. But the improvement is mostly illusory. Campaign issues—or a candidate's charm—are often of fleeting importance. Meanwhile, Congress is hobbled by the erosion of already weak party discipline. Party leaders cannot easily control their representatives, because the parties don't offer them much. With members of Congress concentrating "so completely on making sure the voters know them and like them," writes analyst William Schneider, "the institution cannot make tough choices," because (of course) tough choices offend. But paralysis also offends, because it highlights the gap between promise and performance. "The central irony of American politics," Schneider notes, "is that politicians are ineffective [and, he might have added, unpopular] because they have to work so hard at being popular."[10]

In part, this may explain the regularly lamented drop in voter turnout. Some potential voters may sense that elections don't matter much. Why, then, vote? For many, nonvoting is surely a sign of political alienation. But for others, it may not be. Nonvoters can still invest their time and money in a cause of their choosing by supporting the relevant interest group, whether the Children's Defense Fund or the National Rifle Association. Nonvoters can still write or phone senators or their representative. Politicians have no way of knowing whether these pesky constituents have or haven't voted; more important, complaining constituents are always potential voters. Just possibly, the loud nonvoter may be more influential than the silent voter. Whatever the case, there has been an inverse, though loose, relationship between government's growth and voter turnout. While government has grown, turnout has shrunk. As the following table shows, the decline has been 8 to 10 percentage points since 1960. (The table gives the average percentage of eligible voters who actually vote in presidential elections. The trends for off-year congressional elections are similar, though turnouts are lower.)*

Presidential Voter Turnout Since 1960[11]

Year	Percent
1960	63
1964	62
1968	61
1972	55
1976	54
1980	53
1984	53
1988	50
1992	55

Whatever the impact on voter turnout, these broad trends—the breakdown of parties, the rise of television, the growing independence of individual candidates, the explosion of issues—have made government seem increasingly disconnected from and unresponsive to popular will. Elections are supposed to provide the mechanism by which popular will can be translated into governmental actions. But elections routinely exaggerate the possibility of change and create ex-

---

*I don't want to leave the impression that I consider this to be the only cause of the decline in turnout, which dates to at least the late nineteenth century, when turnouts were as high as 80 percent. For a fuller discussion, see note 11, page 271.

pectations that cannot be met.* The best recent example of this was the so-called Reagan revolution. His election in 1980 inspired a widespread belief—which he encouraged and which was echoed by critics, political reporters, and academic commentators—that American politics had undergone a huge upheaval. "Government is not the solution to our problems," as he said in his first inaugural address, "government is the problem."[12] This seemed a total rejection of the postwar philosophy of government. And yet, the "revolution" was mainly rhetorical. Reagan did not dismantle government. As previously noted, Congress discontinued only two major federal programs (general revenue sharing and urban development action grants) during the 1980s. And Reagan's tax "cuts" merely prevented the tax burden from continuing to rise. When he left office in 1989, the scope of federal activities and the tax burden were essentially what they had been when he arrived. His presidency surely made a difference, especially in shifting the tone and content of political debate. But the actual difference was much less than his rhetoric, or conventional political wisdom, implied. There was no revolution.

Of course, it's possible that Reagan was a hypocrite and never believed half of what he said. This is a convenient but overly cynical theory. The truth is that Reagan lacked the power to put his ideas into action. It was not simply that Congress was always at least partially controlled by Democrats and that most Democrats did not share his distaste for government. (The Senate had a Republican majority between 1981 and 1986. In the House, Democrats enjoyed a consistent majority between 1955 and 1995.) Even if Republicans had run Congress, Reagan probably could not have drastically streamlined government. At the time, there was little public taste or demand for it: Congressional Republicans might have revolted out of fear for their political lives. No one was clamoring for major reductions in Social Security, Medicare, federal college loans, farm subsidies, or a host of other "entitlement" programs that constitute the bulk of federal spending. Reagan was sensitive to these limits. He was content to play

---

*Again, the 1994 Republican congressional triumph will test these generalizations anew. But the Republican campaign promises included many commitments that many observers (including me) found inconsistent: lower taxes, a balanced budget, higher defense spending, and a pledge not to touch Social Security. All of them will be hard to meet.

on the public's expressed suspicion of Big Government without demanding that the public prove its sincerity by embracing sweeping
cutbacks in government. But the discrepancy between his rhetoric
and performance inevitably nurtured the sense of dishonest politics.
Other presidents, before and after, have inspired more disillusion, because Reagan at least maintained considerable personal goodwill.

In a broader sense, discontent is fed by the notion that government is increasingly the captive of undemocratic special interests. It
may be true that many (perhaps most) Americans support or belong
to one or another of these special interests, whether it be the AARP
or the NRA. Yet, although these seem (to their members) to be highly
worthy causes, most Americans are somehow able to overlook their
personal affiliations when concluding that government is becoming
less democratic. Even the most sophisticated observers have argued
that government decreasingly seems to reflect public wishes. Again,
political scientist James Q. Wilson:

> Popular beliefs cannot explain the vast increase in the govern-
> ment's debt, the ascendancy of affirmative action programs, the
> continuance of foreign aid programs, the deregulation of civil avi-
> ation, or the resistance to economic protectionism. The public has
> steadfastly opposed all of these policies, and in many cases—such
> as affirmative action or deficit financing—on grounds of deeply
> held principles. . . . I wish to suggest . . . that many of the largest
> changes of the last century [in government] have occurred not
> because of popular demand but because of elite interests.[13]

What Wilson has actually identified are the political consequences of bigger government. The distinction between elites and
special interests is blurred, and both gain power from government's
expansion. Government's growth removes more of its work from the
visible platform of electoral politics and relegates it to the darker
realm of governing or legislative politics. Experts of all manner—in
and out of government and, often, with their own agendas—become
more important. Government would break down if this did not
occur. But the fact that it does occur gives government and politics a
momentum all their own, which seems unchecked by popular consent. There is a vicious circle. Government that grows must do more

of its work in obscurity; otherwise, it could not function at all and would inevitably fail in many of its missions. But government that works in obscurity will become increasingly dominated by narrow groups, which will bend it to their own purposes and make government seem more removed from popular will. To succeed, government must become more exclusionary, but as it does, it becomes more suspect. Its general direction may well be set by public opinion, but many of its details will be determined by the micropolitics of interest groups, bureaucrats, experts, and elites.

EVERY POLITICAL SYSTEM has its imperfections and inconsistencies. Ours always has and always will. The important (and unanswerable) question is whether the defects of modern government will ultimately prove crippling to the basic purposes of government. Among these are: advancing the "national" or "public" interest, including—most obviously—providing for the nation's security; providing a political mechanism for mitigating economic and social conflicts; and maintaining the trust—the consent—of the governed. Each of these tasks affects the nation's long-term survival and well-being, because successful government and successful nationhood go hand in hand. Government sets society's rules and symbolizes the collective willingness of any group of people to come together and take common action for the common good. Government's growth has in many ways advanced these objectives. It has made capitalism more compassionate and socially acceptable; it has reduced discrimination and helped assimilate new immigrant groups into American society. But government's growth also complicates and compromises its ability to fulfill its basic tasks.

The difficulty lies, as it always has, in defining what truly national and public interests are. The more government does, the harder this becomes. Our political vocabulary has been debased. Every group (and its members) that receives something from government believes or asserts that its benefits somehow serve the larger public interest. When everyone uses the same language, the language becomes useless. (No one, after all, defends a governmental benefit on the ground that it is an unjustified enrichment of a small and unworthy clique.) Government's growth may also harm genuine public interests by cre-

ating a scarcity of resources. As the number of claimants for governmental dollars rises, it becomes harder for those that might serve truly
national interests to get an adequate share. Defense poses a special
problem. As social spending has grown, military spending has become
the "principal sufferer," as one former defense secretary has put it.
Judging future defense needs is subjective, especially after the Cold
War, when global threats are more murky than ever. But defense may
be shortchanged, because no one can say precisely how much of it is
desirable and because its constituencies (defense contractors, veterans'
groups, and the like) focus mainly on their own particular programs.*[14]

Government's growth has also reduced its capacity to conciliate.
Politics and government are not simply processes by which collective
benefits and burdens are decided upon and distributed. They are vehicles through which society creates rules for itself. Devising these rules
forces government to mediate among different interests and points of
view. The thrashing out of differences is one way by which society de-
fuses social, economic, and cultural tensions. Those who disagree are
forced to confront one another peacefully. They are compelled to
search for ways to agree or, at least, to limit their disagreements. Indeed, if there were no disagreements, rules—and government itself—
would be unnecessary. To play this role, government (though clearly
not all the individuals in it) must be seen as "fair." It has to have moral
authority and cannot be viewed mainly as an instrument to advance a
set of interests or groups. But as government has been enlisted to solve
more problems, its conciliatory role has suffered, because it *is* increasingly seen as an instrument that's being used to help some at the expense of others. Government is seen as taking sides, and the more this
happens, the more its moral authority to act as a neutral arbiter is undermined. Government itself becomes a source of contention.

Quite obviously, most social and economic conflicts exist independently of government. But when government intervenes, it makes
enemies and certifies one party or position as superior. Consider tax
policy. When the tax burden is low, tax policy is not controversial.
When the tax burden rises, different taxpayers (families, companies,

---

*In 1995, defense spending was 18 percent of total federal spending, the lowest since
1940, when it was also 18 percent. By the year 2000, the defense share of the federal budget is projected to drop to about 14 percent.[15]

industries) may feel they are treated unfairly. Their villain is "the government," not some amalgam of groups acting through government. Government can help resolve conflicts when there is an overwhelming social consensus by, in effect, smothering the opposition. Consider the Civil Rights Act of 1964. Most Americans felt discrimination in employment and public accommodations should be illegal as a moral principle; the law simply codified this consensus and disregarded those (mostly in the South) who felt otherwise. But when no such consensus exists, mobilizing government's authority on one side may fail to settle the conflict while also alienating large numbers of people from government itself. A good example is the recent controversy over permitting homosexuals in the military; government didn't settle the issue but offended those on both sides. It is one thing to feel unhappy about something. It is quite another to think that government is the source of unhappiness. The first condition is a private or personal matter; the second is a source of political discord.

The ultimate threat here is to government's legitimacy. If government is seen to abuse its power too often, it will no longer command public respect. Popular consent will erode, and consent is the lifeblood of successful democracies. It is the capacity of a political system to command the loyalty of the vast majority of its citizens, even when it produces (as it must) policies with which many people disagree. They are willing to accept these unwanted policies because they believe that the process by which the policies were reached was essentially fair and that the importance of the system as a whole outweighs the outcomes (distasteful as they may be) of any single issue or even of many issues. Consent is an amorphous quality that, as long as it exists, is barely noticed and almost never discussed. This is surely true in the United States, where Americans feel a strong pride in their political system even as they grow more critical of their political leaders. One public poll asked whether "Whatever its faults, the U.S. still has the best system of government in the world." About 85 percent of respondents agreed. Yet, confidence in Congress and political leaders has steadily eroded.[16] Americans love their system of government, even while increasingly detesting the people who run it.

In some ways, the two trends are not as contradictory as they appear. Americans hold their political system in such high (and perhaps romantic) regard that they tend to see most fallible politicians as unworthy heirs to the country's great traditions. Another poll question asked whether "The system [of government] is good but the people in government are not doing their jobs well enough." Nearly 70 percent of respondents agreed.[17] Although the deep confidence that most Americans feel in their system is not easily shaken, government's growth poses threats. Government will increasingly be dismissed as corrupt and illegitimate if, somehow, it is seen as breaking the nation's traditions and ignoring its long-term interests. For example, Americans may not agree on how government budget deficits should be ended, but they do seem to agree that persistent deficits are unhealthy. A political system that routinely generates more demands and expectations than it can reasonably fulfill is trifling with its own future. By trying to do too much, it risks doing little well and sowing mass disappointment. Government that is overused undermines its own competence and subverts consent.

It is an illusion to think these failings exist apart from mass beliefs and yearnings. Our political system ultimately responds to public opinion and suffers from its weaknesses. "The accepted theory of popular government," Walter Lippmann wrote in 1925, "rests upon the belief that there is a public which directs the course of events. . . . This public is a mere phantom. It is an abstraction. The public in respect to a railroad strike may be the farmers whom the railroad serves; the public in respect to an agricultural tariff may include the very railroad men who were on strike. The public is not, as I see it, a fixed body of individuals. It is merely those persons who are interested in an affair and can affect it only by supporting or opposing the [political] actors."[18] True in 1925, it is far more true today. Public opinion is not a monolith, because "the public" is not a coherent body on all issues. It is a constantly changing collection of groups that provide contradictory signals as to what they think government can and should do. Congress and the President do not defy or ignore public opinion, but they do not accommodate it either, because it is impossible to accommodate fully. Politics confounds and confuses, because public opinion confounds and confuses. It is in this sense that we may have gotten the government we want and, perhaps, deserve.

Epilogue:
After Entitlement

13

History's Cycles

☙ ☙ ☙ ☙

THE HISTORIAN ARTHUR SCHLESINGER, JR., among others,
has noted that the American story moves in cycles. So it does.
But Schlesinger mischaracterizes the cycles when he says that they reflect a "continuing shift in national interest . . . between public purpose and private interest." The underlying rhythms are more
complicated than that and really engage a ceaseless conflict between
Americans' unchanging ideals and the ever shifting circumstances
that prevent those ideals from being realized. The cycle is one of exertion and exhaustion, of romantic assault and ugly accommodation.
This is hardly, of course, the sum total of our history, because the history of any country or people is a mosaic of blinding complexity. It is
an interlay of an infinite number of events and trends, personal tri-
umphs and tragedies. The understanding of history involves the selective viewing of the mosaic in an effort to discover some order and
pattern, and the existence of these broad rhythms—driven by contradictions between ideals and reality—is one such recurring pattern.[1]

We can detect it from the earliest days of the republic in the journey between the Revolution and the Constitution. Here was the original collision between Americans' thirst for liberty and freedom, on the one hand, and the need to have order and authority, on the other. The Constitution was the by-product of this collision: an effort to find some acceptable middle ground between anarchy and tyranny. We can also see the same rhythm operating in the events that climaxed in the Civil War. Slavery was so anathema to the central concept of America—that all people are born equal in their humanity and dignity—that it could not coexist with that belief. We can see the rhythm arise again from the tension between the accelerating industrialization and urbanization of the late nineteenth century and the early ideals of Jeffersonian republicanism, with its emphasis on a citizenry composed of self-sufficient and responsible farmers. In each of these cases, Americans struggled to sustain their ideals against the insistent pressures that seemed to imperil them. A good part of our history is captured by these struggles, which, despite their variety, continually buffet us between hope and disillusion.

What I have called the Age of Entitlement is simply another episode in this chronicle. As before, we have believed that we were making the one, last ferocious assault against the glaring evils and shortcomings of American society and that, once the attack was completed, we would have arrived at the place where we were always intended to be. That is, we would have created a society worthy of and consistent with America's most admirable values and traditions. It would preserve liberty, allow "the pursuit of happiness," and, by protecting the unfortunate, advance equality. Not only did we believe that we could attain this new and improved America; after a while, we came to believe that we were entitled to it—that the very desire to bring it into being, coupled with our deliberate efforts to do so, gave us a right to its realization. The wish became the reality and, inevitably, the seed of disappointment and discontent. With hindsight, we know that the wish ran afoul of numerous practical obstacles. It presumed that we could orchestrate continuous, rapid economic growth, when we couldn't; it placed too much faith in the power of prosperity, by itself, to guarantee social peace and personal happiness; and it attributed more power to large organizations—government, corporations, schools, universities, research enterprises—to solve economic and social problems than they possess.

To Schlesinger, the oscillation "between public purpose and private interest" flows in part from natural lapses in national stamina. "Sustained public action . . . is emotionally exhausting," he writes. "A nation's capacity for high-tension political commitment is limited. . . . People can no longer gird themselves for heroic effort. They yearn to immerse themselves in the privacies of life. . . . Weary of ceaseless national activity, disillusioned by the results, they seek a new dispensation, an interlude of rest and recuperation."[2] There is doubtless much truth in this, but it is at best an incomplete truth. The discontents that Americans feel today are not merely (or even mainly) the consequences of exhaustion. Americans still have—and constantly exhibit—ample energies in many aspects of national life, including politics. Nor are today's discontents directed only at government or at politics, though these are the easiest and most obvious targets. More than emotional fatigue, the source of these discontents is simple disappointment.

The problem-solving personality—which characterizes much of the American population, regardless of people's position along the political spectrum or social ladder—craves solutions. Lacking them, it becomes embittered, confused, and disillusioned. It disparages old authorities and leaders and anoints new. It seeks to assess blame and to find scapegoats. It searches hungrily for new "solutions" and, in its frustrations, is often undiscriminating in its choices. We are now clearly in this phase of the cycle, which I call the "ugly accommodation" to reality. It is the dawning recognition, accompanied by a parallel ill temper, that the goals and aspirations that we pursued so avidly not only remain unattained but are probably unattainable. There is anger, letdown, and a void. In this sense, the Age of Entitlement is drawing to a close. Imperceptibly and perhaps unconsciously, Americans are beginning to grasp that they are not entitled; and the recognition has inevitably led to both recriminations and a search for a new set of organizing ideas.

We should not be surprised, therefore, at the ferment that animates so much of our political life and commentary. It is, of course, most obvious in politics, where beginning with the election of Ronald Reagan in 1980 and continuing with the Republican capture of Congress in 1994, old appeals and coalitions seem to be disintegrating. It also surfaces in the explosion of radio and TV talk shows (from Larry King to Rush Limbaugh), the controversies over "multiculturalism" and "diversity," the ongoing self-doubt about our present and future economic well-being, and the unending frustration over federal budget deficits. Most of these conflicts stem from the feeling that some or all of us are being denied whatever was (or is) our due and that someone else has orchestrated this felony of our income, values, or sensibilities. Entitlement denied is a breeding ground for resentments and suspicions, which are now played out daily in our political debates, newspaper and magazine columns, and electronic media of all sorts.

Yet, the appearance of discontent and change exaggerates the reality. Most Americans continue to believe that the United States is a pretty good place to live in and that our ideals, even if they remain unfulfilled, still remain worthy beliefs around which to construct a society. We are a phenomenally prosperous nation and, better yet, are now at peace. If the future were to be as placid as the present, we would have ample cause for national rejoicing. For all their shortcomings and contradictions, the last fifty years of our national life have generally been constructive ones, and most Americans—including me—continue to see them that way. Some of today's complaining and contention derive from objective conditions: economic setbacks, crime, disagreements on political or moral issues. These are all legitimate subjects of concern and debate. But much of our discontent also flows from a feeling of arrested progress and unrealized ambitions: a frustration over what might have been and a bewilderment over why it isn't.

COMPOUNDING OUR BAFFLEMENT is a growing sense of social and economic fragmentation. In the 1950 and early 1960s, everything seemed to foster greater national cohesion. Postwar affluence narrowed the gap between the rich and poor. New technologies (TV, jet travel, interstate highways) shrank social distance and favored "mass" markets. Almost all adults shared the experiences of the Depression and the Second World War. Politics widened the "mainstream" to include those—notably, blacks and the poor—who had been most removed. But since then, everything has seemed to emphasize our differences. Income inequality has increased. Group consciousness (whether by women, blacks, ethnic groups, gay people, the disabled, or different generations) has risen. Popular culture has been further splintered by new technologies. Advertising targets smaller "niche" markets through cable TV, computer-sorted direct mail, and specialized magazines. In 1970, fewer than 7 percent of households received cable TV. Now, more than two thirds of households have cable and its many stations. The prime-time evening audience of the three original TV networks has dropped from 90 percent of those watching in the early 1970s to about two thirds.

Mass culture is receding before niche culture. Although this is in many ways healthy, because it offers people more choices, it also fosters social distance, as historian Paul Croce of Stetson University has written:

> The breakdown of mass culture is not the only cause of [social] polarization, and in fact sometimes it is less a cause than a symptom. But no matter the ultimate source, the difficulties of a society of separate subcultures mount. An evangelical Christian can read Christian books and newspapers, watch Christian TV, and even go to a Christian theme park. A radical feminist can learn and have fun from another wholly separate set of institutions. Each feels comfortable in his or her setting, but each learns less and less from the other. They learn what they already know.[3]

All these developments are real; but the sense of disappointment they inspire is artificially heightened by other factors. One is the press and the other media. It is not true, I think, that Americans have suddenly become more noisy or contentious than they ever were before. Our political rhetoric has always contained a fair amount of invective and viciousness. There has always been a resort to prejudice, notes Kathleen Hall Jamieson of the University of Pennsylvania. In the 1840s, the Know-Nothings (a transient party that opposed immigration, most of it from Catholic nations) charged that the Pope was contemplating summoning his followers to slaughter all Protestants. In the 1850s, street gangs in Baltimore dunked Irish immigrants in tubs of blood obtained from butchers to discourage them from voting. In the 1920s, the Ku Klux Klan, which had five million members, called for barring immigrants and inveighed against blacks, Catholics, and Jews. Before the Second World War, it was not uncommon for southern politicians to thrill audiences, as one Georgia senator did in 1938, with "anti-Negro, anti-Semitic, anti-Labor and anti-Yankee" rhetoric that incited rebel yells and cries of "Let 'em have it." In the 1950s, there was McCarthyism. In the 1960s, the strident rhetoric of the radical left denounced police as "pigs" and its opponents as "fascists." Indeed, some of today's invective seems fairly tame by past standards.[4]

The difference today is that the nature of the modern press gives the worst side of us much more exposure and respectability than ever before. We are constantly immersed in our imperfections and failings, and the effect is to convince us that we are worse off than we actually are. Politics, the most consistently strident part of our national life, is no longer experienced in occasional bursts (campaigns) or filtered through the relatively dry medium of newspapers and magazines. Our leaders constantly perform for us—on network news, CNN, C-Span—and the knowledge of this affects their behavior. They become more critical, more hostile, and more uncompromising. Television and radio (over a multitude of channels and in a multitude of ways) in general feed us a steady diet of our disagreements and depravities. Increasingly, the print media ape their electronic cousins, and the effect is to project a picture of America that is strikingly at odds with the way life is experienced by most Americans most of the time. Most of us are not victims of unemployment, crime, or child abuse—to take three common story themes—and even those of us who are often manage to overcome them and go on with life. It is hardly novel that the press shuns the ordinary. But what the press finds novel now has unprecedented prominence. A selective and distorted reality, if repeated often enough, becomes its own reality.

The critical bias of the press has another counterpart in politics. Modern advocacy groups derive their power from their ability to arouse popular passion and indignation. Political scientist Peter Skerry, among others, has pointed out that such groups often have little genuine political base. Their formal membership may be small or nonexistent; or the requirements of membership may be so slight (say, only annual dues) that the mutual ties between members and leaders are also slight. These groups, writes Skerry, tend to have a "headquarters driven operation that allows, and expects, scant input from members." To overcome the absence of a firm political base—

voters, for example, that could be delivered in the fashion of big-city political machines—these organizations adopt "publicity-seeking agendas" that "are often highly emotional and divisive." Without the inducements of old political organizations (jobs, party advancement), the advocacy groups must stir a sense of grievance that, combined with plausible remedies, cements loyalties and creates a credible claim to political influence. (This type of organization, incidentally, exists all along the political spectrum.) Put simply, these groups traffic in discontent.[5]

THIS MIXTURE—ENTITLEMENT PSYCHOLOGY, a quarrelsome press, and a discontent-based politics—casts almost everything in the worst possible light. It produces what social critic Robert Hughes has aptly termed the "culture of complaint." The entitlement society exaggerated governmental and corporate competence and, thereby, encouraged unrestrained individualism. Because all wants could (ultimately) be satisfied, all wants were (ultimately) legitimate. And any unsatisfied wants were, therefore, a reasonable cause for resentment. Self-fulfillment and "liberation" were increasingly worshiped and pursued, and in the process, these impulses nurtured heightened group consciousness. People were encouraged to convert individual desires into group demands, because group demands could more easily find standing before government, courts, or companies, which were seen as instruments to satisfy individual wants—whether of workers, the elderly, blacks, women, gay people, working mothers, or almost anyone. Everyone demands something from someone; rhetoric becomes inflamed. Entitlement abets social segmentation because benefits are encoded and delivered to groups.

The culture of complaint sustains itself by demeaning or even denying success. In effect, the problem-solving personality becomes a parody of itself, finding more and more problems of greater and greater gravity, even if the problems are often wildly exaggerated and gains are sometimes considerable. In a recent book, the writer Gregg Easterbrook gives a telling illustration of this tendency in environmentalism. By almost all indicators, as Easterbrook shows, the environment has dramatically improved in recent decades. Air pollution has declined sharply. (In 1992, the number of Americans living in cities that didn't meet federal air standards was about half its 1980 level—and the number is dropping.) Forests have expanded. Acid rain has decreased. Many dire predictions—for example, the mass extinction of birds from pesticides—have failed to materialize. "Yet our political and cultural institutions continue to read from a script of instant doomsday," observes Easterbrook. Environmentalists overstate some genuine problems and risk "their credibility by proclaiming emergencies that do not exist." Environmentalism is no exception. The intellectual and social respectability of finding and highlighting problems often creates a false sense of failure. A few years ago, a Harvard economist wrote a well-received book claiming that Americans—at home and on the job—were working more hours. No doubt, many Americans feel "overworked" and stressed. But a careful examination of the statistics used to justify longer working hours showed that the conclusion was simply wrong. Women work more on jobs, but the increase is fully offset by doing less housework. Men's working hours have remained roughly stable.[6]

When all these complaints are magnified (as they are) in the popular media and when they are mixed (as they also are) with a general bafflement about the country's direction, they produce a sense that America is coming apart at the seams and that it is riven by ever worsening social schisms. This belies our actual condition, which is fairly solid and united. A 1994 poll asked, "Earlier in American history, many people thought the U.S. was the very best place in the world to live. Do you still think it is, or not?" About 80 percent of the respondents still thought it was. Nor were there huge differences by race; 82 percent of whites agreed, as did 74 percent of blacks. Similarly, differences by education were modest; 81 percent of high school graduates and 84 percent of college graduates agreed. (Interestingly, the greatest dissent occurred at the ends of the educational spectrum; only 74 percent of non–high school graduates agreed, as did 75 percent of those with graduate degrees.)[7]

Now obviously, we are not a society without genuine tensions and conflicts. But many of these result precisely from the breakdown of old social roles and divisions. In many ways, the mixing of races, ethnic groups, and sexes has never been greater. When social conditions are fixed—and apparently unchangeable—hardly anyone comments or complains. It is typically change that triggers unease and protest, because people feel disoriented and sometimes threatened. The change, though, has been mostly for the good. Consider race, which remains the largest dividing line in American society. The shift in attitudes has been enormous. In 1944, a survey asked whether blacks "should have as good a chance as white people to get any kind of job." Less than half (45 percent) of Americans said yes. By 1972—the last time the question was apparently asked—almost everyone (97 percent) said yes. Put another way, most whites a half a century ago felt that blacks should only get jobs whites didn't want. Now, almost no one feels that way. Prejudice remains among both blacks and whites, but virtually all studies show it is much less. Surveys ask blacks and whites whether they have a "close personal friend" of the other race. In 1981, 69 percent of blacks and 54 percent of whites said yes; by 1989, those percentages had risen to 80 and 66 percent.[8]

In many other ways, too, American society smooths and accommodates differences. "Assimilation has become America's dirty little secret," writes sociologist Richard Alba. Early twentieth-century immigrants (Italians, Eastern Europeans) have been decisively integrated into the wider society, he shows. Intermarriage rates are high. In 1990, only a fifth of white married couples had husbands and wives of the same ethnic background. More educational opportunity has enabled children of immigrants to take jobs once barred to their parents. And suburbanization has reduced many ethnic urban neighborhoods. Even Bensonhurst in New York, the largest Italian-American neighborhood in the country in 1980, had lost a third of its ethnic population by 1990. It is quite possible that, with time, new immigrants will be absorbed in much the same way. Similarly, prejudice against homosexuals and women is probably near historic lows— though plenty of it still exists—which is why many once unmentionable issues (women in combat, the legitimacy of homosexual marriages) can actually be debated.[9]

These debates do grate. And the influx of immigrants does create social strains, especially in states (California, Texas, Florida, New York) where inflows have been greatest. The stresses resonate loudly in part because they offend our postwar sensibility, which foresaw ever greater social harmony and economic security. But they also resonate loudly because modern politics constantly broadcasts them. Politics has always mirrored social conflict. That's hardly new. What is new is the extent to which modern political groups must exploit conflict to survive. Villains not only exist, they are required. Group grievances not only exist, they must be nurtured. These campaigns, full of pessimism and condemnation, feed on one another and are reflected in the press, including the "new media" such as talk radio. The result is a picture of America which, though containing many elements of truth, is ultimately a caricature of life as it is lived and experienced by most Americans most of the time. It serves political and journalistic purposes, which require conflict and drama, while also swamping routine realities. Life is pretty good for most Americans, and most people get along fairly well. The caricature, though, can become a self-fulfilling prophecy if it is projected often enough and, by making more and more Americans feel they are preyed upon by some sinister force or group, aggravates popular anxiety and alienation. In the caricature, we become a society of rising stridency and falling satisfaction. Everything is fraying, and civility is collapsing.

WHAT THE PERCEPTION and rhetoric of disintegration do signify is the progressive breakdown of the postwar vision. The social glue that bound Americans together in the 1950s, 1960s, and even 1970s—when much else actually divided us—was a common vision of our imagined future: of the type of society that we were slowly building. Progress had a shape, it was a shape that intuitively appealed to most people, and it was what I have called entitlement. As a grand concept, it was the idea that we could consciously control our future; in its tangible manifestations, it was all the guarantees, from job security to food stamps, that people thought would ensure and improve their own futures. But now this vision of the future is blurred almost beyond recognition. Americans cling to the entitlements they have (or believe they deserve) not only because it is human nature to do so but also because they still want to believe in the broader promise of the entitlement society. But not all these entitlements—whether government benefits or more general expectations—can be enjoyed; by now, that is clear. The tension between entrenched entitlement and unforgiving reality spawns popular confusion and political conflict. It also poses the obvious question: If entitlement is dead, what's next?

The answer isn't obvious, and until now, I haven't tried to provide it. The main purpose of this book is to describe our predicament, not to cure it. This reflects my own background as a reporter and my political values. As a reporter, I seek to understand how the world works and changes. Politically, I believe that the success of American democracy ultimately depends upon the wisdom of the "people," even if the people repeatedly make mistakes, as they do. The value of freedom of the press is that information lubricates democratic debate; if this book deepens public understanding, however modestly, it will have done some good. But it would be dishonest to stop there, because it implies that I have no other views and that I make no further connections between parts of my analysis. This is, of course, untrue. Not only do I have views, but as a columnist in *Newsweek*, *The Washington Post*, and a few other papers, I make those views known all the time. To leave readers dangling would be unfair. Broader connections can be made, and I will now say what I think they should be.

14

Responsibility, Not Entitlement

ﹰﹰﹰﹰ

THERE IS NO "after entitlement" in the sense of a coherent and self-contained national vision. The fatal flaw of entitlement, in fact, is its utopianism: its presumption that we are inexorably working our way toward a perfect society. As individuals and as a society, we must take life as it comes. We can't know what awaits us each day, and on many days, the world will give us a fairly bad battering. But that doesn't mean we can't do anything to affect our destiny. The same is true of the nation. Just because we can't anticipate—or solve—all problems doesn't mean that we can't anticipate and solve some of them. What comes after entitlement is, or ought to be, responsibility. It ought to be the animating ideal of public conduct and private behavior. People ought to do more for themselves and expect government to do less. We need to curb our casual use of government—especially, the federal government—as the problem solver of last resort. It has clearly failed in this role, and unless we narrow its responsibilities, we can expect the failure to continue and worsen. We need to recognize that society can be strong only if its many constituent parts—families, private businesses, community, religious, and professional organizations, as well as government—are strong.

Rhetorically at least, the transformation has already occurred. Politicians of both parties now routinely invoke "personal responsibility," "leaner government," or "reinvented government." But responsibility is behavior, not rhetoric, and politicians proclaim it more than they practice it. Being responsible means facing up to your own problems. Preaching responsibility for someone else is not being responsible; neither is making blatantly inconsistent promises. Unfortunately, this behavior—overpromising, as I have put it—now dominates our political culture. It differs from mere demogoguery, which has always existed but which typically was considered deviant and often stigmatized. Overpromise is respectable and often passes for serious political discourse. It is part of the legacy of entitlement: a denial of choices and an expression of the pious hope that every problem can, somehow, be solved. But, of course, not every problem can be solved. If political leaders expect ordinary Americans to behave more responsibly, then they must behave more responsibly by acknowledging social and political choices as they actually exist.

THE FIRST REQUIREMENT is to balance the budget. It is not that balancing the budget is the country's only problem or, in some ways, even its most important. But it is something that elected officials can affect, and their refusal to do so condones and perpetuates overcommitted—and irresponsible—behavior. Resurrecting the discipline of a balanced budget does not mean that the budget must be precisely balanced every year. In an economic downturn or national crisis, the budget can swing into deficit. But it does mean reasserting a standard of conduct that will apply in most years: government services worth having ought to be worth paying for with taxes. People should see and feel what government gives and takes. Gain and pain should be calibrated; it is the only way to impose a crude discipline on government, to compel it to make choices. This was the standard that prevailed in the nineteenth and early twentieth centuries, and although it was far from perfect, it was superior to what we have today. It saw the budget primarily as an adjunct to politics, as a way to set government's priorities, and not primarily as an instrument of economic policy.

It is a myth that balancing the budget now would require wrenching changes. Consider some basic arithmetic. The deficit runs about $200 billion a year. Ineffective or unnecessary programs (farm subsidies, Amtrak) total perhaps $40 billion to $50 billion. Some federal grants to states and localities for many things—schools, law enforcement, mass transit—that are mainly local responsibilities could be canceled. (Federal aid, for example, only constitutes about 6 percent of public school spending and has never exceeded 10 percent.) The official inflation index (the consumer price index, or CPI) used to adjust benefits for Social Security and other programs, as well as for changes in tax brackets, slightly overstates inflation; a defensible change is slicing half a percentage point from the adjustment (a 3 percent change in the CPI would become 2.5 percent). That would save about $25 billion. Medicare and Medicaid costs could be cut by $40 billion annually. Higher taxes, including a 12-cent-a-gallon oil tax, could raise about $50 billion. Together, all these steps would shave the deficit about $165 billion; interest savings—because the government would borrow less—would amount to about $40 billion. Such a budget wouldn't cause severe social dislocation or personal suffering. Food would still be grown without farm subsidies. Social Security beneficiaries wouldn't perish if their benefits rose 2.5 percent instead of 3 percent. The tax burden would be only slightly higher than it is now.*[1]

What is harder is coming to grips with the long-term problems of an aging America and spiraling health care spending. The great budgetary transformation of our time has been the shift from defense to old-age support and health care. In 1955, defense was 62 percent of federal spending; in 1995, it is 18 percent. In 1955, Social Security and health care spending were 7 percent of federal spending; by 1995, they were 40 percent. Through Medicare (which provides hospital and doctors' insurance for the over-sixty-five population) and Medicaid (which, in addition to providing health coverage for the poor, also provides some long-term nursing-home care), health spending is heavily skewed toward the elderly. Until now, this increased spending has been heavily financed by lower defense spending. But this drop has gone almost as far as it can—and perhaps further than it should. In 1996, defense spending will be at its lowest point, as a share of

---

*As this book goes to press, Congress is debating a plan with deeper spending cuts.

GDP, since 1940. (In 1996, it is projected to be 3.5 percent of GDP; in 1940, it was 1.7 percent.) Worse, the aging of the baby boomers means that many present programs can't be afforded in the future without huge tax increases or implausibly vast budget deficits.[2]

The table below crudely depicts the dimensions of the impending pressures. It gives Social Security and Medicare spending as a share of GDP between now and (as projected) 2030. Almost certainly, these projections won't come true, because before they could, changes will be made to prevent them. Still, the pressures are of tidal-wave proportions. As the table shows, Social Security and Medicare, which consumed less than 1 percent of our national income in 1950, now consume about 7 percent and might—under present programs—consume nearly twice that much in 2030, when all of the baby boomers will have passed sixty-five. Consider now that our present budget deficit equals about 2.5 percent of national income (GDP) and taxes equal slightly less than 19 percent of GDP. To finance the projected increases in Social Security and Medicare would require a nearly 50 percent increase in the tax burden (about $650 billion in today's dollars) or more than a tripling of the deficit. Even these unsettling statistics may understate the case, because they exclude spending by other retirement and health programs that face similar pressures.

Social Security and Medicare as a Percentage of GDP[3]

	Social Security	Medicare	Total
1950	0.3	0	0.3
1970	3.1	0.6	3.7
1993	4.8	2.1	6.9
2010	4.6	4.3	8.9
2030	6.0	7.0	13.0

That these pressures won't truly materialize for another ten or fifteen years is no reason to ignore them. Just the opposite: the needed changes should be made soon so that people who are now middle-aged or younger can sensibly prepare for their retirements. The longer we wait, the more abrupt (and, hence, unfair) the changes will be. Nor, in my view, is it hard to decide what ought to be done. First, we should gradually raise the normal retirement age, now 65. Under present law, it is scheduled to rise in small steps to 66 in the year 2009 and, then after a hiatus of a few years, to increase slowly again to 67 in the year 2027. I would increase that to 70 by the year 2015; people all along the way would have higher retirement ages than at present. Under present law, people can receive reduced Social Security benefits as early as 62; I would raise that to at least 64, again gradually.*

At the same time, more well-to-do elderly ought to be treated less generously than they are today. There are many ways to do this. Social Security benefits could be fully taxed, meaning that older and younger taxpayers with similar incomes would be treated more alike. (I favor this.) Wealthier retirees could be charged more for Medicare. Or all government benefits could be "means tested"—that is, limited by income. Today younger and poorer workers increasingly support (through payroll taxes) older and wealthier retirees. (I have been writing about these issues for almost twenty years and have often been accused of "bashing the elderly." The charge is that I have favored lower benefits for them to provide tax relief for me. As this is written, I am approaching fifty. These proposals imply modest changes for present retirees but major changes for me and my contemporaries.) Government needs to adapt to social change, not resist it. People live longer; they ought to work longer. As a society, we need to maintain our productive base. In 1930, average life expectancy at birth was 58 years for men, 61 years for women (and at age 65 life expectancy was an additional 12 years for men and 13 for women); by 1990, life expectancy was 71 years for men, 79 years for women (and at age 65, an additional 15 years for men and 19 for women).[4] When Social Security was enacted in 1935, it was presumed that most older people were needy, because personal savings were meager and private pensions were few. But none of this is true any longer. New retirees are relatively well off. Americans ought to be more responsible for their own well-being as they age.

---

*Under present law, the normal retirement age remains at 65 until 2003—that is, for anyone born in 1937 or earlier. In 2003, it begins rising two months a year until it reaches 66 in the year 2009—that is, for anyone born in 1943 or later. It stays at 66 until 2021, when it begins rising again by two months a year until it reaches 67 in the year 2027. Anyone born in 1960 or later has a retirement age of 67; anyone born between 1955 and 1960 has a retirement age between 66 and 67.

Making such changes, of course, will be enormously difficult. Older Americans are a huge constituency, and many elderly feel indignant about possible cutbacks in Social Security or Medicare, believing that their past payroll taxes are simply being returned as benefits. This is simply wrong. Both Social Security and Medicare are financed largely on a pay-as-you go basis; this year's taxes pay for this year's benefits. Even if the taxes of present retirees had been invested, they wouldn't have accumulated enough interest to pay for the benefits of most retirees.[5] These difficulties emphasize the inertia of entitlement politics. What people have they expect to keep. Promises were made (it's said)—no matter whether the promises were more imagined than real or whether social conditions have since changed dramatically.

Raising retirement ages and trimming benefits for the well-off elderly would probably go halfway toward controlling the budget pressures of an aging population. The other half requires subduing health care spending, another daunting problem, because older people use more medical care than younger people (average per capita health care spending for someone over sixty-five is more than three times that for someone nineteen to sixty-four), and worse, health care costs have outpaced inflation or economic growth for years. The combination, if continued, would be crushing.[6] We need to contain this spiral, because the extra social good of higher health care spending is dwindling. That is, we spend more on people about to die or with chronic or incurable diseases. Or, we overtest, overprescribe, or overtreat many ordinary patients, because all of us (quite naturally) want the best that's available, even when the best usually isn't necessary. Health care illuminates the dilemma of an individualistic culture that adopts a welfare state. What we all want for ourselves as individuals may end up hurting all of us as members of the larger society.

How to control health care spending? Again, the central issue is responsibility. Who has it, and who should? Today, there is splintered responsibility. Government pays about two fifths of health care costs directly, mainly through Medicare and Medicaid, and heavily subsidizes private insurance, mainly through a tax subsidy for employer-purchased insurance. But doctors and patients make most spending decisions; the split of responsibility between who pays and who spends has encouraged spiraling costs. There are really only two ways to alter this. One is to make government more responsible; the other is to make the "market"—meaning individuals or employers—more responsible. Each has advantages, drawbacks, and practical problems.

Government control involves, somehow, imposing strict spending limits. Ultimately, this would probably mean nationalizing all insurance, instead of tolerating the present quasi-nationalization. Most Americans would have roughly comparable coverage, though the rich would presumably still be allowed to buy additional coverage. Government, being the major buyer, could set prices and avoid wasteful duplication. It could monitor procedures and not reimburse those that didn't provide much benefit. By imposing tough controls, it might force hospitals, doctors, and health plans to be more efficient. The disadvantage is that cost controls would probably involve rationing and, moreover, might succumb to political pressures. Congress (or health care agencies) might promise people more benefits than could be provided under spending ceilings. Spending would then either exceed the ceilings (and be financed by higher taxes or deficits) or some health care services would be denied. Waits would be longer; some services simply wouldn't be available; the quality of others might deteriorate. Health care might become even more tangled in bureaucracy.

Relying on the market might solve some of these problems, while creating others. First, we would have to decide what "relying on the market" means in practice. It would almost certainly not mean what it seems to mean: allowing people to buy as much health care as they could afford. Almost no one supports such draconian discipline, which implies that Medicare and Medicaid would be eliminated and that many people might go without all but emergency medical care. But relying on the market could mean ending—or limiting—the tax subsidy for private insurance and converting both Medicare and Medicaid into vouchers. These programs would no longer allow open-ended reimbursement; instead, recipients would receive a fixed amount of money and would have to purchase their own insurance coverage (presumably with minimum required benefits) or health plan. Workers and government beneficiaries would be given an incentive to shop for health coverage that offered the best value for their money. Doctors, hospitals, and health maintenance organizations (HMOs) would compete on the basis of price and quality. But of course, health plans might skimp on service to hold down costs. Similarly, more workers might go without insurance, and those who didn't might still buy inadequate coverage. Finally, richer Americans would almost certainly do better than poorer, because they would be able to buy better insurance coverage.

I prefer the second approach to the first, because it better accords with American individualism and also stands a better chance of promoting cost-effective medicine. But either approach—depending on how it's designed and implemented—might succeed or fail. The point is not that one approach is clearly superior to the other. The point is that both approaches require judgments and choices to be made. This is what responsibility means in practice. As a guiding precept, it is the mirror image of entitlement. Responsibility poses choices, recognizes limits, and clarifies accountability. Entitlement denies choices, ignores limits, and muddles accountability. Properly construed, responsibility is a fundamental issue that all modern societies must answer in their own way. How much should people do for themselves and how much should government—that is, the people acting as a collective—do for them? What are the respective roles and competences of individuals, families, social organizations, profit-making enterprises, and government? What answers best fit our traditions, values, and common sense?

AS RHETORIC, RESPONSIBILITY has yet to achieve this broad meaning. Rather, it has been focused more narrowly on the poor or upon families. Teenage girls (the refrain goes) shouldn't bear children before they are ready to be responsible mothers; young men shouldn't father children if they aren't prepared to be responsible fathers. Parents ought to spend more time raising their children. All these moral exhortations make sense. Who could disagree? But these familiar incantations are too constricting and too convenient. They imply that government spending can be easily curbed if only the poor behave more responsibly, allowing programs that help them to be reduced. Not so. Though these programs are costly, they still constitute a relatively small fraction of federal spending: about a seventh.* Moreover,

*In 1994, total "means-tested" programs—that is, those programs that provided benefits only for those with incomes below certain certified minimums—cost about $177 billion in a federal budget whose total spending was $1.4 trillion. This was about 13 percent.[7]

these familiar sermons about responsibility imply that it's always someone else's affair: either the poor or lazy parents. In practice, the rhetoric is aimed heavily toward blacks, whose rates of out-of-wedlock births are highest. But as I have shown, broader questions of responsibility engage much of the middle class. How much shall Americans be responsible for themselves in older age, and how much shall they rely on government? How much shall government be responsible for health care, and how much shall individuals? On budget deficits, what do we really want government to do for us, and who should bear the burden of paying?

Responsibility is sober, understated, and flawed. It means not expecting someone else (government or a benevolent corporation) to rescue us from all of life's jolts. By contrast, entitlement is romantic, exaggerated, and utopian. It assumes that, somehow, society can solve every possible problem and create a seamless safety net against any conceivable mishap. Government simply isn't up to this grandiose task; it can't substitute for all the failings of other social units. The argument for the two-parent family, for example, is not that it is perfect. It isn't. Some two-parent families are indifferent, abusive, or alcoholic—and some single parents are heroic. The argument is, simply, that on average two-parent families better provide the time, love, skills, and income that help children develop. "Adolescents who have lived apart from one [parent]," report sociologists Sara McLanahan and Gary Sandefur, "are twice as likely to drop out of high school, twice as likely to have a child before age twenty, and one and a half times as" likely to be out of school and work in their early twenties. (These comparisons adjust for parents' education, race, and place of residence.)[8]

The entitlement society strayed from a sensible social division of labor. One obvious danger of overusing government is that, at some point, its weight—in taxes, laws, and regulations—will overburden the economy. No one knows whether we have yet reached this point; my hunch, as I have said, is that the economic slowdown since the early 1970s stems mainly from other causes, such as high inflation and poor management. But I doubt we can continually expand government without risking economic harm. Prosperity is not everything— that is a central theme of this book—but it still is a great deal. If our economy permanently deteriorated, many other problems would get worse. As growth slowed, the demand for government benefits would rise while the tax base to support them would erode. Government would then face distasteful choices. It could cut benefits dramatically, alienating those who had expected them. It could raise taxes sharply, alienating taxpayers and risking further economic harm. Or it could gamble with bigger budget deficits. By striving to improve everyone's welfare, the modern welfare state may ultimately jeopardize everyone's welfare. All modern societies grapple with this paradox. America is no exception.

The other great defect of the entitlement society is that, by catering to group needs, it encourages separate group political—and cultural—identities. Affirmative action epitomizes the problem. In my view, it has outlived its usefulness, because what was once defensible—that is, aggressive recruiting of qualified blacks, women, and other minorities for jobs and college openings—has turned into something that is not defensible: preference. (Indeed, the original concept is still defensible and desirable. Why shouldn't companies or colleges look aggressively for good candidates?) By one count, the federal government now has 168 separate programs involving some sort of preference, including "goals and timetables" and "set-asides" for federal contracts.[9] These programs contain an untenable contradiction: that to cure past discrimination, new discrimination—against people who usually had no part in past discrimination—must continue indefinitely. By law, this separates individual effort from reward. (That is the critical point. Those who work hard or who have talent don't always get what they deserve. They may be frustrated by bad luck or a bad boss. But it is one thing to be mad at your luck or your boss and quite another to feel that government, supposedly impartial, has done you in.)

As a result, affirmative action now generates more ill will than social justice. It is a bad bargain. It does its intended beneficiaries much less good than they suppose, while it probably harms others less than they think—that is, reverse discrimination is probably less widespread than complaints about it. But the bargain is hard to undo, because affirmative action is a government benefit: an entitlement that, once bestowed, cannot easily be withdrawn. It has acquired a symbolic importance. Taking it away is an affront, whatever its real value. In this sense, affirmative action merely epitomizes the larger issue of coping with all America's official and semiofficial entitlements. The central task of the post-entitlement society is to revise our political and social handiwork, discarding the unrealistic and excessive while retaining the sensible and worthwhile, without getting too many people too angry at one another.

MUCH OF THE POLITICAL turmoil of recent years signals that this messy process has already begun. No one can know how it will turn out: whether this political reconstruction will do more harm than good and whether it will promote social peace or the opposite. But however it proceeds, we can be sure that it will not do either of the two things that its advocates and opponents proclaim.

First, it will not repeal Big Government.

And second, it will not create utopia.

Although we may dismantle parts of government and redesign others, the end result will still be—by any historic standard—a huge federal government that spends about a fifth of our national income and regulates much of our national life, from banking to drugs. (Recall that in 1929, federal spending was 3 percent of national income.) There is no public demand or taste for anything else. The din to "get government off our backs" is more an abstraction than a pointed criticism of specific programs. Even if existing programs were sharply cut, countervailing pressures might enlarge government. Aside from the demands of an aging society, these include the possibility that defense spending may have to be raised. Since 1985, it has been cut about 25 percent, adjusted for inflation. Between 1987 and 1994, the number of Army divisions dropped from 18 to 12, the number of active Air Force tactical fighter wings declined from 24 to 13, and the number of active military personnel decreased from 2.2 million to 1.6 million. These reductions rest on optimistic assumptions about world order that, if confounded, might require costly rearming.[10]

In practice, it is doubtful that many large federal programs, even if substantially revised, will be totally repealed. Most Americans do not reject the basic ideas that have given us bigger government—the idea that government should provide a "safety net" for the poor and dependent, or that it should regulate business, or that it should promote some activities (such as education or research and development) for the national good. There is no clamor to end federal college student loans, nor is there a clamor—despite dissatisfaction—to end environmental regulation.* The difficulty of defusing public discontents occurs precisely because Americans' demands are often so inconsistent. Government's benefits are not resented, but the burdens (more taxes, intrusive regulations, and bureaucrats) are. Ideally, government needs to become more focused to be more effective. It will not, for instance, be able to maintain a satisfactory "safety net" unless it becomes more discriminating about who deserves public aid. Sweeping invocations of "equality" ought to give way to more narrow goals that can be explained, evaluated, and defended.

But even making government more focused will not put us on the path to utopia. I have written approvingly of a new emphasis on personal and private responsibility, as opposed to government responsibility. In my view, this would be healthy, because it recognizes that any society succeeds mainly because most of its parts work and not because a few powerful elites know what everyone should do. National success builds up more than it builds down. It rests on the solid foundations of family, private groups (churches, professional societies, clubs, Scouts, Little Leagues, self-help groups, neighborhood organizations), and productive enterprises. It is in these realms that competences are developed and pleasures enjoyed. If these foundations are weak, then society is wobbly. By assigning too much responsibility to government, we weaken the reasons people have to assume responsibility for themselves and for the private associations—economic and social—so critical to the nation's well-being. Americans believe that a free society is a superior society, because people are the best custodians of their own well-being. Freedom enables people to tap their own potential and creativity. All this is true, but it is not the whole truth.

Another truth is that there are no clear solutions for many of our most pressing social problems, especially those involving race and

*Federal college student loans, though, do present an interesting example of a program that ought to be revised to promote more responsibility by those using it and to make it more effective. As it exists, the program imposes no academic standards on recipients. To get a college loan, they don't have to demonstrate they're capable of doing college work. The easy availability of this money encourages colleges to accept many unprepared students and, at the same time, tends to inflate tuition costs. If students had to pass a qualifying exam to receive a federally backed loan, more of them would work harder in high school, and there would be fewer college dropouts.

poverty. The postwar record on race balances spectacular success and spectacular failure. On the one hand, we outlawed legal segregation, and millions of black Americans have moved decisively into the middle class. Since the mid-1960s, the proportion of black households with incomes exceeding $50,000 (adjusted for inflation) has roughly doubled, rising from 6 to 13 percent; another 26 percent have incomes exceeding $25,000.[11] But against these successes are enduring poverty, soaring rates of out-of-wedlock birth, and high crime rates. Family breakdown is worst among blacks; unemployment among black men remains roughly twice the level among whites, and many blacks are stuck in low-skill, poorly paid jobs. Racial resentments often lie just beneath the surface, buttressed by persisting black-white gaps of incomes and living conditions. But no one has a ready answer to these problems. Vast social spending has at best helped modestly, and the availability of welfare (Aid to Families with Dependent Children) with food stamps and Medicaid may have promoted debilitating dependency and single parenthood. Toughening welfare eligibility might reverse those trends, but even those who believe that doubt the effect would be instant or dramatic. Some new approaches in local programs might help poor black youth. The sociologist William Julius Wilson has suggested that their job prospects might be improved if there were more shuttle buses between inner-city neighborhoods and suburbs, where jobs are more plentiful. He also argues that schools should give greater emphasis to language and grammar as basic job skills. But again, the potential gains would be modest and gradual.[12]

And there is a still larger truth: responsibility invests people not only with freedom's benefits but also with its burdens. Given freedom, many people abuse it. They do not realize their potential; they destroy it. They do not bring themselves contentment, but misery. Freedom and unrestrained self-interest often degenerate into meanness and exploitation. The dilemma is unavoidable. America is an inventive, productive, and satisfied society because it is free; it is also a messy, violent, and dissatisfied society, because it is free. Our means of social control are, compared with those of many societies, modest. Moreover, life is full of inequality and unfairness; the more people are left to their own devices, the more these differences will assert themselves. The resort to government in the postwar era was an effort to erase some of the worst forms of inequality and unfairness, and if the effort is now choking on its excesses, we should not think that all un-fairness and inequality will miraculously vanish if we implore people to be more responsible. Some people can't or won't be more respon-sible; some economic, social, or personal conditions defeat the great-est individual exertions. Responsibility is a worthy ideal, but it is not a panacea.

15

Crisis or Consensus?

☙ ☙ ☙ ☙

A<small>LTHOUGH A RESPONSIBLE SOCIETY</small> would not be a perfect society, it could be a better society. By a better society, I mean one in which some of our worst problems diminish, though they do not disappear. They would diminish because a society that demands more from all its members—whether in their public or private roles—will get more. Government that is more disciplined in its spending, taxes, and regulations would help the economy. A clearer split of responsibilities among the federal, state, and local governments would encourage better government at all levels, because voters would know who to blame for failures. Stronger families would mean less poverty and less crime: mostly because children from more stable families would succeed more in school and the job market. And, finally, a responsible society might be less shrill than today's, because it would emphasize common obligations instead of self-interested entitlements. But all these improvements would occur gradually, and great societal blemishes would remain. The economy would still experience periodic slumps; companies would still suffer setbacks. Government would still

be messy and often ineffective. Sizable pockets of urban poverty would survive. Crime would still be too high.

The advantage of a responsible society is that it recognizes that some types of human organization are better suited for some tasks than others. Government cannot do everything. Corporations cannot do everything. Voluntary groups (churches, clubs, professional societies) cannot do everything. Families cannot do everything. Individuals cannot do everything. Our society won't work well if it asks more of its parts than they can accomplish. Nor will it work well if it asks too little. The entitlement society lost the crude balance between responsibility and competence, and our prospects depend heavily on restoring a better balance. But whether we can raises a hard question: Does America adapt by crisis or consensus? Do we spontaneously change because we see we must, or must we be coerced by events that leave us no choice? All my practical suggestions can be dismissed as hopelessly naïve; their prospects would founder (it can be argued) on the opposition of all those who have a stake in the status quo. Perhaps we can't adapt; perhaps we respond only to crisis.

On this question, American history offers no conclusive answer. An optimist will find much evidence to argue for quiet consensus. Just as the entitlement society was a slow adaptation to experience, so may the post-entitlement society evolve gradually without fanfare. The dominant idea of our political heritage—freedom—does not require that every major social change be preceded by a debate over winners and losers. If it did, little change would occur. Instead, our freewheeling culture lets things happen. Individual reputations and fortunes are made and lost. Companies rise and fall. Places thrive and decay. People move to opportunity or flee from failure. They climb up or slide down the social ladder. Our politics are similarly pragmatic. By and large, Americans are not strict ideologues. Not every political debate pits irreconcilable philosophies. Politics is an arena to get things done. Although this can make government open-ended, it focuses debates on the matter at hand. America's politics values answers, not questions. Politicians seek common ground and the mainstream. Similarly, the fragmentation of power sometimes abets consensus; unless people work together, nothing gets done.

Unfortunately, our history can also be read another way. Some conflicts run so deep or arouse passions so fierce that they can be settled only by cataclysm, or something close to it. There is no plausible middle ground; only an outside event, sometimes tragic, compels change. This pattern dates to at least the Constitution, which was fundamentally a reaction to the breakdown of the Articles of Confederation. Similarly, only the Civil War could end the horror of slavery. Our most important social programs—Social Security, unemployment insurance, welfare—were not calm responses to increased urbanization and industrialization; rather, they were hasty reactions to the Great Depression, the worst economic crisis in American history. Nor did Americans anticipate or prevent, as they conceivably might have, the Second World War; only Pearl Harbor could end our shortsighted isolationism. In our own era, modern civil rights legislation was not the outcome of a dispassionate recognition of the injustice of segregation. Instead, we needed sit-ins and marches to make us see the injustice and shame us into outlawing it. Time after time, we are prisoners of events and trends that proceed to some shattering climax that changes us forever.

If our history is thus distilled, the future is shrouded. The case for consensus assumes that Americans—as individuals and as a nation—learn from their mistakes. We see that we have overused government; so we begin to use it more sparingly. We see that family breakdown (more divorce, more out-of-wedlock births) brings neither personal happiness nor societal well-being; so we begin to be more careful in our personal relations. The best evidence that this is, in fact, what happens comes from the economy. It has been pronounced dead or dying so many times by so many reputed authorities that hardly anyone grasps that just the opposite is true. The economy is stronger now than it has been in many years. Some statistics cited at the outset of this book bear repeating. The U.S. economy produces more than twice as much as the next largest (Japan's), is 15 to 20 percent more efficient per worker, remains the world's largest exporter, and retains leadership in many critical technologies (aerospace, computer chips, software, and fiber optics, to name a few). More important, productivity gains are accelerating. After averaging about 1 percent annually in the 1970s and 1980s—well below the 3 percent average of the 1950s

and 1960s—gains have risen to and are now in the range of 1.5 to 2 percent. This means that, over a decade, average incomes might rise 15 or 20 percent instead of 10 percent.

What's interesting is how the change occurred: not by a few large leaps, but by many small steps. Arguably, America's economy faltered in the 1970s and early 1980s because it suffered from a series of problems: high and rising inflation, which increased uncertainty and disguised inefficiency; overconfident management, which led to rigid, bureaucratic, and excessively diversified companies; and a general complacency—a feeling that prosperity was a perpetual sure thing—that infected both managers and workers. Slowly, all of these problems abated, though with much suffering. High inflation collapsed under the pressure of several recessions, one of which (1981–1982) was truly severe. These recessions, plus intensified competition—both foreign and domestic—and a surge in corporate takeovers, chastened overconfident managers and stripped everyone of the illusion of total and permanent economic security. In the end, Americans adjusted to change, and despite the difficulties, were ultimately better off for it. What happened to the economy could happen (and may already be happening) to politics and family life.

EVEN AS I WRITE, the first Republican Congress since the mid-1950s is beginning to shift the terms, tone, and substance of political debate. Government is being cut. Questions of federal responsibility are being discussed with more seriousness than has occurred in decades. Some programs may actually be eliminated, because they are deemed ineffective, outdated, or, just simply, improper for the federal government. Others are being shifted to states. Similarly, open-ended regulation is being questioned: it is increasingly recognized that regulation, though worthwhile, can descend into the petty pursuit of trivial gain. Nor is this merely a partisan shift. Many Democrats echo similar concerns. None of this means that all changes will be for the good. Mistakes will be made; rhetoric about change will exaggerate the reality of change; and these shifts will clearly hurt some Americans. But political discussion is becoming more realistic. Similarly, family life might spontaneously strengthen. Expert opinion, which

once decreed that divorce and sexual freedom were healthy ways to achieve self-fulfillment, has shifted. Family breakdown is now seen as having bad effects. Discussion of family values, once considered hopelessly prudish or old-fashioned, is now conventional and even clichéd. Popular behavior could follow; social norms do change. Divorce rates have already dropped slightly. (Between 1980 and 1992, the crude divorce rate [divorce per 1,000 people] dropped from 5.2 to 4.8. The rate per 1,000 children under 18 declined from 18.7 in 1981 to 16.4 in 1988.[1])

All this seems plausible—but perhaps no more plausible than a grimmer picture. In this view, the inertia of our present situation is so powerful that it cannot be stopped short of some tidal-wave event. Government is inherently undisciplined, because it conforms to deep contradictions in public opinion. People dislike big government, especially its taxes; but they like the things that big government does for them. Politics succumbs to "demosclerosis," as Jonathan Rauch has written. The "broad public never care about eliminating any given program as much as its beneficiaries care about saving it," he observes.[2] The fight, then, is always uphill and usually futile. Political paralysis ultimately overwhelms the private economy with high taxes, spending, and regulation. The welfare state's dilemma is fatal: satisfying the public's demand for public benefits depresses economic growth, but denying promised public benefits breaks a public trust.

Deteriorating social conditions and race relations compound disillusion. The full force of family breakdown hits only in the early twenty-first century, as more children of divorce and single-parent families become adults. Racism rises; so do tensions among whites, blacks, and new Hispanic and Asian immigrants. In a chilling prophecy in their book, *The Bell Curve*—a prophecy the authors didn't endorse—Charles Murray and the late Richard Herrnstein speculated that the frightened majority might construct a "custodial state" that, with harsh policing and welfare rules, would create a "high-tech and more lavish version of the Indian reservation for some substantial minority of the nation's population, while the rest of America tries to go about its business."[3] America becomes progressively more and more balkanized and more and more embittered.

———

HISTORY CANNOT BE FORETOLD. I have no idea which of these imagined futures might come closer to eventuality—or whether, as is probable, something else entirely will happen. I have sketched both of them because each seems possible and neither seems certain. It seems possible that Americans will gradually recognize that their situation is not as dire as it's constantly portrayed. They will see that their economy remains fairly robust and that, although it can't eliminate inequality, it can slowly raise most people's incomes. It seems possible that the long-range problems of an aging society will prudently be addressed: that retirement ages will be increased and benefits trimmed. It seems possible that Americans will build thicker walls between public and private spheres, so that every disagreement over private values (sexual orientation, religion) does not become political combat. But none of this is certain, and it is surely possible that our present inertia will triumph. In such a society, recriminations and competition for mutually exclusive entitlements would escalate. Groups—for various reasons—would feel more victimized and would search more vigorously for villains to explain their victimization. "Culture wars" would intensify and perhaps be accompanied by a "generation war" and a "class war." Civility and our sense of national cohesion would further fray.

What ultimately binds together a country such as ours—so large and composed of so many people of different religions, races, and ethnic backgrounds—are ideas and ideals. America is defined by its distinctive bedrock beliefs, which, if widely discredited, would shake society to its foundations. Perhaps we are being hurled toward some future crisis, whose shape we cannot perceive and whose occurrence would permanently change us. Perhaps that crisis will be domestic, but it might also be foreign, because there is an obvious connection between how Americans handle themselves at home and how they conduct their affairs abroad. An America at war with itself internally will probably shy away from engagements abroad, even if they serve our national interests; and a confident America will be better able to evaluate its foreign interests and then act on them. Our capacity to deal with such threats—whether they involve nuclear proliferation, terrorism, a threat to world oil supplies, or a global financial crisis—will depend heavily on how strong and cohesive we are at home.

American "competitiveness," to use a fashionable term, mostly reflects the economic vitality, political wisdom, and social stability of Americans in America.*

AS A NATION, we have been through these economic, political, and psychological upheavals before. We present Americans flatter ourselves by thinking that we live in an era of unprecedented change. We don't. In scanning history, the period that most resembles our own occurred roughly a century ago. But in many ways, it encompassed more change. Imagine Americans born in 1850 and 1950 and assume that they survived to, respectively, 1895 and 1995. Our nineteenth-century predecessors witnessed a greater national transformation. It was not just the Civil War. In 1850, only one city (New York) had more than 250,000 people, and about 85 percent of Americans lived on farms or in rural towns. By 1890, the country's population had nearly tripled (to 63 million), and the urban population was a third of the total. Three cities exceeded 1 million, and eight more surpassed 250,000. Increasingly, Americans experienced astonishing industrialization. Between 1860 and 1900, annual steel production rose from 13,000 to 11 million tons. Dozens of industries were expanding rapidly: railroads, oil refining, meatpacking, electric utilities, telephones, cigarette making, and food canning, to name a few. Between 1850 and 1900, the number of factory workers more than quintupled, to 5.5 million.[4]

The fabric of everyday life altered in countless ways. The influx of immigrants was pronounced. In the Gilded Age, visible wealth dis-

---

*I have mainly ignored foreign affairs, because this book is mostly about postwar American society. Much has been written on the post–Cold War world, very little of it illuminating, because most reasonable generalizations are fairly obvious. Although the United States may be the world's richest and most powerful nation, it cannot act as the world's bank, cop, or priest. We cannot impose our views and values on others, willy-nilly.

In this world, neither unrestrained internationalism nor seductive isolationism will suffice. Economically, we should not mistake a proper nationalism—looking out for ourselves—for a false protectionism. Trade still represents a relatively small part of our economy, and protecting U.S. companies usually doesn't protect American living standards or incomes—mainly, it protects a specific set of firms and workers. Competition, whether foreign or domestic, generally invigorates the economy. The critical question about the new global economy concerns its stability: whether it harbors some mechanism (akin perhaps to the Depression-era gold standard) that threatens collapse. But to gauge that and defend against it require global engagement.

parities became greater. Americans were connected, by railroads and telegraph, as never before. Between 1850 and 1900, the rail network grew from 9,000 to 259,000 miles. "In a quarter of a century," wrote the *Omaha Republican* in 1883, "[railroads] have made the country homogeneous, breaking through the peculiarities and provincialisms which marked separate and unmingling sections." What joins this era with our own is the profound political and psychological pressures that accompanied economic and social change. Ever since the Revolution, Americans had believed that their democracy required self-reliant farmers and craftsmen. Freedom flourished not only because we had democratic institutions but also because America cultivated independent citizens. By the 1890s, these Jeffersonian ideals were besieged. The "frontier"—the possibility of free or cheap land for anyone who wanted it—had been closed. Workers and farmers depended on large corporations for jobs and supplies. Independent craftsmen were being eliminated by huge manufacturers.[5]

People felt less and less in control of their lives, and protest movements mushroomed. In the late nineteenth century, there was agrarian populism, which rebelled against railroads and eastern banks. In the early twentieth century, there was the Progressive movement, which attempted to regulate away the evils of industrialization and urbanization. Beyond these movements, there was a palpable uneasiness. Mark Sullivan, a perceptive popular historian of the time, once aptly summarized the climate:

> There was in America, during the years preceding 1900 and for many years thereafter, a prevailing mood. It was a mood of irritation. The average American in great numbers had the feeling that he was being "put upon" by something he couldn't quite see or get his fingers on; that somebody was "riding" him; that some force or other was "crowding" him. Vaguely he felt that his freedom of action, his opportunity to do as he please, was being frustrated in ways mysterious in their origin and operation, and in their effect most uncomfortable; that his economic freedom, as well as his freedom of action, and his capacity to direct his political liberty towards results he desired, was being circumscribed in a tightening ring, the drawing-strings of which, he felt sure, were being pulled by the hands of some invisible power which he ardently de-

sired to see and get at, but could not. This unseen enemy he tried
to personify. He called it the Invisible Government, the Money Interests, the Gold Bugs, Wall Street, the Trusts.[6]

The forces of economic and social change that produced this
mood could not be denied or, apparently, stopped. Somehow, they had
to be reconciled with Americans' basic beliefs, which were associated
with an economy and society that were rapidly disappearing. There
was a collision between beliefs and social conditions that had, somehow, to be survived. In some ways, America's history from the late
nineteenth century through the early decades of the twentieth century
represents an effort to come to terms with this conflict. It involved
placing new restrictions on business (through the courts, antitrust laws,
workers' compensation programs, child labor laws), while also recognizing that many of America's fundamental values were strong
enough to withstand urbanization and industrialization. The accommodation process was haphazard, prolonged, sometimes inconsistent,
and often inconclusive. But, grudgingly, America moved on.

There are strong parallels with our predicament today. Over the
past half century, America has built institutions that now seem increasingly at odds with many basic values. Government has grown to
dimensions that would astonish not only the Founders but also Americans in the 1920s. Corporate business has similarly expanded, and together these twin titans dominate modern America. At its core, the
idea of entitlement aimed to reconcile these institutions with Americans' traditional beliefs in individuality and freedom. To be entitled
meant that the power of these immense institutions was ultimately
put at the disposal of individuals, to satisfy their needs and wants, as
they might see fit. Thus deployed, these institutions would become
benign and benevolent. But we now see that such entitlement was a
mirage. We are left with the inevitability of our institutions and the
permanence of our beliefs, which war with each other.

In the Age of Entitlement, we thought we had settled this conflict. But instead we simply transformed it. A culture that celebrates
the individual exists uneasily with the modern welfare state and the
modern corporate world. As long as we believed that our beliefs and
institutions could be made thoroughly compatible, we remained
oblivious of the deeper tensions of postwar society. But the contra-

dictions could not be obscured forever, and as economic and social conditions changed, the impossibility of building the future we imagined became more and more obvious. We have now arrived at that future, and it is not what we visualized. So the Age of Entitlement fades into history, a victim of its successes and illusions. If the past is prologue, Americans will grope their way to a new future, making it up as they go along and—as always—trying to advance their ideals against the unrelenting pressures that seek to deny them.

Notes

1. See Frederick Lewis Allen, *The Big Change: America Transforms Itself, 1900–1950* (New York: Harper & Brothers, 1952), p. 234.
2. Press release, Luntz Research Companies, Arlington, Va., "Americans Speak on What 1994 Was All About," November 1994. The poll, taken just after the 1994 congressional election, asked: "How often do you discuss politics with your friends and family?" The answers were:

Twice a day or more	13 percent
Once a day	16 percent
One or two times a week	31 percent
Rarely	32 percent
Never	8 percent
Don't know/Refused	1 percent

3. See Ronald Steel, *Temptations of a Superpower: America's Foreign Policy After the Cold War* (Cambridge, Mass.: Harvard University Press, 1995), pp. 1, 21. In fairness to Steel, his book is clearly concerned with foreign policy, and his

main point is that the end of the Cold War has been disorienting. But he also argues—wrongly in my view—that the Cold War was the overwhelming influence on postwar America. It "defined our government and how we lived our lives" (p. 13), and until President Clinton, foreign policy "always came first. How we lived with each other—whether we were rich or poor, segregated or integrated, united or divided—always came second." In my view, this is a complete misreading of history. The Cold War was important, but it occurred during a period of enormous change and ferment in domestic politics that was by no means secondary. The postwar era witnessed the largest permanent growth in domestic government in our history, the most important changes in race relations since the Civil War, the most systematic government attempt ever to foster U.S. economic growth, and the most concerted effort in our history to promote more income equality. How all this could be described as coming second is baffling to me. The postwar era was one of major domestic and international developments. In my view, it is impossible to describe one as primary and the other as secondary, though such distinctions may usefully apply to earlier eras in our history.

4. See Office of Management and Budget, *Historical Tables, Budget of the United States Government, Fiscal Year 1996,* table 6.1, January 1995.

5. The graduation rates are from National Center for Education Statistics, Department of Education, *Digest of Education Statistics, 1994,* table 8, 1994. The share of spending for "payments to individuals" is from *Historical Tables, Budget . . . 1996,* table 6.1. The hypothetical decline in defense spending of $150 billion is based on its drop, as a percentage of all federal spending, of about 10 percentage points over the last decade, from 27 percent in 1985 to about 17 percent in 1995. With total federal spending of more than $1.5 trillion, defense spending would have been about $150 billion higher if it had stayed at 27 percent.

6. Statistics on industrial production from *Economic Report of the President,* table B-49, February 1995. Statistics on income penetration rates provided by the U.S. International Trade Commission. Data on the U.S. market share of world exports from the International Trade Administration in the Commerce Department.

7. Data on relative productivity levels, from the Organization for Economic Cooperation and Development (OECD) in Paris, make comparisons among twenty-four wealthy members, which include all major Western European countries, Japan, Australia, and New Zealand. The data indicate the amount of economic output per person (per capita gross domestic product). Only one country, Luxembourg, ranks higher than the United States. This table shows some of the main countries, based on an index using average per capita GDP in the OECD countries as 100.

GDP per Capita, 1993

Luxembourg	149
United States	128
Switzerland	122
Japan	108
Canada	101
France	98
Germany	97
Italy	92
United Kingdom	89
Sweden	88

In theory, the higher U.S. GDP per capita could reflect more Americans (proportionately) working longer hours than in other countries. In some cases, that is a source of some difference, but the main difference is higher U.S. productivity.

The review of technologies is found in White House Office of Science and Technology Policy, *National Critical Technologies Report,* March 1995.

8. See Bureau of the Census, *Statistical Abstract of the United States, 1994,* table 100.

9. See James Truslow Adams, *The Epic of America* (Boston: Little, Brown, 1931), p. 374. For a short history of the phrase, see Anthony Brandt, "The American Dream," *American Heritage,* April–May 1981, pp. 24–25.

I. THE POSTWAR PARADOX

1. For opinion data supporting these points, see surveys by ABC News/*Washington Post* on whether the country is going in the right direction or is on the wrong track. The question was first asked in October 1973, when 16 percent of the respondents thought the country was going in the right direction. In 1985 and 1986, nearly half the public (49 and 45 percent, respectively) felt the country was going in the right direction. Otherwise, the readings tend to be in the low 30s or high 20s, sometimes dipping into the teens. The Gallup Poll regularly asks the question: "In general, are you satisfied or dissatisfied with the way things are going in your own personal life?" Between 1979 and 1990, the low occurred in July 1990, when 73 percent said they were satisfied; the high was registered in October 1990, when 87 percent said they were satisfied. A similar question is asked about whether people are "satisfied or dissatisfied with the way things are going in the United States at this time." The highest level of satisfaction occurred in March 1986 (66 percent); the low was in July 1979 (12 percent). Of twenty-one surveys during this period, the

percentage saying they were dissatisfied exceeded 50 percent eleven times, and another five were over 45 percent. See *Gallup Poll Monthly*, July 1990, p. 13. More recent corroborating survey data come from Frank L. Luntz, "The State of the American Dream: A Study for the Hudson Institute," October 1994. Luntz finds, for example, that 88 percent of respondents said that they are "personally" going in the "right direction," while 60 percent thought the country was on the "wrong track."

2. The Whyte quote is from his *The Organization Man* (New York: Touchstone, 1956), p. 4. The quote from the banker is on page 14.

3. For flush toilets, see Stanley Lebergott, *Pursuing Happiness: American Consumers in the Twentieth Century* (Princeton, N.J.: Princeton University Press, 1993), p. 202; the share of rents is from Bureau of the Census, *Historical Statistics of the United States: Colonial Times to 1970*, 1975, series N238–245, p. 646. The Lebergott quote is from p. 106 of *Pursuing Happiness*, and the statistics on running water are from ibid., p. 101.

4. For fifty-hour workweek in the 1920s, see *Historical Statistics*, series D830–844, p. 172. On rising times and shift hours, see Robert S. Lynd and Helen Merrell Lynd, *Middletown: A Study in Contemporary American Culture* (New York: Harcourt, Brace, 1929), pp. 53, 33–34, 11. For figures on government spending on various programs, see Social Security Administration, Department of Health and Human Services, *Annual Statistical Supplement, 1993, to the Social Security Bulletin*, pp. 13–15. The figure for Social Security includes old-age insurance (29.3 million), survivors insurance (7.3 million), and disability insurance (4.9 million). Most Medicare recipients also receive Social Security, so these two figures should not be added.

5. The information about the first black in the NBA is cited in *A Common Destiny* (Washington, D.C.: National Academy Press, 1988), p. 68; first black network TV reporter is on p. 85. The number of black elected officials is cited in Anthony Lewis, "Brown v. Board," *New York Times*, May 16, 1994, p. A-17. Poll on anti-Semitism is in John Brooks, *The Great Leap: The Past Twenty-five Years in America* (New York: Harper & Row, 1966), p. 302. The decline in the social and economic power of white Anglo-Saxon Americans is described in Robert C. Christopher, *Crashing the Gates: The De-WASPing of America's Power Elite* (New York: Simon & Schuster, 1989). The quote is from pages 9–10.

6. Quote from the doctor is found in Michael B. Katz, *In the Shadow of the Poorhouse: A Social History of Welfare in America* (New York: Basic Books, 1986), p. 266. Data on food stamps is in House Ways and Means Committee, *1994 Green Book: Overview of Entitlement Programs*, 1994, p. 777.

7. "The American Century" appeared in the February 17, 1941, issue of *Life*. See also Charles S. Maier, "The Politics of Productivity: Foundation of American International Economic Policy After World War II," *International Organization*, Autumn 1977.

8. Figures on postwar economic growth are from "The Postwar Economic Achievement," in *World Economic Outlook, October 1994* by the staff of the International Monetary Fund (Washington, D.C.: IMF, 1994), pp. 86–97.

9. See Joseph A. Schumpeter, *Capitalism, Socialism and Democracy* (1942; reprint, New York: Harper Torchbooks, 1975), chapter 7.

10. Data are from the American Iron and Steel Institute—1980 data from its *1984 Annual Statistical Report*, table 7, and 1992 data from *Steel Works: U.S. Steel Industry at a Glance*. The later data on production are from the same sources; for 1980, table 1B.

11. I am indebted to political scientist Robert Shapiro of Columbia University for pointing out to me the first question in the Gallup Poll. See *The Gallup Poll: Public Opinion 1935–1971*, vol. 1, *1935–1948* (New York: Random House, 1972), p. 1.

12. See especially the introduction to Whyte, *The Organization Man*, and p. 7 for the quotes.

13. See Geoffrey Kollmann, *How Long Does It Take New Retirees to Recover the Value of Their Social Security Taxes?* (Congressional Research Service, January 3, 1994). And also, Geoffrey Kollmann, *Social Security: The Relationship of Taxes and Benefits for Past, Present and Future Retirees* (Congressional Research Service, updated December 16, 1993).

14. The Roosevelt quote is cited in Robert Y. Shapiro and Tom W. Smith, "The Polls: Social Security," *Public Opinion Quarterly* 49, Winter 1985, p. 561.

15. See Richard Hofstadter, *The Age of Reform* (New York: Vintage, 1955), p. 16.

16. Studs Terkel, *Hard Times: An Oral History of the Great Depression* (1970; reprint, New York: Washington Square/Pocket, 1978), p. 76.

2. HISTORY'S CHASM

1. Frederick Lewis Allen, *The Big Change: America Transforms Itself, 1900–1950* (New York: Harper & Brothers, 1952), p. 158.

2. Bureau of the Census, *Historical Statistics of the United States: Colonial Times to 1970*, 1975, series D85–86, p. 135.

3. I am indebted to Michael Barone for this point.

4. The price drop between 1929 and 1933 was actually 28.8 percent—see *Historical Statistics*, table E1–22, p. 197. The data on postwar business cycles is from Robert J. Gordon, ed., *The American Business Cycle: Continuity and Change* (Chicago: National Bureau of Economic Research/University of Chicago Press, 1986), pp. 44–45. Unemployment data are from *Historical Statistics*, p. 134. For the drop in industrial production, see *Historical Statistics*, table P13–17, p. 667; the decline in industrial production (20 percent) is in annual averages; the peak-to-trough decline would be greater.

5. Wheat prices from *Historical Statistics,* p. 208. The incident about U.S. Steel and its customer is cited in William Manchester, *The Glory and the Dream* (New York: Bantam, 1975), p. 34. On the twenties' boom, the increase in cars comes from *Historical Statistics,* p. 716; the increase in radios comes from Frank Freidel and Alan Brinkley, *America in the Twentieth Century,* 5th ed. (New York: Knopf, 1982), p. 174. The quotes from the banker and Schwab both appear in Frederick Lewis Allen, *Since Yesterday: The 1930s in America, September 3, 1929–September 3, 1939* (1940; reprint, New York: Perennial Library/Harper & Row, 1972), p. 58.

6. Most quotes and figures are from Allen, *Since Yesterday,* pp. 47–48, 59. The age of the average person on relief and the quote from the national study are in Michael B. Katz, *In the Shadow of the Poorhouse: A Social History of Welfare in America* (New York: Basic Books, 1986), pp. 211–12. I am indebted to Michael Barone for pointing out the high level of household servants in the 1920s. In 1930, they constituted about 2 million of a nonfarm labor force of 31 million (see series D182–232, p. 139, and series D233–682, p. 144, of *Historical Statistics*).

7. See Alistair Cooke, *A Generation on Trial: U.S.A. v. Alger Hiss* (1950; reprint, New York: Penguin, 1968), p. 24. For the son's quote about his father repainting the house, see Studs Terkel, *Hard Times: An Oral History of the Great Depression* (1970; reprint, New York: Washington Square/Pocket, 1978), p. 128.

8. See Robert S. McElvaine, ed., *Down and Out in the Great Depression: Letters from the Forgotten Man* (Chapel Hill, N.C.: University of North Carolina Press, 1983), p. 75.

9. Figures on relief and other economic impacts of the New Deal programs are cited in Michael Barone, *Our Country: The Shaping of America from Roosevelt to Reagan* (New York: Free Press, 1990), pp. 95–96. For the quote, see Cooke, *Generation on Trial,* p. 32.

10. The quote is from economist Alvin Hansen and is in Alan Brinkley, "The New Deal and the Idea of the State," in *The Rise and Fall of the New Deal Order, 1930–1980,* ed. Steve Fraser and Gary Gerstle (Princeton, N.J.: Princeton University Press, 1989), p. 85.

11. The drop in construction time for cargo vessels is cited in Manchester, *Glory and the Dream,* p. 295. The Barone quote is from *Our Country,* p. 156.

12. The estimate of the proportion of arms that were exported comes from *The First Report of the Office of War Mobilization and Reconversion, December 30, 1944,* p. 32. Unemployment figures come from *Historical Statistics,* series D85–86, p. 135. Farm production figures are from ibid., p. 31. The wartime production figures in the table are reproduced from Manchester, *Glory and the Dream,* p. 296.

13. The Manchester quote is from *Glory and the Dream,* p. 290. The Gallup Poll results are from *The Gallup Poll: Public Opinion 1935–1971,* vol. 1, *1935–1948* (New York: Random House, 1972), p. 488.

14. This paragraph relies heavily on William L. O'Neill, *A Democracy at War: America's Fight at Home and Abroad in World War II* (New York: Free Press, 1993). It may be the best single-volume treatment of the war effort both at home and abroad. For U.S. deaths, see *Historical Statistics*, table Y856–903, p. 1140. I was unable to find any agreed-upon total for fatalities for the entire war and doubt that any really exists. I've seen estimates in the 40 million to 60 million range.

15. This paragraph and its predecessor rely heavily on Paul Fussell, *Wartime: Understanding and Behavior in the Second World War* (New York: Oxford University Press, 1989). The quote about the letters soldiers didn't write home is found on p. 145. The figures (derived from a government survey) on the proportion of soldiers who vomited or soiled their uniforms is on p. 277, as is the estimate of the number of combatants in the Army. The discussion of "chickenshit" is on p. 80, and the quotes from the anonymous soldier and Keegan are on p. 83. The 1943 survey is "What the Front-Line Infantryman Thinks," December 21, 1943, and was on display in the National Archives, January 1995.

16. See Richard Polenberg, *War and Society: The United States, 1941–1945* (Philadelphia: Lippincott, 1972), p. 138, for the estimate of mobility. Polenberg estimates that between Pearl Harbor and mid-1945, 12 million men went into the military and more than 15.3 million civilians moved across county lines. The material on California relies heavily on Gerald D. Nash, *The American West Transformed: The Impact of the Second World War* (Bloomington, Ind.: Indiana University Press, 1985). See p. 4 for "colonial status," p. 62 for the figure of 17 percent of wartime contracts to California, and p. 217 for the rise in manufacturing output. The figure of about 10 percent of California's population consisting of migrants is from *First Report of the Office of War Mobilization and Reconversion*, p. 26.

17. The increase in aluminum production is taken from *First Report of the Office of Mobilization and Reconversion*, p. 9. The background on race relations comes from Polenberg, *War and Society*, pp. 116–17.

18. The survey on home canning is reported in *The Gallup Poll: Public Opinion 1935–1971*, vol. 1, (New York: Random House, 1972), p. 426. The Perret quote is from his *Days of Sadness, Years of Triumph: The American People 1939–1945* (1973; reprint, New York: Penguin, 1974), p. 433.

19. Depression fears reported in *The Gallup Poll*, vol. 1, p. 594. In a poll done for *Fortune* at the same time by the Roper Organization, about 45 percent of respondents felt there would be a depression within a decade (January 1946, p. 221). The Truman quote is in *Public Papers of the Presidents of the United States: Harry S. Truman, 1947* (Washington, D.C.: GPO, 1963), p. 13. The Senate action on the proposed legislation and the two Gallup Polls are cited in O'Neill, *Democracy at War*, p. 393. The Gallup Poll about the need for the government to provide jobs is reported in *The Gallup Poll*, vol. 1, p. 526.

20. For the Blum quote, see his *V Was for Victory* (New York: Harvest/Harcourt Brace Jovanovich, 1976), p. 145. For the quote from the bombardier, see Brendan Gill, "Young Man Behind Plexiglas," *The New Yorker*, August 14, 1944, reprinted in *The New Yorker Book of War Pieces* (New York: Schocken, 1947).

21. See Alan Brinkley, *The End of Reform: New Deal Liberalism in Recession and War* (New York: Knopf, 1995), p. 265.

3. THE CULT OF AFFLUENCE

1. Unemployment data from *Economic Report of the President*, 1994, table B-33, p. 306.

2. See James Q. Wilson, "A Guide to Reagan Country: The Political Culture of Southern California," *Commentary*, May 1967, pp. 37–38.

3. For the figures on white-collar and service workers, see Bureau of the Census, *Historical Statistics of the United States: Colonial Times to 1970*, 1975, series D182–232, table on p. 139. See Frederick Lewis Allen, *The Big Change: America Transforms Itself, 1900–1950* (New York: Harper & Brothers, 1952), pp. ix–x.

4. See John Brooks, *The Great Leap: The Past Twenty-five Years in America* (New York: Harper & Row, 1966), pp. 11, 131–32, and Allen, *The Big Change*, p. 213.

5. Quoted in Raymond Arsenault, "The End of the Long Hot Summer: The Air Conditioner and Southern Culture," *The Journal of Southern History* 50, no. 4 (November 1984), pp. 619–20. Data for the South's per capita incomes are from *Historical Statistics*, series F287–296, p. 242.

6. The sources for the list are:

Television: Stanley Lebergott, *Pursuing Happiness: American Consumers in the Twentieth Century* (Princeton, N.J.: Princeton University Press, 1993), p. 137. The 1994 data are from the Electronic Industries Association, Marketing Services Department, Washington, D.C.

Jet travel: The passenger figures for recent years come from the Air Transport Association in Washington, D.C. The figure for 1940 is from *Historical Statistics*, table Q577–590, p. 769. All figures are for domestic travel only.

Air-conditioning: Arsenault, "End of the Long Hot Summer," p. 611. The recent estimate of two thirds of households with air-conditioning comes from Bureau of the Census, *Statistical Abstract of the United States, 1994*, table 1223, which lists 30.1 percent of households with window units and 38.9 percent with central units in 1990 (the proportion has almost certainly increased since then).

Long-distance phone service: See *Historical Statistics*, table R1–12, p. 783, for the percentage of households with telephones; the origins of direct dialing for long distance are discussed in John Brooks, *Telephone: The First Hundred Years* (New York: Harper & Row, 1975), p. 244. Data on the share of long-distance calls occurring through direct dialing were supplied by the American Telephone and Telegraph Co. The number of toll calls is taken from *Historical Statistics*, table R1–12, p. 783, for 1940 and 1970; I could locate no current data. The latest data I could find on the actual number of calls were for 1985, when the number of toll calls was 102 million (see table 888 in *Statistical Abstract . . . 1994*). Calling rates were then increasing by more than 10 percent a year; assuming a rate less than half that would put the current total over 150 million.

Interstate highways: See Federal Highway Administration, *Our Nation's Highways: Selected Facts and Figures*, 1984, p. 2. For current accident statistics and usage of interstate highways, see table 1017 in *Statistical Abstract . . . 1994*.

Automatic washers and dryers: Lebergott, *Pursuing Happiness*, p. 115. For the latest data, see table 1223 in *Statistical Abstract . . . 1994*. In 1990, 76.3 percent of households had washing machines and 68.8 percent had dryers.

Antibiotics: See *I'll Buy That! 50 Small Wonders and Big Deals that Revolutionized the Lives of Consumers* (New York: Consumer Reports Books, 1986), pp. 11–16.

Social Security and private pensions: See table 582 of *Statistical Abstract . . . 1994*. The actual number in 1992 was 41.5 million, of which 25.8 million were retirees. But these figures have increased since then. For private pensions, see Pension and Welfare Benefits Administration, Labor Department, *Trends in Pensions, 1992*, table 4.2 on p. 76.

Health insurance: Data on health insurance coverage provided by the Health Care Financing Administration.

The Pill: See *I'll Buy That!*, pp. 129–32. Indeed, this entire list draws heavily on *I'll Buy That!* and a column I did on the book, "The Consumer Hit Parade," *Newsweek*, October 6, 1986, p. 44.

7. See National Center for Education Statistics, Department of Education, *Digest of Education Statistics, 1992*, tables 3 and 8.

8. Data obtained privately from the Air Transport Association.

9. See *I'll Buy That!*

10. The Eisenhower quote comes from Stephen E. Ambrose, "An Early Champion of Unity," *U.S. News & World Report*, October 15, 1990.

11. The $13.3 billion figure for the Marshall Plan is found in Bureau of Public Affairs, Department of State, *The Marshall Plan: Origins and Implementation*, April 1987, p. 11. My estimate of more than $300 billion was calculated as follows: the $13.3 billion over four years was roughly 1.2 percent of the U.S. economy's cumulative output between 1948 and 1951. Today's output (gross domestic product) is nearly $7 trillion; over four years, that's $28 trillion, and

1.2 percent of that is $336 billion. The conversion here is one of effort—not simply a conversion for inflation. The figure for the increase in European industrial production is from table 1 in Barry Eichengreen and Marc Uzan, "The Marshall Plan: Economic Effects and Implications for Eastern Europe and the Former USSR," *Economic Policy*, April 1992, pp. 13–75.

12. For background on the Marshall Plan, see Charles P. Kindleberger, *Marshall Plan Days* (Boston: Allen & Unwin, 1987), especially pages 245–65. The argument minimizing the Marshall Plan's importance is made in Alan S. Milward, *The Reconstruction of Western Europe, 1945–51* (Berkeley, Calif.: University of California Press, 1984). See also Eichengreen and Uzan, "The Marshall Plan."

13. For polling data on the Marshall Plan, see *American Enterprise*, March–April 1993, p. 98. See Sanford, *American Business Community*, (New York: Garland, 1987), chapter 5, for the various quotes of Americans and Europeans.

14. See Alfred E. Eckes, "Trading American Interests," *Foreign Affairs*, Fall 1992, pp. 135–54, for numbers on the 1947 GATT negotiations and the quote from Dulles. The quotes from the National Security Council on Japanese policy are from Stuart Auerbach, "The Ironies That Built Japan Inc.," *Washington Post*, July 18, 1993, p. H-18.

15. See Neil Sheehan, *A Bright Shining Lie: John Paul Vann and America in Vietnam* (New York: Vintage, 1989), pp. 7–8.

16. "Aspirations of an American Century," excerpts of a speech by Tom Wolfe to the American Association of Advertising Agencies; in *Advertising Age*, June 12, 1989, p. 44.

17. William Safire, "On Language: Cap the Entitlement," *The New York Times Sunday Magazine*, January 9, 1983, p. 9.

18. Norman Ornstein, "Roots of 'Entitlements,' and Budget Woes," *Wall Street Journal*, December 14, 1993, p. A-16.

19. See Charles Reich, "Individual Rights and Social Welfare: The Emerging Legal Issues," *Yale Law Journal* 74, no. 5 (April 1965), p. 1255.

20. See Daniel Yankelovich, *New Rules: Searching for Self-Fulfillment in a World Turned Upside Down* (1981; reprint, New York: Bantam, 1982), p. xvi.

4. PROSPERITY'S BROKEN PROMISE

1. See Daniel Bell, *The Cultural Contradictions of Capitalism* (1976; reprint, New York: Basic Books, 1978), pp. 23, 233.

2. Data provided by Karlyn Bowman of *American Enterprise* magazine from polls by Louis Harris and Associates, New York.

3. See Nicholas Lemann, *Out of the Forties* (Austin: Texas Monthly Press, 1983), pp. 30–31.

4. Home computer and answering machine data are from the Electronic Industries Association.

5. See Christopher Jencks, *The Homeless* (Cambridge, Mass.: Harvard University Press, 1994), p. 84.

6. For housing data, see Bureau of the Census, *Statistical Abstract of the United States, 1994,* tables 1204 and 1220.

7. See Jean Bethke Elshstain, *Democracy on Trial* (New York: Basic Books, 1995), p. 48. Elshstain cites—critically—writer Susan Schechter.

8. The 1980 VCR penetration rate is from Bureau of the Census, *Statistical Abstract of the United States, 1993,* table 900. The 1994 figure is from the Electronic Industries Association. See also Fred Hirsch, *Social Limits to Growth* (Cambridge, Mass.: Harvard University Press, 1976).

9. For murder statistics, see *Health Affairs* magazine, Winter 1993, p. 12.

10. For 1960 and 1970 data, see Bureau of the Census, *Statistical Abstract of the United States, 1980,* table 95. See *Statistical Abstract . . . 1994,* table 100, for more recent data.

11. This paragraph draws on Neely's *Tragedies of Our Own Making* (Urbana, Ill.: University of Illinois Press, 1994). The quote is on p. 13.

12. See *Statistical Abstract . . . 1994,* tables 80 (children living with mothers), 728 (children living in poverty), 315 (arrests), and 306 (murder victims).

13. For income data, see Bureau of the Census, *Money Income of Households, Families and Persons in the United States: 1991,* series P60, table xx. See also Ellis Cose, *The Rage of the Privileged Class* (New York: HarperCollins, 1993); the book was excerpted by *Newsweek,* November 15, 1993, pp. 56–63. My summary is from that excerpt.

14. Data in December 1993 from the National Opinion Research Center at the University of Chicago, personal communication, for NORC's most recent survey. See also Robert E. Lane, "Does Money Buy Happiness?," *The Public Interest,* Fall 1993.

15. See Steven Waldman, "The Tyranny of Choice: Why the Consumer Revolution Is Ruining Your Life," *The New Republic,* January 27, 1992, pp. 22–25.

16. See *American Enterprise,* January–February 1994, p. 93. For the 1939 poll, see *Public Opinion,* September/October 1978, p. 40. In calculating the "80 percent wrong" figure, I combined two answers on the original poll—"wicked" and "unfortunate."

17. See Andrew Cherlin, *Marriage, Divorce, Remarriage,* rev. ed. (Cambridge, Mass.: Harvard University Press, 1992), pp. 15–16.

18. For shares of global output, see International Monetary Fund, *World Economic Outlook,* October 1994, p. 112.

19. See Samuel P. Huntington, "The Clash of Civilizations," *Foreign Affairs,* Summer 1993, pp. 22–49.

20. See Richard Hofstadter, *The Age of Reform* (New York: Vintage, 1955), p. 17.

5. THE APOSTLES OF CONTROL

1. Historic data provided by the Income Branch of the Bureau of the Census. More recent data (going back to the late 1960s) are published annually in *Money Income of Households, Families and Persons in the United States,* also by the Census Bureau. Although data for median income are available through 1993, I have not used the most recent information in the text for two reasons: first, I wished to present long-term comparisons over convenient and equivalent time periods (1950–1970 and 1970–1990); and second, the more recent data seem unduly distorted—at least in terms of making historic comparisons—by changes in sampling techniques, statistical adjustments, and demographic changes. For example, median family income shows a sharp drop between 1990 and 1993, from $39,086 to $36,959 (in constant 1993 dollars). Some of this drop is clearly the onetime adjustment of the population base as a result of the 1990 census. The share accorded to Hispanics was increased, depressing median incomes because Hispanics—many of them recent immigrants—have lower than average incomes. The rapid increase in Hispanic families is also having a depressing effect; for example, the number of families in poverty rose 2.2 million between 1990 and 1993, but half the increase (1.1 million) was accounted for by Hispanic families, whose numbers increased almost 20 percent. There is also a lingering effect from the 1990–1991 recession on reported incomes. All these factors would tend to distort long-term comparisons.

2. Data from the Productivity Division of the Bureau of Labor Statistics provided by Larry Fulco.

3. In 1950, the bottom 60 percent of the population commanded 33.8 percent of total family income; by 1970, its share was 35.3 percent. (Although the increase was modest, it occurred during a period when most people's incomes were rising rapidly). By 1991, its share had dropped to 31.4 percent. For the 1950 and 1971 figures, see Bureau of the Census, *Statistical Abstract of the United States, 1974,* p. 384; for the 1992 figures, see *Money Income of Households, Families and Persons in the United States: 1992,* series P60–184, p. B-13.

4. Calculated from data provided by the Income Branch of the Census Bureau. Similar tables are provided annually in the *Money Income of Households, Families and Persons* reports.

5. See Arthur M. Okun, *The Political Economy of Prosperity* (Washington, D.C.: Brookings Institution, 1970), p. 33.

6. The article was reprinted in book form. See Melvin Anshen, "The Management of Ideas," in *Strategic Management,* ed. Richard G. Hammermesh (New York: John Wiley, 1983), pp. 50–63. The quote can be found on pp. 51–52.

7. For the Tobin quote, see Arjo Klamer, *Conversations with Economists* (Totowa, N.J.: Rowman & Allanheld, 1984), p. 98. For the Samuelson quote, see George R. Fiewel, ed., *Samuelson and Neoclassical Economics* (Hingham, Mass.: Kluwer-Nijhoff, 1982), p. 205.

8. For background on Heller's role, see his *New Dimensions of Political Economy* (Cambridge, Mass.: Harvard University Press, 1966). Monthly unemployment data can be found in *Labor Force Statistics Derived from the Current Population Survey*, a periodic volume published by the Bureau of Labor Statistics. My data come from the volume covering 1948–1987. For the Kennedy quote, see *Public Papers of the Presidents: John F. Kennedy, 1962* (Washington, D.C.: GPO, 1963), p. 473.

9. *Time*, December 31, 1965, p. 67B.

10. For background on the social development of large companies, see Neil J. Mitchell, *The Generous Corporation: A Political Analysis of Economic Power* (New Haven, Conn.: Yale University Press, 1989), especially chapter 2. See also Sanford M. Jacoby, *Employing Bureaucracy: Managers, Unions, and the Transformation of Work in American Industry, 1900–1945* (New York: Columbia University Press, 1985), which is a thorough and well-written account of changing employment practices at large manufacturing firms. The ad from the *New York Times* is quoted in Francis X. Sutton et al., *The American Business Creed* (New York: Schocken, 1956), pp. 35–36.

11. For basic inflation data, see *Economic Report of the President*, 1992, tables B-56 and B-59. For historic price data, see table E52–63 on p. 201 of Bureau of the Census, *Historical Statistics of the United States: Colonial Times to 1970*, 1975. Recent budget statistics can be found in Office of Management and Budget, *Historical Tables, Budget of the United States Government*, published annually. The historic data cited can be found in James Savage, *Balanced Budgets and American Politics* (Ithaca, N.Y.: Cornell University Press, 1988), appendix 3, pp. 287–91.

12. Data on diversification in Richard P. Rumelt, *Strategy, Structure and Economic Performance* (Cambridge, Mass.: Division of Research, Graduate School of Business, Harvard University, 1974), p. 51.

13. See Glenn D. Rudebusch and David W. Wilcox, "Productivity and Inflation: Evidence and Interpretations," Federal Reserve Board, Washington, D.C., 1994 (mimeographed).

14. The figures for farm real estate values come from Bureau of the Census, *Statistical Abstract of the United States, 1984*, table 1156.

15. See *The Origins and Causes of the S&L Debacle: A Blueprint for Reform* (Washington, D.C.: National Commission on Financial Institution Reform, Recovery and Enforcement, July 1993). See p. 29 for the estimate that by 1981, 85 percent of the S&Ls were running losses (these S&Ls held an even larger share of the industry's assets—about 90 percent). See p. 4 for the estimates of the ultimate losses, which the commission put between $150 billion and $175 bil-

lion in then current dollars. See p. 2 for estimate that 1982 cost would have been $25 billion.

16. See William Greider, *Secrets of the Temple: How the Federal Reserve Runs the Country* (New York: Simon & Schuster, 1987), pp. 16–17.

17. The quote from *The Nation* is cited in D. A. Wells, *Recent Economic Changes* (New York: D. Appelton and Co., 1890), p. 16. A good summary of postwar and prewar business cycles can be found in two short, excellent reports presented in the *Federal Reserve Bank of San Francisco Weekly Letter*. The data on the frequency and duration of slumps are in "Have Recessions Become Shorter?," number 93-33, October 1, 1993; the unemployment data are cited in "Postwar Stability: Fact or Fiction?" in the October 13, 1989, letter. Such historic comparisons can also differ slightly depending on the exact time periods that are being used.

It is worth noting, however, that some economists dissent from the view that recessions have become less frequent and milder. The argument for this position is that much of the apparent improvement in postwar business cycles is a statistical mirage. Prewar statistics, it's said, were simply more primitive; when adjustments are made for the differences, the argument goes, much of the postwar improvement disappears. Although this is conceivable, I have accepted the old wisdom—which still seems to be the majority position among economists—for three reasons.

First, even when the new statistical adjustments are made, postwar recessions have been shorter and less severe than prewar slumps. The major proponent of the argument that business cycles have not changed much is economist Christina Romer of the University of California at Berkeley. But much of her own data leave prewar slumps worse than their postwar counterparts. The standard GNP (output) series show the prewar slumps to be about twice as severe as their postwar counterparts. Romer's data show them to be about a third more severe. See "The Postwar Business Cycle Reconsidered: New Estimates of Gross National Product, 1869–1908," *Journal of Political Economy* 97, no. 1 (February 1989), table 3. Other economists who have reworked the data conclude that, despite shortcomings, the old data are more accurate. See in the same issue of *Journal of Political Economy*, "The Estimation of Prewar Gross National Product: Methodology and New Evidence," by Nathan S. Balke and Robert J. Gordon. Indeed, Balke and Gordon think the old data may have slightly understated the differences between the prewar and postwar periods. In addition to the severity of the slumps, Romer has challenged the traditional dates of business cycles—the ends of expansions and recessions—as developed by the National Bureau of Economic Research. Her own measures provide somewhat different dates. This table shows her results, giving the average duration (in months) of both economic expansions and recessions since the late nineteenth century.

Duration of Recessions and Expansions
(Months)

Period	AVERAGE LENGTH OF RECESSIONS		AVERAGE LENGTH OF EXPANSIONS	
	NBER	*Romer*	*NBER*	*Romer*
1887–1917	17.7	9.7	24.2	32.2
1918–1940	18.0	13.1	26.0	28.0
1948–1992	10.7	10.9	51.5	51.4

The same pattern is apparent here. Even if Romer's new dates are accepted, they show a huge difference between prewar and postwar business cycles. In the postwar era, expansions are roughly five times as long as recessions, whereas (according to her data) they were only twice as long between 1918 and 1940 and three times as long between 1887 and 1917. The major difference that arises from her dating is that postwar recessions do not appear significantly shorter than their prewar counterparts. (The table is drawn from Romer's "Remeasuring Business Cycles," *Journal of Economic History* 54, number 3 [September 1994].)

The second reason that I am skeptical of the view that business cycles haven't changed much is that today's younger economists (who have championed the new theories) didn't personally experience both prewar and postwar business cycles, while the older economists—many of them now dead—who devised the earlier wisdom had personally experienced both. Thus, what they saw in the statistics was buttressed by their own personal observation. This is a crucial difference and (for me) counts for a lot. In a famous speech given to the American Economics Association in late 1959, entitled "Progress Towards Economic Stability," Arthur Burns—a specialist in business cycles who was then president of the AEA and later became chairman of the Federal Reserve Board—put it this way: "More than twenty-five years have elapsed since we last experienced a financial panic or a deep depression of production and employment. Over twenty years have elapsed since we had a severe business recession." And by that time, there had been three postwar recessions. See *American Economic Review* 50, no. 1 (March 1960), pp. 1–19.

Finally, milder and less frequent postwar recessions are consistent with higher postwar inflation. It is hard to believe that had the prewar cycles simply been perpetuated in the postwar period, inflation would have been nearly so great. In theory, it is possible, but it seems unlikely that if we had suffered recessions with similar frequency and ferocity as in the prewar period, inflation in the postwar period would be so much worse. The advocates of the new view, it seems to me, will have to not only develop much more convincing statistical proof but also advance some plausible explanation for why business cycles should have remained constant in the face of so much change in the structure of the economy, the financial system, and governmental policy. By contrast, there are plausible (if not airtight) explanations for why business cycles now should be less violent.

18. For story on stable job tenure, see Albert Crenshaw, "The Myth of the Mobile Workers," *Washington Post*, December 28, 1994, p. A-1. Another study showing that job tenure has remained fairly stable is Francis X. Diebold, David Neumark, and Daniel Polsky, *Job Stability in the United States*, Working Paper no. 4859 (Cambridge, Mass.: National Bureau of Economic Research, 1994).

19. For data on health insurance, see Employee Benefit Research Institute, "Sources of Health Insurance and Characteristics of the Uninsured," Washington, D.C., January 1993, table 2. For data on pensions, see Pension and Welfare Benefits Administration, Department of Labor, *Trends in Pensions, 1992*, table 2.5, p. 34. For job tenure, see press release, Bureau of Labor Statistics, "Employee Tenure and Occupational Mobility in the Early 1990s," June 26, 1992. For Jacoby quote, see *Employing Bureaucracy*, p. 204.

20. See Claudia Goldin, *Labor Markets in the Twentieth Century*, Working Paper Series on Historical Factors in Long-Term Growth, Historic Paper no. 58 (Cambridge, Mass.: National Bureau of Economic Research, 1994), pp. 24–25.

21. Data on 1900 farming and factory employment calculated from *Historical Statistics*, table D75–84, p. 134, and table D127–141, p. 137. Modern data computed from *Economic Report of the President*, 1993, tables B-30 and B-41.

22. See Mark Sullivan, *Our Times*, vol. 3, *Pre-War America* (1930; reprint, New York: Charles Scribner's Sons, 1971). Banking panics in general do not seem to have triggered recessions, though they made them worse. According to a study by economists Charles Calomiris and Gary Gorton, the major banking panics in the so-called national banking era (the end of the Civil War until the creation of the Federal Reserve) occurred only if there had been at least an 8 percent decline in the stock market and a 50 percent increase in bankruptcies in the preceding quarter. See their "The Origins of Banking Panics" in *Financial Markets and Financial Crises*, ed. R. Glenn Hubbard (Chicago: University of Chicago Press, 1991). I am indebted to Calomiris for pointing this out to me and for discussing a number of other points about the nineteenth-century monetary system.

6. CHEERY ECONOMICS

1. This argument is made lucidly and in great detail in Robert H. Nelson, *Reaching for Heaven on Earth: The Theological Meaning of Economics* (Savage, Md.: Rowman & Littlefield, 1991).

2. See *Economic Report of the President*, 1994, table B-40, p. 314, for the unemployment figure; the Heller quote is from his *New Dimensions of Political Economy* (Cambridge, Mass.: Harvard University Press, 1966), p. 3.

3. Forecasting errors cited in Alfred L. Malabre, Jr., *Lost Prophets: An Insider's History of the Modern Economists* (Cambridge, Mass.: Harvard Business School Press, 1993), pp. 118–19. A more detailed record of economic forecasting can be found in Victor Zarnowitz, *Has Macro-Forecasting Failed?*, Working Paper no. 3867 (Washington, D.C.: National Bureau of Economic Research, October 1991). Zarnowitz noted that "when inflation was rising and high, it was clearly underpredicted, as in 1962–76 and especially 1969–76. Finally, inflation peaked in 1980–81 and decreased markedly in the following five years. Predicted rates moved down with a lag." However, Zarnowitz also argues that forecasting has generally improved over time—despite many continued errors—and that it is better now than it was in the earlier years of the postwar era. Presumably, it is also considerably better than in the prewar period. The decline in economists' reputations for accurate forecasting, he contends, has occurred because there were "unrealistically high prior expectations."

4. The unemployment/inflation trade-off of the Phillips Curve is taken from a chart on p. 95 of *Economic Report of the President*, 1969.

5. See *Economic Report of the President*, 1994, table B-62. These changes in prices are measured by comparing prices in December with prices in the previous December. Thus, in December 1961, consumer prices (the consumer price index) were 0.7 percent higher than in December 1960; in December 1969, prices were 6.2 percent higher than in December 1968. Comparing average prices for the full year shows the same trend with slightly different figures. In 1961, average prices were 1 percent higher than in 1960. In 1969, average prices were 5.5 percent higher than in 1968.

6. For a good summary of recent thinking on the Depression—though one placing less emphasis on the importance of the gold standard than I do—see Christina D. Romer, "The Nation in Depression," *Journal of Economic Perspectives* 7, no. 2 (1993), pp. 21–39; the figures on the amount lost by bank depositors and shareholders and also on the decline in wholesale prices are drawn from p. 32 of this article. The drop in the loan-to-deposit ratio is drawn from Charles W. Calomiris, "Financial Factors in the Great Depression," in the same issue of the *Journal of Economic Perspectives*, p. 59. For data on the number of bank failures, see Bureau of the Census, *Historic Statistics of the United States: Colonial Times to 1970*, 1975, vol. 2, series X588–609, p. 1021.

7. On the Fed's reaction to Britain going off the gold standard, see Barry Eichengreen, *Golden Fetters: The Gold Standard and the Great Depression, 1919–1939* (New York: Oxford University Press, 1992), pp. 295–98. My inter-

pretation of the Depression is heavily borrowed from Eichengreen's superb account.

8. See Milton Friedman and Anna Schwartz, *A Monetary History of the United States, 1867–1960* (Princeton, N.J.: Princeton University Press, 1963); Peter Temin, *Lessons from the Great Depression* (Cambridge, Mass.: MIT Press, 1989); and Eichengreen, *Golden Fetters.*

9. See Herbert Stein, *Presidential Economics,* 2d ed. (Washington, D.C.: American Enterprise Institute, 1988), p. 182.

10. See *Economic Report of the President,* January 1973, table C-26, p. 223.

11. Stein, *Presidential Economics,* p. 186.

12. For the number of credit cards, see Bureau of the Census, *Statistical Abstract of the United States, 1994,* table 817. The estimate is for the year 1991; the number of actual cards today undoubtedly exceeds 1 billion by a wide margin.

13. For a good summary of monetarist ideas in an accessible form, see Allan H. Meltzer, "Monetarism," in *The Fortune Encyclopedia of Economics,* ed. David R. Henderson (New York: Warner, 1993), pp. 128–34. In this essay, Meltzer— an economist whom I generally admire—seems to blame monetary policy for all post-1960 recessions.

14. For a good summary of tax changes in the 1980s, see C. Eugene Steuerle, *The Tax Decade* (Washington, D.C.: Urban Institute, 1991). One reason the effect of tax changes may have been muted is that the decline in the marginal tax rate (the rate on the last dollar of income) and average tax rates (the overall proportion of income paid as taxes) did not drop nearly as much as the nominal rates for the wealthiest taxpayers. For families with income twice the average, the drop in marginal rates was from about 40 percent in 1980 to 27 percent in 1987 (p. 135). The controversy over the promises of supply-side economics is discussed in Robert M. Dunn, Jr., and Joseph J. Cordes (economics professors at George Washington University), "Revisionism in the History of Supply-Side Economics," *Challenge,* July–August 1994, pp. 50–53. I don't think there is any doubt that, informally and sometimes formally, the advocates of supply-side economics made large claims for the beneficial effects of their policies. For example, here is a quote in 1978 from Paul Craig Roberts, who became an assistant secretary of the treasury in the Reagan administration, making the case in the *Wall Street Journal* for cuts in tax rates: "If government spending in real terms could be held to current levels for about two years, the Kemp-Roth [tax-cut] bill would get us out of the high deficit, high inflation, low productivity, low growth doldrums, and save transfer programs like Social Security" ("The Economic Case for Kemp-Roth," *Wall Street Journal,* August 1, 1978). On the other hand, it's also true that opponents of the supply-siders consistently cast their arguments in the worst possible light. The Niskanen quote is from his *Reaganomics: An Insider's Account of the Policies and the People* (New York: Ox-

ford University Press, 1988), p. 326. The quote about Reagan's policies being a blend of supply-side, monetarist, and traditional Republican ideas is from Paul Craig Roberts, *The Supply-Side Revolution* (Cambridge, Mass.: Harvard University Press, 1984).

7. THE MYTH OF MANAGEMENT

1. See Peter F. Drucker, *The Practice of Management: A Study of the Most Important Function in American Society* (New York: Harper & Brothers, 1954), p. 4.
2. See J. K. Galbraith, *The New Industrial State,* 4th ed. (Boston: Houghton Mifflin, 1985), p. 64. The book was originally published in 1967, so this statement dates from then. The outline of the postwar faith in large corporations and modern management largely follows Galbraith's logic. But the optimism was widely shared, though not all observers bought every detail in his argument. Economist Paul Samuelson, writing in the mid-1950s, said: "To keep the tremendously creative abilities of the modern large-scale corporation working towards the public good—that is the goal for the years ahead" (*Economics: An Introductory Analysis,* 3d ed. [New York: McGraw-Hill, 1955], p. 94).
3. See John F. Love, *McDonald's: Behind the Arches* (New York: Bantam, 1986), pp. 14–15, for the quote from McDonald. See also pp. 6 and 47 for details on Kroc.
4. The details on the founding of Federal Express can be found in Oliver E. Allen, "Absolutely, Positively Overextended," *Audacity* 3, no. 2 (Winter 1995).
5. The actual figure for 1989 was 77.9 percent. Firms with fewer than 1,000 workers do only 9 percent of commercial R&D. See *Science and Engineering Indicators,* 1991 ed. (Washington, D.C.: National Science Board, 1991), table 6-16, p. 418.
6. For a good history of the Xerox machine, see David Owen, "Copies in Seconds," in *The Man Who Invented Saturday Morning* (New York: Villard, 1986), pp. 132–57.
7. The story of executive jets and golf course subsidies is told in John Strohmeyer, *Crisis in Bethlehem: Big Steel's Battle to Survive* (Washington, D.C.: Adler & Adler, 1986), chapter 2. For General Electric, see Noel Tichy and Stratford Sherman, *Control Your Destiny or Someone Else Will: How Jack Welch Is Making General Electric the World's Most Competitive Corporation* (New York: Currency/Doubleday, 1993), pp. 37, 6. I am indebted to Tichy for providing me with excerpts from the Blue Books and with insights about their significance.
8. See Judith Bardwick, *Danger in the Comfort Zone: From Boardroom to Mailroom— How to Break the Entitlement Habit That's Killing American Business* (New York: American Management Association, 1991), p. 9.
9. See Alfred D. Chandler, "Organizational Capabilities and the Economic History of the Industrial Enterprise," *Journal of Economic Perspectives* 6, no. 3 (Summer 1992), pp. 79–100.

10. For the buyout premiums of recent corporate acquisitions, see "1991 Mergerstat Review," Merrill Lynch Business Brokerage and Valuation, p. 77.

11. See Dennis C. Mueller and Elizabeth Reardon, "Rates of Return on Corporate Investment," *Southern Economic Journal* 60, no. 2 (October 1993), pp. 430–53. Other similar studies have reached comparable conclusions. See Ben C. Ball, Jr., "The Mysterious Disappearance of Retained Earnings," *Harvard Business Review*, July–August 1987, pp. 56–63, and Michael Jensen, "The Modern Industrial Revolution, Exit, and the Failure of Internal Control Systems," *Journal of Finance* 48, no. 3 (July 1993), pp. 831–80.

12. See Richard Austin Smith, *Corporations in Crisis: How Big Companies Get into Big Trouble—The Drama of Management Under Stress* (1963; reprint, New York: Anchor, 1966), p. 2.

13. Data from the Bureau of Economic Analysis, Commerce Department, supplied by Ken Petrick.

14. There are various ways of calculating corporate debt burdens, depending on whether debts and the company's assets are recorded at their historic value (purchase value less depreciation) or at market value. Most calculations indicate a substantial rise in indebtedness since the 1960s. For example, this table shows the ratio of debt to total corporate assets for selected years.

Corporate Debt/Assets

1945	26%
1950	25
1960	26
1970	31
1980	28
1985	33
1990	39
1993	36

Data provided by Steve Oliner of the Federal Reserve from the Fed's "flow of funds" statistics. The figures cited in the text about increased corporate debt service involve a sample of more than 800 large companies. The median ratio of interest expense to corporate cash flow (profits before taxes plus depreciation) went from 9 percent in 1969 to 17 percent in 1988. For the same companies, the median debt/asset ratio calculated using market prices went from 30 percent in 1969 to 41 percent in 1988. See Mark J. Wahshawsky, "Is There a Corporate Debt Crisis? Another Look," in *Financial Markets and Financial Crises*, ed. R. Glenn Hubbard (Chicago: University of Chicago Press, 1991), tables 6.3, 6.6.

15. See Robert Hayes and William Abernathy, "Managing Our Way to Economic Decline," *Harvard Business Review*, July–August 1980, pp. 67–77.

16. See "A Note on the Boston Consulting Group Concept of Competitive Analysis and Corporate Strategy," a Harvard Business School Note, 9-175-175. There were many other related techniques—for example, PIMS, or profit impact of market strategy. This was a database of the performance of corporate business groups from which (it was argued) consistent relationships between profitability and strategy could be derived. See Robert D. Buzzell and Bradley T. Gale, *The PIMS Principles: Linking Strategy to Performance* (New York: Free Press, 1987).

17. See Jonathan Welsh, "Binge of Stock Buybacks Makes 1994 a Record Year," *Wall Street Journal*, December 19, 1994, p. C-1.

18. See Margaret M. Blair, ed., *The Deal Decade: What Takeover and Leveraged Buyouts Mean for Corporate Governance* (Washington, D.C.: Brookings Institution, 1993), p. 222.

19. Michael Jensen, "Agency Cost of Free Cash Flow, Corporate Finance, and Takeovers," *American Economic Review* 76, no. 2 (May 1986), p. 323.

20. The Ford data are from studies by Harbour and Associates, Inc., in Troy, Michigan.

21. See *About Your Company*, pp. 21–22. There is no date on my version of this book, which runs 154 pages and contains detailed description of IBM's benefits—everything from pensions to aid for adoptions. I picked my copy up at IBM while conducting interviews there in the early 1980s. It contains a report on the financial status of IBM's pension plans dated March 1981.

22. The figures about IBM and Sears are taken from "When Slimming Is Not Enough," *The Economist*, September 3, 1994, pp. 59–60.

23. The quote is from Clifford J. Ehrlich, senior vice president for human resources at the Marriott Corporation, in a 1993 letter to the author. More systematic surveys have revealed similar and widespread changes among big companies. See "The New Social Contract," by James E. Post, professor of management at Boston University; the paper was delivered at a conference on Global Concepts of Corporate Responsibility, April 11–13, 1994, at University of Notre Dame, Notre Dame, Ind. For evidence of changing corporate practices, see the *1994 AMA Survey on Downsizing* (New York: American Management Association). For corporate pay practices, see annual surveys by Buck Consultants, New York. The 1994 survey is reported in a press release of August 30, 1994. Similar results come from a survey by Hewitt Associates in September 1994.

8. THE REAL ECONOMY

1. The point about change and continuity in the American economy is also made in Herbert Stein, *On the Other Hand* (Washington, D.C.: American Enterprise Institute, 1995), pp. 27–56.

2. The Volcker quote is from his "The Triumph of Central Banking?" (The 1990 Per Jacobsson Lecture, mimeographed), p. 15. Inflation figures from *Economic Report of the President*, 1995, table B-62, p. 345.

3. For evidence of disagreement over the natural rate of unemployment, see "Business and Academia Clash over a Concept: 'Natural' Jobless Rate," *Wall Street Journal*, January 24, 1995, p. A-1.

4. For one example of the ambivalence about the importance of resisting higher inflation, see Louis Uchietelle, "Who's for More Inflation," *New York Times*, October 2, 1994, sec. 4, p. 1.

5. For a good summary of the problems and data, see *The OECD Jobs Study: Facts, Analysis, Strategies* (Paris: Organization for Economic Cooperation and Development, 1994).

6. See Wesley Clair Mitchell, *Business Cycles and Their Causes* (Berkeley, Calif.: University of California Press, 1963 [originally published 1913]).

7. Productivity data from Larry Fulco, productivity division of the Bureau of Labor Statistics, Department of Labor. See William J. Baumol, Sue Ann Bakey Blackman, and Edward N. Wolff, *Productivity and American Leadership: The Long View* (Cambridge, Mass.: MIT Press, 1989) for an elaboration of the argument that the productivity slowdown may really be a nonevent and that the exceptional event was the previous speedup; p. 2 gives their estimate of 1.5 percent for annual productivity increases since the early nineteenth century.

8. For data on immigrants, see Bureau of the Census, *Statistical Abstract of the United States, 1994*, table 54, p. 52. For a detailed discussion of trends in inequality, see Frank Levy, *Incomes and Income Inequality Since 1970*, Industrial Performance Center Working Paper 94-001 (Cambridge, Mass.: MIT Press, 1994). See also Robert Frank, "The Winner-Take-All Economy," *The American Prospect*, Spring 1994, pp. 97–107.

9. The possibility that greater inequality results mainly from a change in the general economic outlook—and its impact on business hiring and pay practices—is explored at slightly greater length in a column by the author in the *Washington Post* of August 31, 1994 ("Casualties of the 'Rising Tide,' " p. A-25). Subsequent studies that support this point of view include Peter Gottschalk and Robert Moffitt, *The Growth of Earnings Instability in the U.S. Labor Market*, Brookings Papers on Economic Activity, no. 2 (Washington, D.C.: Brookings Institution, 1994), and a study by Census Bureau economists reported in "Census Bureau Confirms Eroding Wages," *Wall Street Journal*, January 25, 1995, p. A-2.

10. Data on investment rates provided by the Bureau of Economic Analysis of the Department of Commerce. Averages calculated by the author. The shares of GDP are based on current dollar spending for gross nonresidential fixed investment or, in plain language, business investment. Those who worry about investment being too low usually point to figures on net invest-

ment (that is, total investment minus depreciation, which is the wear and tear on machinery or its obsolescence). The argument is that much of new investment is in short-lived assets, such as computers; what this overlooks is that many long-lived assets—such as buildings or factories—will, by their very nature, last a very long time. Nor do they need to be supplemented unless there is rapid population growth. It is not at all clear that the shift toward assets with shorter lives is bad, even assuming that we know how to measure the actual depreciation on new investment.

11. Data for shopping centers from the International Council of Shopping Centers. In 1980, there were 22,050 shopping centers with 2.96 billion square feet of leasable space; by 1990, there were 36,650 centers with 4.39 billion square feet of leasable space.

12. See *Economic Report of the President,* 1994, table B-51, p. 326, for data on industrial production.

13. See ibid., table B-1, p. 268. For 1993, the precise share of GDP represented by exports was 10.35 percent; imports were 11.39 percent. Exports and imports are here broadly defined and include services such as travel (when Americans travel abroad, that's an import; when foreigners travel here, it's an export) and royalties received by U.S. corporations—or paid by U.S. companies—for their technologies.

14. Data on transatlantic cables and telephone costs provided by AT&T. Farm population for 1910 from Bureau of the Census, *Historical Statistics of the United States: Colonial Times to 1970,* 1975, p. 457; 1850 estimate by the author.

15. For a fuller discussion of relative growth rates over the past century, see Moses Abromovitz and Paul A. David, "Convergence and Deferred Catch-up: Productivity Leadership and the Waning of American Exceptionalism," Center for Economic Policy Research, Stanford University, Stanford, Calif., 1994.

16. See Organization for Economic Cooperation and Development, press release, "How Countries' Economies Compare: New Rankings by OECD and Eurostat Based on Purchasing Power Parities," January 19, 1995.

9. COLLIDING IDEALS

1. See Edward C. Banfield, *Here the People Rule: Selected Essays* (New York: Plenum Press, 1985), particularly "Federalism and the Dilemma of Popular Government." Banfield's essay provides the framework for much of this chapter.

2. Poll results are from *American Enterprise,* March–April 1993, pp. 87–90.

3. For government spending in the 1920s, see Bureau of the Census, *Historical Statistics of the United States: Colonial Times to 1970,* 1975, vol. 2, series

10. The figure for farms for 1935 comes from Bureau of the Census, *Historical Statistics of the United States: Colonial Times to 1970*, 1975, p. 465. The figure for present farms comes from Bureau of the Census, *Statistical Abstract of the United States, 1994*, table 1084, p. 667. The high delinquency rate is cited in Sharon LaFraniere, "Agency Fails to Collect Millions in Loans to Wealthy Farm Owners," *Washington Post*, January 28, 1994, p. A-1.

11. For figures on the share of federal spending accounted for by the elderly, see House Ways and Means Committee, *1993 Green Book: Background Material and Data on Programs Within the Jurisdiction of the Committee on Ways and Means*, table 1 in appendix M, p. 1564. The figure of $13,000 spent for each older American comes from ibid. A good short history of the Social Security increases can be found in John Makin and Norman Ornstein, *Debt and Taxes* (New York: Times Books, 1994), pp. 148–55.

12. Data on the increase in the public debt during the Second World War and its present levels come from *Historical Tables, Budget . . . 1996*, table 7.1. The data for spending and revenue for World War II come from ibid., table 1.3.

13. See James D. Savage, *Balanced Budgets and American Politics* (Ithaca, N.Y.: Cornell University Press, 1988), pp. 4–5. This entire section relies heavily on Savage.

14. Ibid., p. 70.

15. Ibid., p. 93.

Jefferson had no objection to repaying loans to foreigners; but Hamilton wanted to repay all the debts, including those incurred by the states. These debts were owed heavily to Americans themselves, and Hamilton's plan, in Jefferson's view, provided an unwarranted windfall to domestic speculators. In many cases, the debt was no longer owned by the original lenders. Rather, it had been sold to others, often at large discounts from face value. The new debt holders, therefore, stood to make huge gains if the government repaid the full face value. Moreover, the gains to speculators "filched the poor and ignorant," because the government would repay the bonds by raising revenues through tariffs on imports. In turn, these tariffs increased prices for ordinary Americans. Our present understanding of these early disagreements is confused, because the positions of the antagonists— symbolized by Hamilton and Jefferson—confound today's political labels. Hamilton advocated strong central government and showed an occasional tolerance of deficits; these are positions now most commonly identified as "liberal." Yet, Hamilton is usually seen as a "conservative," because his strong government would promote the nation's economic development and, in the process, help business interests. By contrast, Jefferson is now usually cast as a liberal, because he saw himself as an egalitarian and champion of the common man as opposed to the pro-business, elitist Hamilton.

16. The Jefferson quotes are in C. Northcote Parkinson, *The Law and the Profits* (New York: Penguin, 1965), pp. 75–76.
17. See Savage, *Balanced Budgets*, p. 127.
18. Ibid., appendix 3, p. 289.
19. Ibid., p. 169.
20. Quoted in Raymond J. Saulnier, *Constructive Years: The U.S. Economy Under Eisenhower* (Lanham, Md.: University Press of America, 1991), p. 20.
21. For background, see "The Budget Process and Deficit Reduction," pp. 83–93 of Congressional Budget Office, *The Economic and Budget Outlook: Fiscal Years 1994–1998,* January 1993.
22. The CBO estimates are contained in *The 1990 Budget Agreement: An Interim Assessment,* December 1990, p. 6, and *The Economic and Budget Outlook: An Update, September, 1993,* p. 29.
23. The $500 billion estimate is based on the work of economist Thomas Hopkins of the Rochester Institute of Technology, details of which are presented in *Costs of Regulation: Filling the Gaps* (Washington, D.C.: Regulatory Information Service Center, August 1992). The number of pages in the Federal Register was provided by the Office of the Federal Register, which is part of the General Services Administration. The examples of the types of regulatory proposals that may appear daily are drawn from the Federal Register of June 23, 1995.
24. The notion that regulatory costs and benefits were, at the beginning of the 1990s, roughly in balance is based on Thomas Hopkins and Robert W. Hahn, "Regulation/Deregulation: Looking Backward, Looking Forward," *American Enterprise,* July–August 1992.
25. The OMB study is reported in Executive Office of the President, *The Regulatory Program of the United States Government, April 1, 1992–March 31, 1993,* p. 28.

II. ELUSIVE EQUALITY

1. Quoted in Lawrence A. Cremin, *Popular Education and Its Discontents* (New York: Harper & Row, 1990), p. 15.
2. See National Center for Education Statistics, Department of Education, *Digest of Education Statistics, 1992,* table 8, p. 17.
3. For SAT scores, see ibid., table 121, p. 125. It is hard to generalize about test scores in high school, because there are so many tests measuring so many things. For reading scores, see ibid., table 103, p. 112. Between 1970 and 1989, the average reading score for seventeen-year-olds on the National Assessment of Educational Progress tests rose from 285 to 290. Scores of those in the bottom 5 percent rose from 206 to 220. Scores of those at the 50th

percentile of seventeen-year-olds rose from 288 to 291, while those at the 95th percentile remained steady at 356. See ibid., tables 118 and 119, p. 123, for the science and civics test results. Spending per student is from table 156. In the 1977 school year, spending was $4,419 in 1991 "constant" dollars; by the 1987 school year, it was $5,553 per student. The student quote is in Chester E. Finn, Jr., *We Must Take Charge* (New York: Free Press, 1991), p. 112.

4. See Karlyn H. Bowman, *Public Attitudes on Health Care Reform* (Washington, D.C.: American Enterprise Institute, 1994), p. 10. Bowman cites a Gallup Poll that asked whether "government should be responsible for providing medical care for people who are unable to pay for it." In 1991, 80 percent of respondents said yes; interestingly, the response was almost exactly the same (81 percent) in 1938. In January 1994, 79 percent of respondents in another Gallup Poll said they would support a health reform plan that "guarantees every American private health insurance that can never be taken away." Support dwindled, however, when qualifications were imposed. In a poll in February 1994, for example, 42 percent of respondents said they opposed universal health insurance if it meant higher taxes; 46 percent favored it.

5. See Willard Gaylin, "Faulty Diagnosis: Why Clinton's Health-Care Plan Won't Cure What Ails Us," *Harper's*, October 1993.

6. For a history of affirmative action, see Hugh Davis Graham, "The Origins of Affirmative Action: Civil Rights and the Regulatory State," pp. 50–62 in "Affirmative Action Revisited" in *Annals of the American Academy of Political & Social Science,* September 1992. The entire issue provides good background on affirmative action. The official quoted is Laurence H. Silberman in "The Road to Racial Quotas," *Wall Street Journal,* August 11, 1977, p. 14. Silberman was under secretary of labor in the Nixon administration.

7. The figures on police, electricians, and tellers come from Andrew Hacker, *Two Nations, Black and White: Separate, Hostile, Unequal* (New York: Charles Scribner's Sons, 1992), pp. 121, 130. Leonard's studies are reviewed in his "The Impact of Affirmative Action Regulation and Equal Employment Law on Black Employment," *Journal of Economic Perspectives* 4, no. 4, pp. 47–63.

8. Poll results quoted on p. 82 of *American Enterprise*, September–October 1991. The Hacker quote is from *Two Nations,* p. 131.

9. See James Madison, Alexander Hamilton, and John Jay, *The Federalist Papers* (New York: Penguin, 1987), p. 124.

10. See Alexis de Tocqueville, *Democracy in America,* vol. 1, (1835; reprint, New York: Vintage, 1945), p. 3.

11. The discussion of "free labor" is drawn from Eric Foner, *Free Soil, Free Labor, Free Men: The Ideology of the Republican Party Before the Civil War* (New York: Oxford University Press, 1970). The quotes are on pp. 14 (Lincoln), 16 (Foner), and 29 (comments on homesteading).

12. This and the next few paragraphs rely heavily on Michael B. Katz, *In the Shadow of the Poorhouse: A Social History of Welfare in America* (New York: Basic Books, 1986). The quotes are on pp. xii, 16, and 19.

13. Ibid., pp. 20, 25, and 47.

14. Ibid., pp. 41–42.

15. See *The Public Papers and Addresses of Franklin D. Roosevelt*, vol. 4, *The Court Disapproves: 1935* (New York: Random House, 1938), pp. 19–20.

16. See p. 637, *Public Papers of the Presidents: Lyndon B. Johnson*, vol. 2, *1965* (Washington, D.C.: GPO), p. 637.

17. See Paul Starr, *The Social Transformation of American Medicine* (New York: Basic Books, 1982), p. 388.

18. The quote is from the late federal judge Skelly Wright and is in R. Shep Melnick, *Between the Lines: Interpreting Welfare Rights* (Washington, D.C.: Brookings Institution, 1994), p. 11. Melnick's own words are from p. 45.

19. For a full discussion of the economics and effectiveness of American schools, see Eric A. Hanushek, *Making Schools Work: Improving Performance and Controlling Costs* (Washington, D.C.: Brookings Institution, 1994).

20. For trends in health care spending, see Bureau of the Census, *Statistical Abstract of the United States, 1994,* table 147. The last reported year (1991) shows health care spending at 13.2 percent of GDP. Subsequent estimates by the Health Care Financing Administration put it around 14 percent for 1993.

21. See Everett Carll Ladd, *The American Ideology: An Exploration of the Origins, Meaning, and Role of American Political Ideas* (Storrs, Conn.: The Roper Center for Public Opinion Research, 1994), pp. 79–80.

22. Ibid., p. 40.

23. See Mary Ann Glendon, *Rights Talks: The Impoverishment of Political Discourse* (New York: Free Press, 1991), p. 14.

24. Vice President Al Gore's ideas on information subsidies are discussed in Alan Murray, "Gore's Data Highway," *Wall Street Journal*, March 31, 1994, p. 1. The quote about Candlestick Park was taken from the transcript of *The MacNeil/Lehrer NewsHour*, April 4, 1994.

12. SUICIDAL GOVERNMENT

1. The figure is from a poll taken by Luntz Research Companies of Arlington, Va., directly after the November 1994 election.

2. James Q. Wilson, "Can Bureaucracy Be Deregulated?," in *Deregulating the Public Service*, ed. John J. Diulio (Washington, D.C.: Brookings Institution, 1994), pp. 42–43.

3. See James A. Smith, *The Idea Brokers* (New York: Free Press, 1991), pp. 1–2.

4. The figures on congressional staff size combine both the personal and committee staffs of Congress. See Congressional Quarterly Inc., *Vital Statistics on Congress, 1989–1990,* tables 5-2 and 5-5.

5. See the *National Journal,* September 14, 1985—a special issue on the "influence industry." The 14,000 figure for Washington representatives is taken from the 1992 edition of *Washington Representatives,* published by Columbia Books Inc. The category includes lobbyists, lawyers, consultants, foreign representatives, and public relations and governmental affairs representatives. The facts on the specific groups come from the same source.

6. See Edward C. Banfield, "Party 'Reform' in Retrospect," in *Political Parties in the Eighties,* ed. Robert A. Goldwin (Washington, D.C.: American Enterprise Institute, 1980), p. 21.

7. The background on Truman's political beginnings and Pendergast is in David McCullough, *Truman* (New York: Simon & Schuster, 1992), pp. 157, 159, and 197.

8. See Norman H. Nie, Sidney Verba, and John R. Petrocik, *The Changing American Voter,* enlarged ed. (Cambridge, Mass.: Harvard University Press, 1979), pp. 53, 58. The discussion of changing voter behavior is drawn largely from this book, though the analysis is not unique.

9. See introduction to Everett Carll Ladd Jr. with Charles D. Hadley, *Transformation of the American Party System: Political Coalitions from the New Deal to the 1970s,* 2d ed. (New York: Norton, 1978), pp. 1–27.

10. For the Ehrenhalt quote, see his *The United States of Ambition* (New York: Times Books, 1991), p. 19. Schneider's comments are in his "Off with Their Heads: Public Resentment of Professionalism in Politics," *American Enterprise,* July–August 1992, pp. 30–37.

11. Turnout figures supplied by Curtis Gans of the Committee for the Study of the American Electorate in Washington, D.C.

In the late nineteenth century, voter turnout was as high as 80 percent. Initially, the declines reflected a variety of specific changes: poll taxes and literacy tests in the South intended to suppress voting by blacks; a huge wave of immigrants, many of whom didn't vote; and other reforms—such as registration requirements—intended to check fraud. The decline in party competition after 1896 is also thought to have reduced turnout. Democrats controlled the South, and Republicans dominated elsewhere. With these trends well established, there was less reason to vote. (Woodrow Wilson excepted, Republicans won every presidential election between 1896 and 1932.)

The New Deal realignment—making Democrats the majority party—only partially reversed these trends. To some political scientists, the long slide in turnout reflects class-conscious politics. The poor don't vote, the argument goes, because they have been marginalized and don't have much stake in government. The voting gap between the rich and poor is huge. In

1988, about three quarters of potential voters with more than $60,000 of income turned out compared with only two fifths of those with incomes of less than $7,500. By this reasoning, complex registration requirements have deterred the poor from voting, and political parties then "turned away from issues and campaign stratagems needed to win lower-class support" (Frances Fox Piven and Richard A. Cloward, *Why Americans Don't Vote* [New York: Pantheon, 1988], pp. 17–18).

Whatever their past relevance, these forces have clearly waned. Voting requirements have eased over the past quarter century. Indeed, some of the recent drop in turnout is explained by the extension in 1971 of the vote to eighteen-year-olds, since younger voters traditionally have lower turnouts. And the poor have hardly been ignored by politics: since 1960, many new programs—from Medicaid to food stamps—have served their needs. Finally, nonvoting has increased among better-educated groups, as political scientist Ruy A. Teixeira points out. In 1972, about 79 percent of the richest one sixth of Americans voted; by 1988, this had dropped to 74 percent. In 1988, about 85 percent of nonvoters had at least a high school diploma, up from 71 percent in 1972. "Clearly, the old stereotype of the non-voter as a high school dropout has become less and less reliable," writes Teixeira (Ruy A. Teixeira, ". . . What If We Held an Election and Everyone Came?," *American Enterprise*, July–August 1992, p. 53). In the 1950s, it was suggested that nonvoting was a sign of approval. Content people don't vote. Perhaps. But this seems less likely now in view of all the public opinion polls that show declining confidence in government.

12. See *Public Papers of the Presidents: Ronald Reagan, 1981* (Washington, D.C.: GPO), p. 1.

13. See James Q. Wilson, "The Newer Deal," *The New Republic*, July 2, 1990.

14. James Schlesinger, "A Sure Way to Gut Defense," *Washington Post*, March 4, 1994.

15. See Office of Management and Budget, *Historical Tables, Budget of the United States, Fiscal Year 1996*, table 6.1.

16. The question was included in a April 9, 1992, ABC News survey. Results supplied by the Roper Center for Public Opinion in Stoors, Conn.

17. Another question from the same ABC survey.

18. Clinton Rossiter and James Lare, eds., *The Essential Lippmann* (New York: Random House, 1963), p. 89.

13. HISTORY'S CYCLES

1. See Arthur M. Schlesinger, Jr., *The Cycles of American History* (Boston: Houghton Mifflin, 1986), pp. 22–48. The quote is on p. 27.

2. Ibid., p. 28.

3. For data and quote, see Paul Jerome Croce, "The Polarization of America: The Decline of Mass Culture," *The Public Perspective* (published by the Roper Center of Public Opinion and Polling), September–October 1992.

4. See Kathleen Hall Jamieson, *Dirty Politics: Deception, Distraction, and Democracy* (New York: Oxford University Press, 1992). All these examples are taken from chapter 3.

5. Skerry's quote and insights are contained in a paper he provided to the author, "The Affirmative Action Paradox: Group Rights and Individual Benefits" (Washington, D.C.: The Woodrow Wilson Center, June 1995). A version is scheduled for publication in *The Public Interest*.

6. See Gregg Easterbrook, *A Moment on the Earth* (New York: Viking, 1995). The book on working hours was Juliet B. Schor's *The Overworked American: The Unexpected Decline of Leisure* (New York: Basic Books, 1992). A convincing refutation of Schor's statistics is found in Kristin Roberts and Peter Rupert, "The Myth of the Overworked American," Economic Commentary Series (Federal Reserve Bank of Cleveland), January 15, 1995. Comparing 1976 and 1988, Roberts and Rupert present the following table.

Working Hours per Week

FOR A MARRIED COUPLE, EACH WORKING FULL-TIME

	1976			1988		
	Total Work	*On Job*	*At Home*	*Total Work*	*On Job*	*At Home*
Both	109.4	83.2	26.2	109.5	86.2	23.2
Husband	50.0	44.0	6.0	52.2	44.8	7.3
Wife	59.4	39.2	20.2	57.3	41.4	15.9

7. This and the following four paragraphs rely heavily on a column of mine, "America, the Caricature," *Washington Post*, July 5, 1995, p. A-23. The poll cited about whether Americans still think their country is the best place to live was done for the *Reader's Digest* in August 1994. Data were supplied by Karlyn Bowman of the American Enterprise Institute.

8. For data on Americans' attitudes toward blacks and jobs, see Howard Schuman, Charlotte Steeh, and Lawrence Bob, *Racial Attitudes in America* (Cambridge, Mass.: Harvard University Press, 1985), table 3.1, pp. 74–75. The survey data on blacks and whites having close friends of the other race are from *American Enterprise*, January/February 1990, p. 100.

9. For a discussion of assimilation, see Richard D. Alba, "Assimilation's Quiet Tide," *The Public Interest*, Spring 1995, pp. 3–18.

14. RESPONSIBILITY, NOT ENTITLEMENT

1. I published a budget plan along these lines in "Here's How to Balance the Budget," *Washington Post,* February 15, 1995, p. A-19. Anything I write now may be out of date by the time this book is published. But it's worth showing where the numbers come from and that they add up. Farm subsidies now total $12 billion to $20 billion annually. Amtrak, which provides less than 1 percent of all intercity travel, costs about $1 billion a year. Maritime subsidies cost about $800 million annually and support high-cost shipyards and about 12,000 well-paid American sailors. Federal job training programs cost about $12 billion, and most have repeatedly been judged ineffective by studies. Medicare and Medicaid costs could be trimmed by cutting reimbursement rates for doctors and hospitals as well as imposing some new co-payments on patients, especially for the booming home health care program. A 12-cent-a-gallon oil tax would raise about $23 billion. Taxing capital gains at death—that is, profits on stocks and bonds when people die—would raise about $9 billion.

From these specific proposals, the basic budget-balancing arithmetic is as follows. All the proposals would be introduced between 1996 and 2000, when the full savings would be realized.

End unessential programs (these include farm subsidies, Amtrak, maritime subsidies, the National Endowments for the Arts and Humanities, public TV subsidies) — $15–$25 billion

End some grants to states and localities for mainly local services (these include subsidies for mass transit, some subsidies for local schools and law enforcement) — $15 billion

End ineffective programs (the only category included here is federal job training, though there are doubtless many others) — $12 billion

Cut Medicare and Medicaid (this involves cutting reimbursement rates to doctors and hospitals and increasing patient copayments for some services, such as home health care) — $40 billion

Trim cost-of-living adjustment (COLA) by 0.5 percentage point — $23 billion

Adopt energy tax and end some tax preferences (the largest single tax preference that would be eliminated would be the exclusion of taxes on capital gains—profits from investments, generally on stocks and bonds—when someone dies, which would raise about $9 billion.) — $50 billion

Interest savings — $40 billion

Now, consider my statement that such a budget wouldn't cause severe social dislocation or inflict unbearable personal suffering. Social Security beneficiaries wouldn't starve if their benefits rose 2.5 percent instead of 3 percent. Food would still be grown without subsidies. The Medicare and Medicaid cuts represent only about 9 percent of projected spending ($435 billion in the year 2000). People wouldn't mothball their cars if gasoline cost 12 cents a gallon more; indeed, they might travel a bit more smartly (more car pools, for example). State and local governments would scream if they lost grants for schools, mass transit, and law enforcement; but these total only 2 to 3 percent of their spending. New taxes of $50 billion to $60 billion sound hefty, but they represent only a 3.5 percent overall tax increase (projected taxes are $1.7 trillion) and would leave the federal tax burden roughly where it was in the 1970s and 1980s: around 19 percent of GDP. In the 1970s, taxes averaged 18.45 percent of GDP; in the 1980s, the average was 19 percent. By my calculations, this proposal would make them 19.2 percent. All in all, balancing the budget wouldn't be fun; but it wouldn't be a social calamity, either. Only years of bipartisan complaining about the difficulties have made it seem a feat beyond mortals.

The statistics for federal aid to education as a share of school spending come from National Center for Education Statistics, Department of Education, *Digest of Education Statistics, 1994,* table 157. Projected taxes in 2000 are from Congressional Budget Office, *The Economic and Budget Outlook: Fiscal Years 1996–2000,* January 1995, table 2-15. Average tax burdens for the 1970s and 1980s are calculated from Office of Management and Budget, *Historical Tables, Budget of the United States, Fiscal Year 1996,* January 1995, table 1.2.

2. Figures from ibid., table 3.1.

3. See C. Eugene Steuerle and Jon M. Bakija, *Retooling Social Security for the 21st Century: Right and Wrong Approaches to Reform* (Washington, D.C.: Urban Institute, 1994), table 3.5.

4. For life expectancy figures, see House Ways and Means Committee, *1994 Green Book: Overview of Entitlement Programs,* 1994, table A.2.

5. For estimates of how quickly beneficiaries would receive the hypothetical return on their Social Security contributions, see Geoffrey Kollmann, *How Long Does It Take New Retirees to Recover the Value of Their Social Security Taxes?* (Congressional Research Service, January 3, 1994). For the Medicare estimate, see Guy King, "Health Care Reform and the Medicare Program," *Health Affairs,* Winter 1994, pp. 39–43.

6. For health care spending patterns by age, see Cynthia M. Taeuber, *Sixty-five Plus in America* (U.S. Census Bureau, Current Population Reports, series P23–178, 1992), table 3-14. For health care spending figures as a share of GDP, see Bureau of the Census, *Statistical Abstract of the United States, 1994,* table 147, which carries the figures through 1991. Later estimates bring data through 1993.

7. See *Economic and Budget Outlook: Fiscal Years 1996–2000,* table E-10.

8. See Sara McLanahan and Gary Sandefur, *Growing Up with a Single Parent: What Hurts, What Helps* (Cambridge, Mass.: Harvard University Press, 1994), pp. 1–2.

9. For a cataloguing of federal programs with racial, sexual, or ethnic preferences, see Congressional Research Service, *Compilation and Overview of Federal Laws and Regulations Establishing Affirmative Action Goals or Other Preferences Based on Race, Gender, or Ethnicity,* February 17, 1995. The evidence on the extent of "reverse discrimination" is skimpy, as is the evidence on the effectiveness of affirmative action. But what little evidence there is suggests it is not as extensive as the rhetoric about it. A study by law professor Alfred W. Blumrosen of Rutgers University found that reverse discrimination cases accounted for less than 3 percent of discrimination cases between 1990 and 1994. See "Affirmative Action: No 'Widespread Abuse' in Job Cases, Few Reverse Bias Claims, Study Says," *Daily Labor Report,* Bureau of National Affairs, March 23, 1995.

10. For defense spending figures, see Steven M. Kosiak, *Analysis of the Fiscal Year 1996 Defense Budget Request* (Washington, D.C.: Defense Budget Project, 1995), table 2. Kosiak estimates that between fiscal 1985 and 1996, annual defense spending dropped 26 percent. The projected drop between 1985 and 2001 is 33 percent. Figures on the force level reductions provided by the Congressional Budget Office.

11. See Bureau of the Census, *Money Income of Households, Families and Persons in the United States: 1992,* series P60–184, table B-2, p. B-4.

12. Some of Wilson's views are summarized in John McCormick, "How to Help the Truly Disadvantaged," *Newsweek,* April 3, 1995, p. 33.

15. CRISIS OR CONSENSUS?

1. See Bureau of the Census, *Statistical Abstract of the United States, 1994,* tables 143 and 146.

2. From a new afterword to the paperback edition of Jonathan Rauch, *Demosclerosis: The Silent Killer of Government* (New York: Times Books, 1995).

3. See Richard J. Herrnstein and Charles Murray, *The Bell Curve: Intelligence and Class Structure in American Life* (New York: Free Press, 1994), p. 526.

4. The statistics in this paragraph are drawn from Bureau of the Census, *Historical Statistics of the United States: Colonial Times to 1970,* 1975. The country's population is from series A1–5 on p. 8. The division between urban and rural America and the number of cities with populations exceeding 250,000 and 1 million is from series A57–72 on pp. 11 and 12. The increase in steel production is from series P231–300 on p. 694. The increase in the number of factory workers is from series P1–12 on p. 666.

5. The increase in the miles of rail track is from ibid., series Q321–328, p. 731. The quote from the *Omaha Republican* is in Thomas J. Schlereth, *Victorian America: Transformations in Everyday Life, 1876–1915* (New York: HarperCollins, 1991), p. 22.
6. Mark Sullivan, *Our Times*, vol. 1, *The Turn of the Century* (1900–1925; reprint, New York: Charles Scribner's Sons, 1937), p. 137.

Index

ABOUT THE AUTHOR

ROBERT J. SAMUELSON has been a reporter in Washington, where, since 1969, he has worked for *The Washington Post*, the *National Journal* magazine, and *Newsweek*. He is now a columnist for *Newsweek* and the *Post* and lives in Bethesda, Maryland, with his wife, Judy Herr, and their children, Ruth, Michael, and John.